tough**LOVE**®

raising confident, kind, resilient kids

Edited by Lisa Stiepock with Amy Iorio
and Lori Gottlieb

simon & schuster paperbacks

new york   london   toronto   sydney   new delhi

Simon & Schuster Paperbacks
A Division of Simon & Schuster, Inc.
1230 Avenue of the Americas
New York, NY 10020

Names and identifying characteristics have been changed
and some individuals described are composites.

First Simon & Schuster trade paperback edition October 2016

SIMON & SCHUSTER PAPERBACKS and colophon are
registered trademarks of Simon & Schuster, Inc.

For information about special discounts for bulk purchases,
please contact Simon & Schuster Special Sales at
1-866-506-1949 or business@simonandschuster.com.

The Simon & Schuster Speakers Bureau can bring authors to your live event. For
more information or to book an event, contact the Simon & Schuster Speakers
Bureau at 1-866-248-3049 or visit our website at www.simonspeakers.com.

Interior design by Ruth Lee-Mui

Manufactured in the United States of America

1   3   5   7   9   10   8   6   4   2

Library of Congress Cataloging-in-Publication Data
Names: Stiepock, Lisa, editor.
Title: ToughLove : raising confident, kind, resilient kids / edited
by Lisa Stiepock with Amy Iorio and Lori Gottlieb.
Description: New York, NY : Simon & Schuster, [2016]
Identifiers: LCCN 2014015010 | ISBN 9781476733265 (pbk)
Subjects: LCSH: Parenting. | Parent and child.
Classification: LCC HQ755.8 .T677 2016 | DDC 649/.1—dc23
LC record available at http://lccn.loc.gov/2014015010

ISBN 978-1-4767-3326-5
ISBN 978-1-4767-3327-2 (ebook)

For Allan and Alcy, Ralph and Trey, and Zachary

contents

introduction: raising great parents

Why does the world need another parenting book? Why do I as a parent need to read this particular parenting book? And what is toughLOVE anyway?

Let's get right to it: Why *does* the world need another parenting book?

We know the parenting world today is not the parenting world it was for our parents. The crazy thing is, it's not even the parenting world it was just yesterday. We've never had more good, interesting, relevant science and research to explore in the realm of child and teen development than we do right now, and we've never had all of this great information coming to us 24-7.

Parents need help getting the best of this information when and where we need it most: at our kitchen tables where our kids are doing homework, on our family room couches where they're Snapchatting and texting their friends. I don't know about you, but perhaps nothing has helped me more in particularly bad parenting moments than being reminded *why* my child is acting the way she is. That, for instance, my thirteen-year-old daughter is throwing a three-year-old-style tantrum for the same reason she did when she was three years old: she's separating from me again and it's no less painful or annoying now, but it's just as necessary. Part of the engaged-parenting-me wants to help her in that quest (the other part needs a time-out with a glass of wine and a hot bath).

Which brings me to: Why this particular parenting book?

Because it's written by the people who can best help us navigate all the developmental science, studies, and surveys. The chapters are by practicing therapists, teachers, and coaches, who are also parents themselves. They are giving us the most practical of advice, in that it comes with real stories from their own home lives and those of their patients (the names changed, of course, to protect the harried and sleepless). It's why I can sleep at night when I realize that while I am a recovering helicopter parent, it's okay for me to show my eight-year-old son crazy amounts of love as long as I also hold strong on limits and boundaries.

One of the earliest things we learn in our roles as our children's first teachers is how much better they take in information when we show them instead of just telling them. It turns out that works when raising parents, too!

In addition, this is one parenting guide that doesn't stop when the going gets toughest: when our kids turn into preteens and teens. They may be pushing us away the hardest now, but they really do need us the most. There's nothing for preschooler parents in here, but there's everything for parents of kids in kindergarten all the way to college.

So what is toughLOVE anyway? It's what scientists and researchers tell us we need in order to raise the happiest, healthiest kids who will become the strongest, most secure adults. It's about being both kind and firm. Setting limits while giving as much age-appropriate freedom as possible. It's about respecting your children for who they are while giving them the consistent boundaries they need to become confident, resilient grown-ups; preparing them for adulthood while protecting them from growing up too quickly. It's about putting an end to power struggles and creating a peaceful, harmonious home life.

You're thinking *easier said than done*? True! This is a guide for parents who honestly believe that parenting is the most important job they'll ever have—which is most parents we know. It's for parents who want to be engaged and informed, without smothering or helicoptering; who are students of parenting in the way they want their kids to be students of the world, curious and critical. It is a parenting GPS, but only if you apply to it your own GPI—gut parental instinct. *Because all this great science is confirming what we've always known: parents know best because they know their kids best.* All this expertise and all these stories simply help guide us to do what we know is best for our own kids; they help our gut instincts be the informed ones that get us through the tricky, trying moments, even the tricky, trying years.

—Lisa Stiepock (mom of Alcy) and
Amy Iorio (mom of Trey)

When Do I Start?

Right now! Here are ten toughLOVE tenets to get you started. And, keep in mind, this book is a tiny piece of the parenting bonanza that is toughLOVE. Take a look at toughLOVE.com and Mom.me, where we are raising great parents with up-to-the-minute information from the contributors in this book and many more. It's a community of parents struggling with the same things you are and sharing their strategies for success, as well as their moments of mind-bending failure!

---

toughLOVE TIPS
Ten toughLOVE tenets

---

1. **Kind and firm go together.** Both kindness and firmness are essential for kids to feel safe and cared for. Research shows that this balance is the most effective way to raise kids who thrive. Studies consistently find that teens who perceive their parents as both kind (responsive) and firm (demanding) are at lower risk for smoking, using marijuana, drinking alcohol, and being violent, and that these kids have a later onset of sexual activity. Other studies have correlated a teen's perception of parenting style (kind and firm versus autocratic or permissive) with improved academic performance, higher self-esteem, independence, and self-reliance.

2. **Parenting isn't a popularity contest.** Many parents today are afraid of doing something—anything—that their kids won't like. As a result, they endlessly negotiate, appease, or just plain ignore bad behavior. What these parents don't understand is that not only is it okay for our kids to hate us at times—it's actually healthy! It shows them that we are there for them, even when they don't like us because we said no.

3. **Setting limits is a sign of love.** Yes, it's hard to see that look on your child's face when you've denied her something she really wants, or when you say no to something he finds tremendously fun. But limits keep children safe and socialized, and kids who have practice dealing with frustration and life's ups and downs are far more capable of managing day-to-day life than those who don't. By empathizing with their frustration or disappointment while also holding the limit, you are helping your children to build up crucial resilience

muscles that will serve them well for life. Authoritative parents set clear standards for their children, so that consequences for crossing those limits are thoughtful, measured, and consistent, not arbitrary, laissez-faire, or overreactive.

4. **Your values become your children's, so practice what you preach.** We believe that parents need to clarify their own values and communicate these to their children in confident, consistent ways. If we want our children to act respectfully, not yell at us, show compassion and empathy, turn off technology during dinner, be flexible, listen to other opinions, and experience life balance, we have to do these things as well. For instance, if you think it's okay to exceed the speed limit while driving "sometimes," but you tell your teenager "never" to speed, guess what he'll do? Once you have kids, it's not just the highway patrol who's watching you.

5. *Discipline* **is derived from the Latin verb meaning "to teach."** Discipline is about teaching, not punishing. That's why it's important to combine clear and consistent boundaries with calm, compassionate messages. If, instead of a loving, nurturing tone of voice, you use a mean tone or end up yelling, you'll be teaching a very different lesson: your children will focus on *your* bad behavior and not on their own.

6. **Parenting is equal parts prevention and intervention.** Creating healthy boundaries in your home puts the prevention piece in place so most struggles are headed off in advance and there's less potential for long drawn-out arguments. If your kids know that no really does mean no, they will most often accept that no means no.

7. **Be proactive, not reactive.** The more up-front time you spend clarifying your family culture and values, the less time you'll spend butting heads with your kids. If you're clear about your expectations for things like curfews, language,

computer time, grades, bedtime, and manners, you won't feel trapped by haphazard consequences and wishy-washy parenting.

8. **Earlier is better, but it's never too late.** The earlier we teach children to own their actions with logical consequences, the better prepared they'll be for life. If your child leaves his baseball bat at the park, he doesn't have a baseball bat anymore, or maybe he needs to buy a new one using his allowance. If your child doesn't follow the rules at a friend's house, he might not be invited back, or perhaps he needs to find a way to earn that family's trust again. But as kids get older, the stakes get bigger and the decisions more complicated: Do I get in the car with my friend who is only slightly buzzed? Do I do this illegal thing even though I probably won't get caught? If you teach your kids early on to think through their choices *before they make them*, they're more likely to anticipate the logical consequences that may occur and make better life decisions. When something doesn't go as they'd like, you can say, "It's not your fault, but it is your responsibility." This avoids shaming them but states clearly that their actions are their own.

9. **It's unfair to unload your parenting responsibility onto your children.** When it comes to adults and children, a more "democratic" household is not necessarily more "fair." There's a reason that people aren't allowed to drive, drink, or vote until a certain age. While children do need to be heard and have choices, they can also become overwhelmed if parents act like peers, there are too few limits, and nobody is in charge. Yes, kids may say they'd like equal veto power, but what makes them feel safe and secure is knowing that there are mature grown-ups in the house who are emotionally ready to take on that role.

10. **Consistency shows reliability, not rigidity.** Consistency means working from a reliable and coherent philosophy so that our kids know what we expect of them, and what they should expect from us. If we can provide a safe, secure environment for our kids, where the boundaries are well thought-out and the expectations are clear, and they are presented with a high degree of nurturing and respect, then we offer our kids the security and reliability that they need to become the best adults they can be.

—Lori Gottlieb (mom of Zachary) for the toughLOVE
Editorial Team and Igal Feibush (dad of Carolina),
toughLOVE CEO

foreword: why we need toughLOVE and why we need it now

BY LISA BELKIN, CHIEF NATIONAL CORRESPONDENT FOR *YAHOO! NEWS*, CREATOR OF THE *MOTHERLODE* BLOG, AND MOM OF TWO (ALMOST) GROWN SONS

Time was when being a good parent meant never carrying your child in your arms—at least not until he was four months old. And it meant not kissing her unless absolutely necessary—and then only on the forehead.

Parenting advice once held that parents should wrap their babies warmly and keep them inside away from the slightest chill. Unless you lived in a time and place where the experts advised that it does a baby good to be outdoors, no matter the weather.

Don't praise children, parents were told, because it will swell their heads. Make sure to praise children, parents were taught, because it will bolster their self-esteem.

Forbid thumb sucking because it leads to feebleminded children. Encourage thumb sucking because it leads to self-confidence. Toilet train at three months, or three years. Feed only liquids for the first year. Begin solids at six months. Breast-feed exclusively. Formula is more nutritious. Hire a wet nurse like all the other good mothers do.

We call it "parenting," and then we add descriptors: "good," "irresponsible," "attachment," "helicopter," "Free Range." Our mistake, though, is treating this as a noun in the first place. There is no such thing as "parenting"—certainly no *one* thing. Yes, it feels like an instinct, a higher calling, a Platonic ideal. (By the way, Plato's view was that children should be raised communally, not knowing their own mothers.) But it is really a reflection and a response, an ever-changing set of absolutes.

For even when we think we are choosing the kind of parent we want to be, ours is a choice constrained and defined by context. We can decide only from among the options we can see, embracing or rejecting what our parents did, what our friends think, what the latest author or study suggests. The parents we want to be, and the parents we actually are (rarely the same thing) are shaped by history and culture. What good parents do depends on where, and when, you stand.

We make these incomplete decisions with the best of intentions. The goal is always to get it right, to wrestle this parenting thing down, to demystify the cosmic plunge into the unknown. That so many parenting choices of previous generations look off the mark in retrospect is not because the passion of parents has changed, but because so many other things have (the speed of absolutely everything these days, say). We're given new facts (the ancient Greeks refrained from carrying infant males because they thought it would cause testicular injury) or new tools (kissing babies was thought to spread diphtheria and syphilis, then immunology came along) or we see the realization of unintended consequences.

It's that last kind of pause that we are taking right now. The hows and ways of parenting have shifted markedly over recent microgenerations, and we are seeing some results of this uncontrolled experiment. Let's start with the causes. Every social trend of the past several decades has made parents more present in their children's lives. The world feels more dangerous, so we are less likely to let them go off to do things on their own. The finish line that is college means their spare time is filled with activities that we need to arrange and manage. With more parents working, there's more guilt over any time not spent on all of the above. For those who step back from work, there's the professionalization of parenting to fill the space. Also, we found we actually liked our kids, and wanted to share in their lives.

So we did. We shared, and supported, and managed, and smoothed. We helicoptered, snowplowed, and roared. We did this because we wanted our kids to be safe and successful, and because everyone else was doing it, and because our parents raised their eyebrows, which we took as confirmation that our choices were modern and right. We pored through bookshelves of philosophies, chose one, or several, and bristled at those who chose differently. We made our children the center of our lives, which was what it meant to be a parent.

Wasn't it?

For every action there is an equal and opposite reaction, Newton tells us. (He had no children, never knew his father, and never forgave his own mother for sending him to live with his grandparents after she remarried, as was common during the 1600s.) Parents react to their times, then children react to their parents, creating new times for a next cycle. The way this current wave of children has responded, it would appear, is to spend longer being children. We have protected them to a fault, we are now being told. They are so accustomed to our help that they can't do without it. They grow into young adults who text us several times a day, won't make decisions without our input, resist becoming adults, and are very likely to live at home. They are more anxious and depressed than other generations at their age. We have gone too far.

It could be, of course, that our children are struggling because of the same chaotic, fast-paced world that we were trying to help them navigate in the first place, rather than because we crippled them with our response. We can't know, because we can't run that race again. All we can do is take on the next one, which means taking what we know, and guess, and suppose, and recalibrating it forward, calling it parenting.

At the moment that means swinging back toward center, to moderation. Finding the sweet spot between doing too much, which we suspect we have been doing, and too little, which we refuse to do. It's a pendulum, this act of raising kids, and while it appears to swing freely, all it's really doing is constantly aiming for the middle. (Galileo, who first proved this, had three children out of wedlock, and sent his two daughters to a convent, which is how parents avoided providing a dowry in seventeenth-century Italy.)

What that center might look like is the subject within these pages. Not a watered-down middle ground that lacks passion. Rather a passionate, informed, involved approach that allows for freedom and exploration, even in this world that seems to be spinning almost faster than we can handle. It's an approach that knows when to pitch in and when to stand back. It's a method of taking in information from experts, observing our own kids, and then trusting our own guts. It's about loving our children enough to be tough about limits, loving them enough to let them tough it out, and simply loving them enough. This is a parenting book for that next race, the speedy one we are smack in the middle of right now.

part one

WHAT IS toughLOVE ALL ABOUT?

is one parenting style best?

BY PEGGY DREXLER, PHD, ASSISTANT PROFESSOR OF PSYCHOLOGY IN PSYCHIATRY AT CORNELL UNIVERSITY, BESTSELLING AUTHOR, AND MOM OF A SON AND A DAUGHTER

Back in the early days of my psychology practice, I remember sitting in my office listening to new mothers talk about feeling tired, about how they hadn't been as responsive to their children as they wanted to be, or about having their reactions colored by having been up all night. They'd talk about decisions they made and later regretted, conversations they wished they could undo, second guesses they were having all the time. Still in my early twenties, I had an almost smug certainty that I understood what it meant to be a mother in your body, your soul, and your bones, and that I knew how these women should mother their children just as I would know how to mother my own. Not until the birth of my son did I fully appreciate just how difficult the job of mothering is, what it calls on in oneself, and how it pulls on every single aspect of your emotional and physical life. And how knowing what to do, and how to do it, is not innate—not always.

There was one mother in particular, Olivia, who came to me to talk about her immense anxiety over deciding what sort of parent she wanted to be. In her own life, Olivia described herself as reactive and impatient, diligent and hyperorganized. She always paid bills on time. She was inclined to be critical and had high expectations for herself and for others. As a mother, Olivia wanted to be absolutely sure she was doing everything right. Her instinct was to establish firm, consistent rules—for the kids as well as for how she and her husband, Jack, parented them—from which no one should ever deviate. Jack, meanwhile, was more spontaneous and inclined to react in the moment to a specific situation at hand. As a result, Olivia was often the stricter parent, which I learned was causing much of her angst, while Jack was the "nice guy." If their son was acting out and refusing to listen, for example, and Jack threatened to take away a toy if that behavior didn't change, he wouldn't always follow through. He was easily charmed into backing off a punishment or reprimand, and it drove Olivia crazy. It also made her question her own parenting approach. "He is reluctant to be the enforcer, which means I'm left to do it," she said. "But maybe, I don't know: Is his way the better way?"

Back then, of course, just as now, there were plenty of opinions on how to raise a child. Many came from legitimate experts, though many did not (your know-it-all cousin, your nosy neighbor). For a long time, the baby-raising bible was *Baby and Child Care* by Dr. Benjamin Spock, first published in 1946. With clear, frank advice designed to put new moms at ease (and reaffirm that they knew more than they thought they did) he paved the way for others— including T. Berry Brazelton, Penelope Leach, and Richard Ferber— to build on, agree with, and challenge his philosophies. But with the ever-growing wellspring of information—lots of it contradictory— parenting advice got confusing. Theories went in and out of style as definitively as hemlines. They still do.

One line of thinking—at least in terms of how we view parenting from a philosophical perspective—has endured, however. In the late 1960s, Diana Baumrind, a developmental and social psychologist in Berkeley, introduced the concept of parenting styles, a way of thinking about, and classifying, strategies parents use in child rearing. Baumrind's three defined styles were based on two key, polar opposite characteristics she observed among parents: responsiveness, or a willingness to foster freedom and individuality, and demandingness, or the exertion of control. Through interviews with more than one hundred preschool-age children and their parents, Baumrind concluded that the majority of parents display one of three parenting styles, each of which calls on different degrees of this responsiveness and demandingness: Authoritarian, Authoritative, and Permissive. (Follow-up to her work by researchers Eleanor Maccoby and John Martin would suggest adding a fourth style, Uninvolved or Neglectful.)

The Authoritarians

In Baumrind's view, a parent's style was determined by his ratio of responsiveness to demandingness. Authoritarian parents, wrote Baumrind, are highly demanding and directive. They establish rigid rules and expect kids to follow them without fail, and often even without explanation. (The "Because I Said So" response is classic Authoritarian.) These parents are usually hyperdemanding about how the child behaves both in the house and out and, according to Baumrind, are "obedience- and status-oriented." Respect for and reverence of authority is paramount. They express love, but only when the child behaves in a manner the parent has deemed appropriate.

Here's an example of an Authoritarian approach. A parent issues the increasingly familiar statement: "We don't eat sugar in this house." The desire to eat healthy is one that many parents are embracing for their families, and is an admirable one, for sure. Through the Authoritarian lens, however, this statement is law. There are no exceptions, and no explanations. An Authoritarian parent who sets forth this edict may tell herself that her child is too young to understand the complexities associated with eating, or not eating, sugar. She may say it shouldn't matter *why* the family doesn't eat sugar beyond the fact that that's the rule. In the Authoritarian's mind, rules are absolutely not made to be broken. When she picks up her six-year-old from a playdate and finds him sucking on a lollipop, she flies into a rage, as upset with the child who accepted the treat as with the parent who's offered it to him. But the Authoritarian style in action isn't always as obvious as it is here.

One mother I met, Alison, admitted that she had a hard time praising her seven-year-old son, Adam. Behaving well—making his bed without being asked, saying please and thank you, keeping quiet, and sitting still during church on Sunday—was behavior she expected. "I just don't think about congratulating him for things he should be doing already," she told me. Whenever he did act out of turn, though, she easily reprimanded him—*that*, she thought, was parenting. And the message Adam was likely picking up from her through all of this? You only do wrong.

The Permissives

Permissive parents, on the other hand—often called "indulgent parents"—are highly responsive to individuality and the child's particular moods, whims, or quirks. They rarely discipline, make few demands in terms of behavior or appropriateness, and generally avoid confrontation. They're nurturing and communicative and often involve their child in decision making. They want to be their child's friend, and are afraid of upsetting her or stifling her creativity and uniqueness. In return, though, the child may become spoiled or demanding. She may throw tantrums or act out in search of boundaries.

Bob was a single dad by divorce, a situation over which he often felt considerable guilt. He tended to respond to that guilt with a Permissive approach to raising his son, Neil. At ten, Neil still refused to learn to tie his own shoes, and Bob didn't press him, believing that Neil would "learn when he's ready." He was constantly making excuses for Neil, protecting him from potential frustrations, and cutting him endless slack. After establishing age-appropriate chores for Neil—and following three weeks of watching those chores go undone—Bob assumed those chores for himself, without a single word about it to his son.

"I just don't want to push him too much, or make his life harder than it already is," Bob told me. "In the end, it's easier for me to feed the cat than to nag him about it or clean up after him when he's done it sloppily. After all, he's only ten." Instead of enforcing rules or otherwise letting Neil know what was acceptable behavior and what wasn't, Bob let Neil decide what was best for Neil. When Bob finally decided to try to enforce Neil's participation in household upkeep, Neil simply refused—because he knew he could.

The Authoritatives

The third category, wrote Baumrind, represents a style of parenting that's somewhere in between Authoritarian and Permissive. Authoritative parents are demanding and responsive in equal measure. They establish rules and guidelines for their children, but are willing to listen to, and address, questions. Their word isn't the end-all, but they don't quite view parenting as a collaborative effort, either; these parents are still very much in charge, but exert their control in a far more democratic manner. They are flexible and interactive. When children disappoint or misbehave, they aim to forgive and understand rather than punish. According to Baumrind, they "monitor and impart clear standards for their children's conduct. They are assertive, but not intrusive and restrictive. Their disciplinary methods are supportive, rather than punitive. They want their children to be assertive as well as socially responsible, and self-regulated as well as cooperative." Their brand of "tough" comes with a lot of love.

Imagine a common kid scenario: the argument over a toy. Parents who take an Authoritarian approach may storm into the room where the children are fighting, confiscate the toy while declaring, "This is what happens when you can't play well with others," and leave. Parents who assume a Permissive approach let the fighting between children continue, viewing it as a form of expression that's part of the natural order of things. Using an Authoritative approach, however, a parent will respond sensitively but firmly. She might interject and say to one child, "I understand how you feel, but your cousin is playing Pokémon right now. In a few minutes, you can have a turn." The parent responds, but also establishes limits. Later, she may initiate with her child a discussion about the concept of sharing.

The Uninvolveds

The later-added final category of parents, the Uninvolveds, are neither responsive nor demanding. While they fulfill a child's basic needs and aim to keep him safe, these parents are emotionally, and sometimes physically, detached and fail to provide not only rules and structure, but also personal connection. Sometimes, these are parents whose work, or focus on money and career, comes first, due to personal ambition or economic necessity. Uninvolved parents often leave the parenting to schools and society; they become strangers in their own home. This form of parenting can be a form of abuse, but not always.

Take Lydia and Quinn, for example. Lydia was the CEO of a

digital tech firm. When we met, she was struggling, in her words, to raise eleven-year-old Quinn, a bright, active, popular boy who, it seemed, had zero interest in connecting with his mother. But when we examined what was happening at home, it became clear that Lydia, who worked sometimes eighty-hour weeks and traveled as many as fifteen days a month, considered parenting secondary to her career, something she reluctantly admitted. She had never established very many rules for Quinn, justifying that fact by declaring him "independent" and "mature." But lately he had been slipping in school. One afternoon, he got in trouble for painting on a rock in Central Park. When Lydia wasn't traveling, instead of agreeing to spend time with her, her son would say he was tired or busy and shut himself in his room. Could you blame him? Lydia had provided Quinn with all the comforts a kid could want—but not, it turned out, much emotional support.

So Let's All Be Authoritatives, Right?

Not necessarily. These four categories outline the vast range of approaches to parenting. You see that the use of such styles isn't confined to an isolated event, such as a disagreement or occasion for discipline, but can be seen in a parent's overall demeanor when engaging a child. And they make a difference in how that child grows. In her later work, Baumrind analyzed how these approaches impact development. She found that an Authoritative parenting style is the most likely to produce happy, confident, and capable children who know how to manage stress and can express their thoughts and feelings. While children reared by Authoritarian parents are typically obedient, they also typically have lower self-esteem, are more likely to be anxious, and tend to be less happy. Those raised by Permissive parents are, as a whole, poor self-regulators, antisocial, and tend to have problems in school. In later studies that took into account the

Uninvolved style, those children whose parents could be categorized as such ranked lowest among all children, and tended to lack self-control, have low self-esteem, and were less competent than their peers. Baumrind concluded that an Authoritative approach to parenting was, then, the most universally desirable. Makes sense, right?

Mostly. Despite the fact that her research was conducted more than half a century ago, Baumrind's conclusion that an Authoritative approach results in the happiest kids largely remains the predominant mode of thinking today, as academic studies—which I'll get to in a bit—continue to reinforce this belief. And yet the suggestion that one parenting style is preferable above all others is a very black-and-white, one-size-fits-all answer. Many believe that Baumrind was too focused on control, and inflexible in her rules, and to some extent I agree. When thinking about what sort of parent you want to be, there's a case to be made for adhering less to rules, guidelines, and definitions and instead embracing your own blended style. Though many would-be parents study up on parenting before they have children—and this is happening more and more as the culture of "experts," and availability of resources, continues to thrive—styles are largely instinctual and unconscious. A parent's adopted style is based on how he was raised, what he observed in his own and in other families, and what he's been taught.

Some parents may still find themselves firmly planted in one camp. Some, like Olivia, may be heavily Authoritarian, where "parent knows best" and obedience is paramount. Others, like Jack, are more clearly Permissive, afraid to upset the kids or reluctant to ruin the good time. But most parents will find themselves developing a style that's a combination approach. When considering your own, it's important to recognize that not everyone is born to be a parent, but that doesn't mean they shouldn't be one. The perfect, all-giving, all-loving every-mother is a myth; in reality, the ongoing process of parenting is how we learn—over and over and over again. The adoption of an effective style is not a matter of which to choose, then—an "either/or"—but of finding a balance that works for you, your family, and your particular child.

One Style Doesn't Necessarily Fit All

As a toddler, Antonia was indisputably difficult, from the breakfast she refused to eat in the morning to the tantrums she'd throw every night when confronted with the prospect of a bath, a teeth brushing, or any other effort at personal hygiene. Early on, her mother, Lauren, had adopted a Permissive approach. She valued what she saw as Antonia's individual personality qualities and quirks, which were very different from those of her older sister, Nicola. Lauren's firstborn had been a comparative breeze: an easy sleeper and constantly smiley kid who'd eat anything put in front of her. Permissive parenting was what came naturally to Lauren, who acknowledged that she'd been raised by a very strict, wholly Authoritarian father who demanded obedience from Lauren and her siblings. As a teen, Lauren had fallen, rebelliously, into what she calls a sort of grungy, tattooed, "whatever, man" phase during which she remembered pushing herself to do things she felt uncomfortable with simply because she knew it would get a rise out of her dad.

"I ended up spending my teens and some of my twenties angry and consumed with exacting a sort of revenge," she said. "When instead I could have used that time to express my desire for creativity and freedom in far more constructive ways."

For her own girls, Lauren wanted to foster a household that was inspiring and nurturing, where they had a say in how the family lived and how they, as kids, turned out. With firstborn Nicola, that approach had worked. Of course, a Permissive approach was easy to adopt with a child who naturally required little discipline. But when Antonia came along, Lauren was challenged with wanting to encourage Antonia's expressiveness and growing increasingly frustrated with the fact that the child just would not listen—especially in public.

At the park, seven-year-old Antonia would strip off layers of her clothes and run around topless. Out to dinner, she was a mess. At first, Lauren would ignore the whispers and stares of other mothers, or occasionally request that they mind their own business, as Antonia streaked the playground or pitched a fit at a restaurant until someone removed her placemat ("She hates placemats," Lauren told me as she relayed one such incident). But eventually, she couldn't help but admit that she, too, was disturbed by Antonia's behavior.

"I felt incredible pressure just being around my friends, who were similarly free-spirited about their approach to parenting. Except, unlike mine, their kids did not run out into the street like wild animals," Lauren said. "Whatever approach I was taking, it wasn't working. And though I believed in my heart that a hands-off approach would serve her well later on, it was hard to argue that her out-of-control behavior, left unchecked, was doing no one any favors, Antonia included."

She was right. Although most parents who employ a strictly Permissive approach do so with the idea that a laid-back outlook and warm, nurturing method help foster creativity and individuality, studies show that children of Permissive parents tend to function poorly in many areas of life. A 1987 study of San Francisco Bay area high school students conducted by the Stanford Center for the Study of Youth Development found that Permissive parenting was associated with lower grades, and in 1991, a study of 4,000 American families published in the journal *Child Development* confirmed that kids with Permissive parents achieved less at school. Two decades later, a 2010 study published in the *European Sociological Review* found that children of Permissive parents were more likely to engage in risky behavior, such as smoking, drugs, and violence.

But here's the thing: a Permissive approach isn't necessarily all bad. Some reports, including one in 1999 by Nancy Darling for the University of Illinois's Clearinghouse on Elementary and Early Childhood Education, have found that children and adolescents from indulgent homes have higher self-esteem, better social skills, and lower levels of depression than other children. A 2009 study in Spain, meanwhile, reported that Permissive parenting in that country is actually associated with strong academic performance and relatively few behavior problems.

So what's the answer? For Lauren, it was to adopt a more fluid approach that had her adding some structure and rules to her Permissive style: rules about how to behave while out to dinner, how to address adults, why it's important to do your homework at the same time every day. She gave Antonia responsibilities around the house and found that though Antonia resisted at first, she grew to like the feeling of being part of the family in this way. With Nicola, meanwhile, Lauren maintained a more purely Permissive approach, recognizing in that daughter a natural independence and ability to thrive under fewer rules. To the girls, she explained that everyone is different, and that what's fair for one isn't always the same as what's fair for the other—therefore, some rules would be different, too. Instead of holding fast to the idea of how she wanted to raise her children, Lauren learned to balance her desire for a more democratic household (and her admitted rebellion against her own upbringing) with the need to treat her very different children as individuals with very different needs.

Sometimes, parenting feels like detective work, and often it is. People talk about the mystery of motherhood. Part of that mystery has to do with the fact that kids are unknowns. They're unpredictable, ever-changing, and situations involving them often call for some willingness to be flexible. That doesn't have to mean bending to accommodate a child's whim or mood. But kids do change. As such, parenting requires constant assessment and adjustment, whether you've got one child or five. What works for one may not work for the next; what works for one today may not work for her next week. Achieving a conscious, helpful, individual parenting style involves ongoing effort—we are who we are, but we can, and should, evolve, too. And in many cases, the best style of parenting is not the easiest.

Of course, no one tells you that, do they? Instead, there's an immense pressure parents feel to "get it right." But the myth of the perfect mother and the perfect family does nothing but promote the perfect setup. Instead of recognizing a need to be flexible, this myth can cause parents to question their abilities and their decisions when a style of parenting doesn't seem to "work" instantly on a child. As in the case of Olivia, who began to wonder if her husband's approach was "better" than her own. And in the case of Lauren, who used to parent as much according to her friends' approval as to her own instincts. "I'd want to stop Antonia from doing something, but then I'd picture her on the shrink's couch twenty years from now, free-associating about every no that was issued to her, and why people keep disappointing her," she told me.

Does It Really Matter What Style We Are?

Then, of course, there are other parents who don't care what everyone else says. Lindsay, mom to eight-year-old Sylvester and six-year-old Leo, knew that she was tough. To other moms, she described herself as "an unapologetic hard-ass." She liked things how she liked them, and raised her boys with an eye toward order. She held them accountable for nearly everything: If they poured their own glass of milk too full, they had to finish every drop. If they forgot their backpacks at school, they had to carry their things in a plastic grocery bag for a month, even though they'd cry and cry about how embarrassing it was. The slightest questioning of the rules was received by Lindsay as a personal attack and, as such, met with a look

quite possibly, a time-out. She'd been known t

two. "I am teaching them what it means to respe

Instead, both boys became so dependent on L

they were afraid to leave the house out of fear that they migh

something wrong. They could not adapt to change, whether it was graduating from one grade to the next or taking down the tree after Christmas. They began to cry at the drop of a hat. "That's when I realized that maybe I was being too harsh on them, and that although I thought I was being firm, I was really being dictatorial," Lindsay told me. "I was stripping them not only of their identity but of their ability to feel secure in the world. They were constantly anxious. To be honest, parenting wasn't getting easier. It was getting harder." Lindsay and her boys were lucky. Many parents who take an Authoritarian approach never make this connection. They only get angrier, push harder, as they see their children growing "weaker."

Authoritarian parents may view other parents' disciplinary efforts as carelessly lax, and indeed the Authoritarian approach can be most dramatic when it comes to issuing discipline. With Authoritarian parents, discipline often has a shaming effect.

When we talk about shaming, we tend to talk about the obvious forms: spanking or other physical punishments, public reprimand. But there are other, subtler, yet still as impactful ways that Authoritarian parents shame their children in the pursuit of discipline. These include making a child feel guilty, deficient, or "bad"; a source of trouble; just plain dumb. It can include belittling a child, or even something as seemingly benign as rolling your eyes at him or sighing in response to something he's done. Comments might include "You're acting like such a baby," or "You'd lose your head if it weren't glued on!" As a form of behavior modification, though, shaming—whether obvious or subtle—is ineffective and even destructive. That's because since most kids can't distinguish between their impulses—

ır actions—and their selves, instead of condemning the behavior, naming ends up condemning the child, and making him feel bad about himself. Children live in fear of punishment or rejection.

Studies confirm this. The *Child Development* study referenced earlier found that while children raised by Authoritarian parents are obedient and prone to conforming to the standards set by adults, their self-esteem and sense of self suffers. Sometimes, their grades do too, as proven in the Stanford Center study, though other reports, such as one presented by the Aspen Education Group, point to Authoritarian-raised children who excel in school as a result of living in a fear-based household marked by high expectations, limits, and boundaries. But because they're used to being told what to do, they may struggle to understand how to be independent, form their own opinions, and find activities they truly enjoy. And so they act out: the *European Sociological Review* case study found that children of Authoritarian parents are more likely than children of Authoritative parents to engage in risky behavior, including being 89 percent more likely to smoke. So much for the benefits of iron-fisted rule.

Here's where it becomes clear that good parenting isn't necessarily about choosing a style and sticking to it. It's about judging what's needed at the moment. Sometimes parents need to enforce rules—and some parents are stricter than others, and that's okay. But sometimes parents need to lay off.

That's in large part where the Authoritative approach comes in. One mother I met, Angela, was a master at this approach. When her daughter, Melanie, was younger, she tried her best to be encouraging and supportive. When Melanie did something to disappoint Angela, she'd sit her down and invite her to talk about what had happened—and why. "Sometimes, she was just rebelling. Other times, she was reacting to some struggle she was going through elsewhere in her life," said Angela. "If I had just punished her, I would have missed the opportunity to have real conversations with her about things she was dealing with at school, or with her friends." She set firm limits for Melanie in terms of behavior, but if Melanie strayed, Angela made sure to take the time to find out why—and how she could help Melanie avoid feeling the need to act out in the future.

Still, she had rules. Even Angela wasn't the completely Authoritative parent. As Melanie got older, Angela would allow the occasional extended curfew—a Permissive gesture—but she would absolutely not agree to let Melanie drive with friends after 11:00 p.m., no exceptions, something quite Authoritarian. "If she wanted to stay out late, that was fine, but either 11:00 was the cap or she should expect that I'd be picking her up myself," Angela told me. "I didn't have a reason for this other than my instinct told me that trouble happens with kids in cars after 11:00 p.m. It was maybe irrational, but I felt very strongly about it." In this, Angela was acknowledging her trust of Melanie while also retaining her parental right, and duty, to help ensure Melanie's safety. It honored the fact that Melanie had proved to be a responsible child, while also indulging one of Angela's few sticking points. It let Melanie be Melanie, and let Angela be Angela.

Mother and Father Do Know Best

Yes, the academic studies are contradictory; academic studies often are. But let's be honest: How many parents these days are poring over and debating academic texts when deciding how to raise their children? Not many. More, I'd speculate that most of the confusion and general angst around adopting a style of parenting, or parenting in general, is social: Parents see what their friends do—or don't do. They read endless "expert" takes. In fact, many parents have grown reluctant to do anything without first getting an expert opinion, or three.

This very American desire to seek out the absolute best wisdom—no matter that there are many definitions of *best*—has led to a boon in parenting professionals, from baby nurses to parenting coaches. The Spocks and Brazeltons of yesteryear have been replaced, or at least supplemented, by countless advice givers, the thousands of mommy blogs out there included, each offering his or her own best-laid plans. Parents call for help with breast-feeding, fussiness, and sleeping. Later, they call for input on everything from what chores to give their children (and when) to what constitutes a healthy dinner. Everyone's an expert on parenting—except, that is, parents themselves. This leads to endless questioning, anxiety, and self-doubt.

Of course, there's nothing wrong with seeking out help. Help is great, and for many parents, necessary. But many child-rearing experts don't account for different personalities, growth patterns, and situations. And that's the fatal flaw in taking their word as gospel. You can find a recipe in a cookbook and expect that if you get the ingredients and follow the instructions, most likely you'll wind up with a decent dish. It's different with kids. And so we have to ask: At what point does all this help compromise our innate ability to parent? When does outside help cause us to question our own instincts?

What's more, it's important to remember that opinions and styles reflect the times. The Authoritarian approach, for example, was particularly popular in the 1940s and '50s when children were "to be seen but not heard," and when spanking and other forms of corporal punishment were more common. In the 1960s, Permissive parenting came into fashion along with free love and women's liberation. Things are different now. The opinions change, and so do we.

Trust Yourself

When seven-year-old Grace was small, her mother, Pamela, chose a pediatrician who advised her to stick to a set feeding schedule so

Grace would not become "milk dependent." Almost overnight, Grace went from being an extremely easy, calm, placid baby to crying non-stop. At first Pamela thought it was colic. Then she didn't know what it was. When she called the pediatrician, he insisted that she stick to the schedule. And still Grace cried. One weekend, beside herself at the changes in her happy baby, Pamela called his office yet again, but he wasn't there. Instead, a different pediatrician was taking his calls. "How much are you feeding her?" she asked when Pamela told her about Grace's nonstop wails. Pamela told her about the schedule and the amounts she was fed. "That baby is hungry!" the pediatrician exclaimed. "Give her more food."

Turns out Pamela had based her good judgment on an authority who knew less about her baby than she did. The "expert advice" of the initial pediatrician was wrong, yet Pamela felt that her instinct as a mother was not quite right either, or else wouldn't she have ignored his advice? Like so many other mothers, she wound up trusting herself less and less.

Confidence can be a rare commodity for first-time parents. Thankfully, confidence, like mothering, can be learned. After the incident with her daughter's pediatrician, Pamela decided she was also done with blindly accepting book advice. She stopped taking advice from other mothers, too, including relatives (however well meaning) and people on the street who'd spontaneously offer her "pointers" on how best to raise her child. Pamela finally realized that, when it came to mothering her own child, she was the expert. But it's not an easy position to hold in a world where everybody is sure they know more about mothering your children than you do.

I have my own story to share about this. Four months after my son was born, I was chatting with an acquaintance about what I had been up to. I mentioned that I'd resumed work part-time. "How dare you?" she scolded. "Don't you know that you're hurting your child by not being at home with him?" The implication that I was more interested in my job or my career than in my child was hurtful—and plain wrong. The fact is that a majority of us do go back to work after bearing children, and it's not a bad thing: Research has shown that work can raise a mother's self-esteem, and a mother's self-esteem is directly correlated to her child's.

But this isn't about fact, is it? It's about everybody and her sister having firm (and vocal) ideas about how to mother *your* child. Sixteen years later, at a family get-together, a relative chided me for carrying my baby daughter over to see her. "Don't you know that you have to put her down?" she exclaimed. "She'll get spoiled."

Mothers are not immune to the criticism bug. Working mothers slander stay-at-home moms as settling for less than equality, and moms at home rant that working mothers are harming their progeny by being away from them for days at a time. There's always someone out there critiquing your parenting performance. It's important to remember that mothering simply isn't an exact science. And that— believe it or not—in most cases, the very best expert is you, even when it comes to knowing where, and when, to go for help and support.

Eventually, Olivia and Jack learned that their different approaches to parenting were something of a gift—when practiced in concert, that is. They made a point to never disagree about parenting in front of the kids and to uphold each other's decisions. It worked for them. Their divergent styles were not only true to themselves as people but entirely complementary. They recognized and respected the idea that kids don't have to have the same relationship with each parent. Their kids, in return, were well prepared for a world of negotiating various types of people. They saw and understood that dissimilarities needn't mean strife. Best of all, everyone learned—the kids, Olivia, Jack—that "different" needn't mean better or worse.

---

toughLOVE TIPS

Take these tenets for good parenting—no matter how
you approach it—and make them your own.

SET AN INTENTION. Compromise is good, and necessary, and no matter your style—chosen, instinctual, or still developing—the best interests of the child should always receive top billing. Discuss with your partner your goals for raising your children, and how each of you would come to those goals. Then work to achieve those goals as a family through structure, limits, compromise, understanding, adaptability, and, above all, unity. For more on this, see "Deciding What Your Family Values" by Ann Corwin on page 177.

LET HIM BE HIM. Accept your child for who he is, rather than trying to mold him into your vision of who you *think* he should be. By allowing your child his own space to move beyond you and establish his own sense of identity, you open him up to a world of possibilities and give him the chance to live up to his potential. Expand—rather than constrict—your child's life by not imposing your own fears or limitations on him. For more on this, see "Raising Resilient Children and Teens" by Kenneth R. Ginsburg on page 62.

ENCOURAGE INDEPENDENCE . . . Do this by letting your child do whatever she can by herself, from sounding out letters to pouring a cup of juice to carrying her dishes to the sink when she's younger, to writing her own book reports and fixing her own dinner when she's older. Help facilitate the process for your child, but don't do the task for her. Encourage responsibility by having your child set—and then live up to—her own goals and expectations. Through this, she will unconsciously examine and develop her own morals and values.

. . . BUT MAKE HER FEEL LIKE A PART OF THE TEAM. Instill responsibility and strength in your children by making them active and engaged members of the household. Expect them to do their share of the chores and other age-appropriate duties. Though they may resist at first, like Antonia, most kids find they like having jobs that are theirs. Give your child the ability to feel like she has a role and is an important part of the team. For more on this, see "Routine Zen: Teaching Independence and Gaining Sanity" by Lynne Kenney on page 186.

ENFORCE BOUNDARIES. Parents whose style can be described as both intense and considered raise reflective, conscious, centered children with a sense of identity. That usually means enforcing firm limits and sticking to clear boundaries, but without harshness. Let them know what's right—and what's not—when it comes to the treatment of other family members, their friends, and strangers. For more on this, see "Setting Limits with Love" by Robert J. MacKenzie on page 36.

HELP THEM NEGOTIATE COMPLEX FAMILY DECISIONS WHILE EXPRESSING A BROAD RANGE OF FEELINGS. Do this by talking to, and with, your children using emotional and empathic language, and discussing morality as it relates to broader social situations. One single mom I met told her kids, "You are my emissaries," keeping them in line by making it clear they represented not just themselves, but her as well, out in the world. For more on this, see " 'Gimme' Kids: The Toxic Cocktail of Entitlement, Narcissism, and Materialism" by Madeline Levine on page 104.

MAKE A COMMITMENT TO CONNECTIVE PARENTING. Over the years, I've learned that a parent's ability to connect with her child—including letting him know how she is feeling, acknowledging her own mistakes, and treating his feelings with respect—helps him extend that sense of connection and closeness to others. For more on this, see "Engaging with Your Kids: What Is Family Time These Days and How Can We Make the Most of It?" by Ellen Galinsky on page 141.

setting limits with love

BY ROBERT J. MacKENZIE, EDD, A FAMILY THERAPIST, EDUCATIONAL
PSYCHOLOGIST, AUTHOR OF THE SETTING LIMITS BOOK
SERIES, AND FATHER OF TWO GROWN SONS

Conner, age twelve, knows he's not supposed to ride his skateboard without elbow pads and a helmet. The last time he was caught, his mother took away his skateboard for the rest of the day. But Conner considers himself an expert. He can ride rails, jump over obstacles, and launch himself more than three feet in the air on a half-pipe. He decides to do it anyway and gets caught.

"Hand over the skateboard, Conner," says his mother matter-of-factly, when she sees him jumping off a platform in the driveway without protective gear.

"But Mom, I was just practicing some tricks before going to Neil's house. Can I have another chance? Please?" Conner pleads.

His mother holds firm. "You can tomorrow," she says as she collects the skateboard for the rest of the day.

Conner's mother is using a logical consequence to support her rule about using protective gear when riding the skateboard. Logical consequences are structured learning opportunities. They are arranged by the adult, experienced by the child, and logically related to the situation or behavior.

In this case, Conner temporarily lost his privilege of riding his skateboard because he chose not to follow his parents' rule for wearing protective gear. No yelling or threatening. No warnings, lectures, or second chances. No loss of unrelated toys or privileges. His mother's message is clear: Use protective gear or you can't use the skateboard. In effect, Conner chose the consequence he experienced.

Children need and require limits throughout their development. They want to understand the social rules of their world. They want to know what's expected of them, who's really in control, how far they can go, and what happens when they go too far. Limits provide this vital information. Limits help children understand themselves and their world and stay on the path of healthy development.

Limit setting isn't rigid. It's a dynamic process that changes as children grow and mature and demonstrate increasing readiness for more freedom, privileges, and control over their lives. The challenge for parents is to continually adjust and expand the limits they establish for their children to keep them on the path of healthy development. To accomplish this balancing act, parents need to set limits that are firm enough to guide healthy testing and exploration, yet flexible enough to allow for growth and maturation.

Why *All* Children Need Limits

Imagine that you recently moved to a new town. You don't know anyone, but you're eager to make new friends and settle into your new community. You invite people to your home and make arrangements to visit them, but each time you do, they give you strange looks and seem annoyed by your behavior.

What did I do wrong? you ask yourself. It's confusing. You're doing the same things you've always done, but you encounter disapproval and rejection. You feel anxious and uncertain. You don't know where you stand or what's expected of you.

Sound like a nightmare? This is what many children experience if they grow up in homes with ineffective limit setting. When they head out into the world, they experience conflict, disapproval, and negative reactions from others.

On the other hand, when children receive clear messages about rules and expectations, they learn how to cooperate and get along with others.

Limits Help Children Do Research

Have you ever thought of children as researchers? Well, they are, and they are remarkably well equipped to do their job. From the time they are very small, children are busy testing, exploring, and collecting data in the form of experience about how their world works. They are astute observers, mimicking the behavior they observe, noting and recording cause-and-effect relationships, and forming beliefs about rules based upon the data they collect.

Their research is a process of discovery, but the data they collect and the conclusions they reach are sometimes different from what parents might expect. Why? Because children's research is more heavily influenced by what they experience than by what they are told. Consider the following example.

Seven-year-old Aaron likes to watch cartoons in the morning while he dresses for school, and his parents allow him to do so. Like many seven-year-olds, Aaron has trouble doing two things at once. The dressing part always seems to happen at the very last moment and only after a great deal of coaxing, prodding, and cajoling from his mother. After several months of this routine, Aaron's frustrated mother announces that he cannot get dressed with the TV on unless he dresses more quickly. Things go better for the first few days, but before long, they are back to the old prodding and cajoling. Sometimes his mother threatens to turn off the TV, and on one occasion she does, but she quickly turns it back on when Aaron starts to cry.

What kind of data does Aaron collect from his experience? What conclusion does he reach about his mother's rule about dressing while the TV is on? Of course, it's okay no matter what she says. This is what he actually experiences. The lesson is not likely to change until his mother gives him different data.

Now, let's contrast Aaron's experience to that of Tim, another seven-year-old who also enjoys watching cartoons while he dresses in the morning. When Tim's mother notices the problems Tim has getting out the door, she gives him a clear message: "Tim, the TV will stay off until you finish dressing." Then she turns it off. Tim fusses and complains that she's not fair, but his mother holds firm as precious TV time slips away. Tim decides to get dressed. Why? Because he wants to watch cartoons, and he knows from his experience that he can't do so until the dressing part is done. When he finishes, his mother tells him what a good job he did and turns the cartoons on.

Tim's mother is setting limits effectively. She expects Tim to test her limits like most kids do. She also understands that limit setting is a teaching-and-learning process, and she gives her little researcher the data he needs to arrive at the right conclusion. Getting out the door at Tim's house won't be a problem.

Limits Define the Path of Acceptable Behavior

Have you ever tried to hike a trail with few trail signs or markers? It's confusing. You're not sure in what direction to travel. Without clear signals to keep you on course, you're more likely to make wrong turns and get into trouble. This is what it's like for children when parents are not clear in their limit setting.

When limits are clear and consistent, the path is easier for children to understand and follow. When limits are unclear or inconsistent, children often steer off course and get into trouble. Shelly is a good example.

When nine-year-old Shelly interrupts her parents, they usually stop whatever they're doing and give her their undivided attention. Sure, they're annoyed with her behavior, but they consider it one of those stages children go through. She'll probably outgrow it by the time she turns ten, they tell themselves.

Like most of us, Shelly's parents expect their daughter to behave acceptably, but Shelly is nine, and she's not a mind reader. She doesn't live in their minds. She lives in the real world, and she knows what she experiences. What she experiences is that interrupting is okay. What other conclusion can she reach when she is permitted to do it time after time? Shelly does not understand the path her parents want her to stay on because their signals are not clear. Do you think Shelly is heading for conflict at school when she interrupts her teacher or friends? You bet.

Shelly needs the same kind of signals nine-year-old Andrew receives from his parents. Each time he interrupts, his parents tell him respectfully that interrupting is not okay, then they teach him what he's supposed to do. They ask him to wait for a pause in the conversation, then to say "Excuse me" and wait to be recognized before he speaks. They practice this skill each time he interrupts. When Andrew remembers on his own, they tell him how much they appreciate it. Andrew is learning valuable lessons about how his parents expect him to behave. How do you think he'll do at school?

Older children and teens also need clear, firm limits to understand the path we expect them to stay on. For example, when sixteen-year-old Gwenn asks to use the family car to return a book to a friend, her mother asks Gwenn to return the car by 7:00 p.m. "I have an errand to run," says her mother. But Gwenn decides to test.

She doesn't return the car until 8:00 p.m. When she does, her mother launches into a long lecture about consideration for others, but other than the annoying lecture, nothing else happens.

To many children and teens, acceptable behavior is defined by whatever the market will bear. What did the market bear for Gwenn? What did she learn about the importance of returning the car on time? Is it expected and required? Or is it optional? Gwenn knows what her mother prefers, but she also knows from experience that she doesn't have to follow that path. Do you think Gwenn and her mother are likely to go through this situation again?

Now, let's replay the scene to illustrate how Gwenn's mother might handle this situation more effectively. This time, when Gwenn arrives late with the car, her mother says, "The car is off limits for the rest of the week. When I say I need the car back by seven, that's what I mean." No lectures or drama or lengthy appeals for cooperation. The message is clear, and so is the path she's expected to stay on.

Limits Define Relationships

How do children know how much authority, power, and control they should have in their relationships with adults? Often they don't, but they do know how to find out. They just go ahead and do whatever they want and observe the outcome. They get their answers through their daily research with adults. They learn from experience what the market will bear, and in the process they discover where they stand with others.

The most important research takes place at home, the training ground for the real world. The lessons children learn from our limit-setting practices provide the answers to their most important questions: Who's really in charge here? How far can I go? What happens when I go too far? The data children collect helps them form conclusions about their power and control relative to adults. When children are given too much control, they often develop an inflated sense of their power and authority.

Collin, age nine, is a good example. When Collin arrives at the table in the morning, the first question his mother asks is, "What would you like for breakfast?"

"I want those skinny pancakes with the strawberries on them. Those are good!"

"Those are crepes," says his mother, "and they are good, but I don't have time to make them this morning. What else would you like? I can make waffles or pancakes."

"I don't want anything else," Collin insists with an irritated tone.

"How about eggs?" offers his mother.

"I'm eating crepes or nothing!" says Collin angrily.

"Come on, honey," pleads his mother. "It's important to eat a good breakfast."

"I'm only eating crepes!" Collin insists.

"Well, okay," says his mother reluctantly as she begins to prepare the crepe batter.

Who's really the kid here, and who's the parent? Who has most of the power, authority, and control in this relationship? Right. It's not Collin's mother. She tries her best to be respectful, but she gives away her power and authority to her nine-year-old son. By compromising her limits, she's actually teaching Collin that his needs come first, that he calls the shots, and that he can wear her down and win power struggles. Collin's mother is teaching a lesson that will set both of them up for a lot more testing, conflicts, and power struggles.

Now, let's contrast Collin's experience to that of another nine-year-old, Derek. When Derek arrives at the table in the morning, his mother informs him that she's serving eggs for breakfast. "How would you like them—poached, fried, or scrambled?" she asks. Derek's mother is clear about her limits and expectations. She's firm and respectful. She's the adult in charge. If Derek's mother takes this approach consistently, Derek won't need to do a lot of testing and power struggling to know where he stands.

Limits Are Yardsticks for Growth and Maturity

Ten-year-old Taylor would like to have the same 9:30 bedtime as her twelve-year-old sister. When Taylor approaches her parents with the plan, they discuss what she needs to do to demonstrate that she is ready to handle this new privilege. "You need to get up on time in the morning, do all of your chores, eat a good breakfast, and get out the door to catch the bus on time," says her father. "If you can handle all of that consistently, your new bedtime will be 9:30. If not, we'll remain with 9:00." The ground rules for earning the new privilege are clear. Her parents agree to try it out for a couple of weeks to see how things go.

Taylor demonstrates her readiness by handling her new bedtime just fine. She feels older and more responsible. She's proud of herself. The new limit becomes a reference point for her increasing maturity and readiness for new privileges.

Limits also can show parents what children are not ready to handle. For example, fifteen-year-old Sharon has complained for months that her curfew should be changed from 11:00 to 12:00 on weekends. "It's not fair!" argues Sharon. "All of my friends get to stay out until 12:30."

Sharon's parents are reluctant to revise her curfew for a good reason. Sharon rarely arrives home by 11:00 as agreed. She always has a good excuse, but she seldom calls or keeps them informed when it appears she might arrive late.

Sharon's parents aren't sure how to proceed. On the one hand, they want to encourage their daughter's independence, but they haven't seen the level of maturity or responsibility they need to feel comfortable that Sharon is ready for this new privilege. They decide to set it up as an experiment and test it out.

"We can try an 11:45 curfew and see how things go," says her father. "If anything comes up that might cause you to be late, we expect a call so together we can figure out what to do. Is that clear?" Sharon nods.

The next weekend, Sharon goes to a party with a group of friends but doesn't arrive home until 12:30. No calls to her parents. No warnings that she might be late. When Sharon returns home, she offers her best excuse. "My friends didn't want to leave," pleads Sharon. "I don't think it's fair that I should be penalized because of them."

The data speaks for itself. The conclusion is clear. Sharon is not ready to handle the responsibility of a later curfew at this point. "We're going to stick with the 11:00 curfew until the end of the semester," says her father. "If things go well, we can discuss a later curfew at another time. If things do not go well, we'll be revising your curfew to 10:30 to see if you can handle that."

Like many teens, Sharon believes she should have a later curfew based upon entitlement, that is, she should have that privilege because many of her friends do. Sharon is more than willing to use that pressure and leverage to get what she wants. But Sharon's parents recognize that the real issues are readiness, maturity, and responsibility, not entitlement. Sure, they feel the pressure Sharon wants them to feel, and they are reluctant to disappoint, but they also recognize that readiness must be earned and demonstrated. Readiness should not be based on entitlement.

Limits Provide Security

Chuck, age eight, leaves his collection of Legos spread out all over the dining room floor. "Are you finished playing with your Legos?"

asks his mother. Chuck nods. "Then it's time to pick them up," she says.

"I don't want to," says Chuck. "You pick them up."

"You made the mess," counters his mother. "You need to pick them up."

"I won't!" says Chuck defiantly. He sits down with his arms crossed.

"Come on, sweetheart," coaxes his mother. "Help me out, please, just this once."

"No way!" insists Chuck.

"I won't let you have any ice cream after dinner if you don't help," threatens his mother. Chuck starts to whine. His mother quickly retracts the threat. Ten minutes go by. Chuck still hasn't made a move to help out. His mother cleans up the mess for him.

"I shouldn't have to do your job," she complains as she puts his toys away.

Put yourself in Chuck's shoes for a moment. You're eight years old. You can't prepare your own meals. You can't manage your own weekly allowance without losing it, and some days, you can't make it through the afternoon without a nap, but when you tell your parents what to do, they do it. And if they ask you to do something you don't want to do, you fuss and complain, and they give in!

How do you think you would feel? Powerful? Yes. In control? Probably. Secure? Not likely. After all, these are the parents you're counting on to protect you and guide you in the right direction. It's unsettling to most children to realize they have more power and authority than their parents.

Children count on their parents to be "parents," that is, they need us to be firm and decisive in our limit setting. Their sense of security and stability depends on it. The act of respectful limit setting alone conveys a powerful set of signals for children: I'm your parent. I'm strong and capable. You can count on me to make decisions in your best interest and guide you in the right direction. These are the signals Chuck was searching for when he pushed hard against his mother's rules and authority.

Limits Must Be Adjusted as Children Grow

Would you set the same bedtime for a seven-year-old that you would for a twelve-year-old? Probably not. Would you set the same curfew for a ten-year-old that you would for a sixteen-year-old? Again, probably not. Still, readiness for new privileges varies from child to child.

As children grow and mature they become ready for increased freedom, privileges, and responsibility. Children need opportunities to explore their world, practice their skills, and develop competence and independence. That's their job, and our job is to provide them with limits that support, rather than hinder, this normal growth and maturation process.

How do we provide limits that support healthy development? We do so by adjusting and expanding those limits as children demonstrate readiness for increased freedom, privileges, and control. The limits we set should be firm enough to guide their exploration yet flexible enough to guide their growth and maturity.

Let's illustrate this principle with an example. For several years, Kira, age twelve, has been permitted to join her friends for an evening movie only when accompanied by an adult. Kira has always handled this privilege responsibly. She leaves and returns at the agreed-upon times and always calls to notify her parents if anything comes up that might affect her return time.

Kira's parents feel comfortable with the responsibility she has demonstrated. They trust her, and because they do, they agree to increase her freedom when she requests to go to a movie with her friends unaccompanied by an adult. They discuss transportation arrangements, agree on pick-up and drop-off times, and try it out. Everything goes well. Kira demonstrates her readiness. If she continues to do her part, she will likely enjoy many more of these opportunities.

As children grow and mature, they need limits that are broad enough to permit healthy testing and exploration, restrictive enough to provide security and teach responsibility, yet flexible enough to allow for growth and change. Sound like a balancing act? It is, and here's how to do it.

Set Up the Experiment and Test It Out

How do parents know when their children or teens are ready for more freedom and privileges? Often, they don't know, and neither do their children. They're both just feeling their way along. But there is a simple and easy way for parents to answer the question of readiness. Simply set it up as a research question and test it out. The child's behavior will answer any questions about readiness. Let's look at how Alan's mom uses this approach.

Alan, age seven, has two friends who live about four blocks from his home, but after school Alan is not permitted to play more than a block from his house. He feels he's ready for more freedom.

"I don't see why Bryan and Jake always have to come to my house after school," complains Alan. "I want to play at their homes too."

"I don't want to have to track you down at 5:00 when it's time for dinner," says his mom.

"I know how to tell time," says Allen, "and I have a bike so I can get home quickly. If you get me a watch, I'll be home on time."

His request seems reasonable, Alan's mom thinks to herself. Maybe he's ready for more responsibility. She agrees to buy him a watch and test out the new arrangement for a couple of weeks to see how things go.

Alan handles his new privilege just fine. He keeps his mom informed when he wants to play outside his immediate neighborhood and arrives home promptly for dinner. The research data is clear: Alan is ready for this privilege.

By testing Alan's readiness as a research experiment, Alan's mom was able to get the information she needed regarding his readiness. So can you when your children press you for increased freedom and privileges. Just set it up and test it out. This process will not let you down. The data you collect will answer the question.

Setting Limits with Words and Actions

You understand the process for determining readiness and adjusting limits as your children grow and mature. A clear limit-setting message has two component parts: your words—what you say—and your actions—what you do. As simple as this sounds, your message can easily break down when either part of the message is unclear or ineffective. Consider the following.

Two thirteen-year-olds, Matt and Thomas, climb the stairs to the top of a raised platform at an amusement park while their mothers watch from a lounge area. All goes well until Thomas decides to show off by jumping off the edge of the platform into a netting area below, narrowly missing several children on his way down. His mother intervenes.

"Thomas! What's wrong with you?" she shouts. "You could have injured those children. Can't you just climb up the platform like other normal children? Do you always have to be such a show-off?" She shakes her head in disgust. "If I see you do that again, I'm going to be really angry. Do you understand?" She shoots him a stern glare. Thomas returns to the play structure.

Did Thomas hear a clear message that jumping off the raised platform is not okay? No. Did he hear that he has to stop jumping off the platform? No. What did he hear? He hears that his behavior makes his mother angry. Does that require stopping? No. What is the worst thing that might happen if he does it again? His mother will become even angrier.

If you were a thirteen-year-old who really enjoys jumping off high structures, would this message deter you? Not likely. You might even be curious how many times you could jump before your mother actually did something to make you stop. The ineffective message sets Thomas and his mother up for testing and conflict.

Now, let's look at how Matt's mother handles the same situation when Matt decides to copy Thomas and jumps off the edge of the play structure into the netting area below. She approaches Matt in a calm manner and gives him a clear message.

"It's not okay to jump off the platform," she says matter-of-factly. "You'll have to get down and find something different to do. If you go up there again, our day at the park will be over. Is that clear?" Matt nods.

This is not a threat. Matt's mother is simply setting up a logical consequence, and she needs to be prepared to follow through if Matt decides to test, even if the consequence affects others. This is a safety issue. The logical consequence is certainly appropriate: play safe or don't play at all.

No shaming. No blaming. No shouting. No drama. The focus of Matt's mother's message is on the behavior—not on Matt's worth as a person. Her words are specific and direct. Her tone is matter-of-fact. She simply tells him what she wants him to do and what will happen if he doesn't.

Matt has all the information he needs to make an acceptable choice to cooperate. He may or may not, but either choice will lead to good learning if his mother follows through as stated. Her message sets up an effective lesson.

Clear with Your Words

ssage begins with your words, and most often that's where communication breaks down because parents say or do more than is needed. Anger, drama, and strong emotion can easily sabotage the clarity of your message and reduce the likelihood of cooperation. It's not only what you say that's important, it's how you say it. As Matt's mother shows us, the key to giving a clear message with your words is saying only what needs to be said in a clear, firm, and respectful manner. Here are some tips to help you get the most out of your messages.

KEEP THE FOCUS ON BEHAVIOR

The primary goal in guidance situations is to discourage unacceptable behavior, not the child performing the behavior. Therefore, parents should begin their message with the focus on the right thing—behavior. Messages that shame, blame, criticize, or humiliate are misdirected and disrespectful. They reject the child along with the misbehavior and obscure the clarity of the message.

For example, if you want your ten-year-old to stop shouting in the house, a clear message would be "Use an indoor voice, please," or "We don't shout in the house." It should not be "Why can't you be considerate?" or "How would you feel if I shouted and disturbed what you were doing?"

BE SPECIFIC AND DIRECT

A clear message should inform children, specifically and directly, what it is you want them to do. If necessary, tell them when and how to do it. The fewer words, the better. For example, if you want your twelve-year-old home for dinner by 6:30, your message should be "Be home for dinner by 6:30, please," rather than "Don't be too late," or "Try to get back on time, okay?" If you use either of these latter two messages, who decides what "too late," or "on time," or "okay?" means: you or your twelve-year-old? These messages are invitations for testing.

USE YOUR NORMAL VOICE

The tone of your voice is very important. A raised, irritated, or angry voice shifts the focus off behavior. This is an unnecessary invitation for a power struggle. Your tone should be respectful, but also convey that you are firm, in control, and resolute in your expectation that your child should do what he or she is asked to do. The best way to communicate this expectation is simply to state your message matter-of-factly in your normal voice.

Sound easy? It is for some parents but not for those who grew up in homes with lots of yelling, screaming, and drama. Over time, the feelings of frustration and anger become deeply ingrained habits and nearly automatic reactive responses. These old habits won't change overnight just because you're inspired to be more effective. You have to work at it. Managing anger and strong feelings is a skill you can learn, but like most new skills, the learning process requires time, patience, and lots of practice.

Do you tend to be a reactive parent who is quickly overwhelmed by emotion when your children misbehave? Join the club. Managing intense feelings and recovering self-control were not easy for me. When my youngest son, Ian, set off my triggers, I reacted almost instantaneously. My face would flush with anger. My voice would get loud and stern, and I'd be ready for battle. I needed a way to restore my composure before I said or did something I'd regret.

Patience is the remedy for overcoming the intense feelings we experience when we encounter misbehavior or resistance from our children. Patience provides us with an opportunity to respond thoughtfully, rather than simply react. Here's the best news: Patience is a skill that can be learned by nearly anyone and applied in challenging situations.

How do you do it? For me, patience usually began with the words "Pal, I'm feeling really angry, and I need a few minutes." Then I would remove myself from the situation, take some deep breaths, and wait for my anger to dissipate.

I found two strategies particularly helpful for restoring self-control. The first involved repeating a comforting phrase to myself to put the big picture back into focus. When I felt like exploding, I would repeat to myself, *I'm the adult. He's the kid. I can handle this.* This seemed to help. Other times, I found it helpful to separate the deed from the doer by saying to myself, *I love my son, but what he's doing is not okay.*

The recovery process gets easier with time. As my sons grew older, and I got more practice, I discovered I needed fewer cooldowns and only an occasional apology when I lost control. I realized that feeling composed was not a prerequisite for mastering the skill of patience. By the time Ian reached elementary school, I was able to start off in a more composed, matter-of-fact manner most of the time. But learning to be patient has always been "a work in progress." I appreciate what parents mean when they tell me they don't feel patient when they act patient. That's okay.

SPECIFY THE CONSEQUENCES FOR NONCOMPLIANCE

Remember, children are natural researchers. They want to know the bottom line or how far they can go when they decide to test your authority and resist your rules. When you ask them to stop misbehaving, many children are wondering, *Or what? What are you going to do if I don't?* Your message will be most effective if you answer their research questions in the beginning before they even decide to test. This is not a threat. You're just being clear. After all, your credibility hangs in the balance.

For example, if you ask your fourteen-year-old to turn down his music and you expect him to test, your message should be, "You need to turn the music down or we'll have to turn it off." Now this is a clear message. Your child knows what you want and what will happen if he decides to test. He has all the information he needs to make an acceptable choice. This doesn't mean he will, but either choice will lead to good learning as long you remain firm and follow through as you stated.

How to Be Clear with Your Actions: Set Logical Consequences

Many children need more than your words to be convinced that following your rules is required, not optional. They need to experience what you're telling them before they'll believe it. This doesn't mean your words are not important. It simply means that your words are only the first part of your total message.

Your child or teen may decide to test even your clearest message, and when this happens, the time for talking is over. It's time to act. Consequences are the second part of your limit-setting message. Consider the following:

Eleven-year-old Chuck takes pride in the fact that his friends refer to him as a master at video games. Unfortunately, Chuck is not a master at sharing, and when his friends come over to play video games, they frequently complain that Chuck won't take turns.

Initially, Chuck's parents decided not to intervene and let the boys work it out for themselves, but nothing improved. The parents agree a different approach is needed.

The next day, when Chuck and his friends are playing video games, the familiar chorus of complaints begins.

"You just had a turn!" protests one of Chuck's friends. "It's my turn now."

"No, it's not," insists Chuck. "It's my house, and I decide whose turn it is."

Chuck's father enters the room and says matter-of-factly, "Chuck, you can share the game and take one turn at a time, or we'll have to put the game away. What would you like to do?"

"Okay, I'll share," says Chuck, but less than fifteen minutes later, the complaints begin again. As Chuck's dad enters the room a second time, he sees his son clutching the controls and trying to persuade his friends that he won a bonus game by making it to the highest level.

"We're going to have to put the game away for now, guys," says Chuck's dad matter-of-factly. "We can try it again tomorrow."

Chuck's dad is using a logical consequence to teach his son a lesson about playing fair and sharing. The message is clear: play fair and share or don't play at all.

Let's say, for the sake of argument, that Chuck decides to protest his dad's consequence by throwing a full-blown, yelling-and-screaming tantrum in front of his friends. How should Chuck's dad handle this? He should hold firm in his resolve that the game is over, then calmly inform Chuck's friends that it's time for them to leave because Chuck needs time to get himself under control. The meltdown is just drama and not worth the attention or reprieve Chuck hopes to achieve.

When parents give in to tantrums, they usually encounter more frequent tantrums. Why? Because the tantrum worked. Chuck's dad held firm and didn't give in to the drama or embarrassment he may have felt over his son's behavior.

When it comes to teaching your rules and expectations, logical consequences are the gold standard. Logical consequences are arranged by the adult, experienced by the child, and logically related to the situation or misbehavior. Chuck's dad understands that consequences are most instructive when they are logically related to the behavior. Chuck temporarily lost his privilege of playing his video game because he chose not to abide by his parents' rule for sharing.

In effect, Chuck chose the consequence he experienced. No shaming. No blaming. No long, drawn-out, or unrelated consequences.

Logical consequences are not punishment; that is, they are not intended to hurt. Logical consequences are intended to teach lessons about acceptable and unacceptable behavior without relying on painful or aversive experiences to get the message across.

A punitive consequence or punishment, on the other hand, is designed to stop unacceptable behavior by applying an aversive or painful consequence, but the consequence is often unrelated to the misbehavior. Sure, you can stop most misbehavior in an immediate situation, but punitive consequences have many limitations. They hurt feelings. They are often personalized by the child as an attack upon their character, rather than an object lesson in how to behave acceptably, and they model hurtful methods of communication and problem solving.

Punitive thinking is not logical thinking. The parents' first reactive thoughts are something like this: What does he care about? I'll show him. I'll take it away. Or, I'll make him pay for his misbehavior. Now, let's replay the scene with Chuck and his friends, but this time, when Chuck's father arrives on the scene, he uses a punitive consequence.

"I knew I couldn't trust you to share the game without fighting with your friends!" Chuck's father shouts, when he sees Chuck clutching the controls and arguing with his friends. "You've lost all your TV and electronic game privileges for the next month and your bike and soccer privileges too. I'm tempted to ground you to the house."

What do Chuck's TV, bike, and soccer privileges have to do with not playing video games fairly with his friends? Nothing. How do you think Chuck is likely to feel about losing his favorite privileges and being humiliated in front of his friends? Angry? Resentful? You bet. Did Chuck learn a positive lesson about cooperating and sharing with his friends? Not likely.

Unlike punishment, logical consequences send clear action messages that children and teens really understand. These effective tools stop misbehavior, teach rules, and answer research questions that were not answered with words without injuring feelings or damaging relationships in the process. When children experience logical consequences, they know where they stand and what their parents expect.

Logical consequences are easy to use when you follow a few simple guidelines:

Use your normal voice. Logical consequences are most effective when carried out in a matter-of-fact manner with your normal voice. Anger, drama, or emotionally loaded messages shift the focus off the behavior and onto the child performing the behavior.

Think simple. Some parents have difficulty using logical consequences because they think too hard and get lost in all the details, or they don't think at all and fly by the seat of their pants. The appropriate logical consequence will usually become apparent when thought of in simple terms. Most incidents of misbehavior involve at least one of the following circumstances: children with other children, children with adults, children with objects, children with activities, or children with privileges. You can arrange a logical consequence by simply separating one child from another, such as a sibling or friend; a child from you; a child from an object, such as a toy; a child from an activity, such as a game; or a child from a privilege, such as TV or electronic games.

Follow through. Remember, the consequence is the second part of your limit-setting message. Your message won't be complete unless you follow through and do what you said you would do. Use these teaching tools as often as needed. If you need to use them repeatedly for the same misbehavior, don't assume the consequence is ineffective. More likely, your researcher has more learning to do and needs to experience your consistency to be convinced that you mean what you say.

Making the Consequence Fit the Crime

For the misuse of toys, play items, or possessions, the logical consequence is temporary loss of the item.

When Danny's mom walks into the backyard, she sees Danny hitting a sprinkler head with a baseball bat. "Danny, that's not how we use bats," she says matter-of-factly. "You can have it back tomorrow if you use it the right way." She takes the bat away.

If your kid has made a mess, the logical consequence is cleaning up the mess.

Tina, age thirteen, arrives home from school, eats a snack at the counter, leaves a mess, then announces, "I'm going to Carol's house." Her mom notices the mess.

"You need to clean up your mess before you go," says her mom.

"I'll do it later," says Tina. "I promise." Her mom holds firm.

"You won't be going anywhere until it's done," insists her mom. Tina rolls her eyes, lets out a big sigh, but reluctantly heads back to do the job.

In the example above, Tina decides to make an acceptable choice to cooperate when her mom holds firm, but let's add a new wrinkle to this scene. Let's say that Tina decides to defy her mom's request and walks out the door. How should her mom handle this?

This is still limit testing with a more dramatic flair. Tina simply wants to register her protest. She'll probably return after a few minutes, and when she does, her mom should hold firm without adding additional consequences. If Tina decides to carry out her protest to the fullest extent and doesn't return in a timely manner, Tina's mom should call Carol's house and ask Carol's parents to send Tina home.

Tina's dramatic protest is not intended for public consumption. The target audience is her mom. When Tina returns, her mom should hold firm and continue to hold Tina accountable.

For misbehavior during an activity, the logical consequence is to temporarily separate the child from the activity.

Jacob, age eight, sits with his family in the living room one evening watching a favorite family TV show when he decides to amuse his younger siblings by making disgusting bathroom sounds. His dad intervenes.

"Jacob, we make those sounds in the bathroom in private, not during TV shows in the living room. You need to head to the bathroom or your room until you're done," says his dad matter-of-factly.

"I'm done," says Jacob with a mischievous smile.

"Well, I'm setting the timer for five minutes to be sure," says his dad. "You're welcome back when the timer goes off." Reluctantly, Jacob heads to his bedroom.

Do you think Jacob deserves a second chance to cooperate rather than being sent directly to his room? Let's try to answer this question with a metaphor.

When we run red lights, do police officers routinely give us warnings or do they give us tickets? What's the message if Jacob's dad lets things go with a warning? Of course, it's okay to do it once. The first time is a freebie. Is that the message you want to send your child? If it is, brace yourself for more testing.

For misbehavior with others, the logical consequence is to temporarily separate the misbehaving child from others.

Tara, age ten, is upset with her younger brother and calls him a butthead. Her mom intervenes.

"Tara, it's not okay to call anyone that name," says her mom. "You need to spend the next ten minutes by yourself in your room." Tara heads to her room for a time-out.

In another example, five-year-old Dennis tries to wear his mom down by whining and fussing to avoid doing his weekend chores before playing. His mom holds firm.

"It's okay to fuss if that's what you want to do, but you're going to have to do it by yourself in your room," says his mom matter-of-factly. "I'm not going to listen to it." She sends Dennis to his room for a five-minute time-out.

For the misuse of privileges, the logical consequence is temporary loss or modification of that privilege.

Dale, age six, is permitted to use his father's expensive new computer only when his father is home to supervise. But Dale really wants to play a new computer game, and his father's computer has the biggest screen. Dale decides to take a chance and gets caught. His mother intervenes.

"Dale, you're not supposed to use your father's computer without his supervision," she says matter-of-factly. "You need to turn if off now. It won't be available for the rest of the day."

For destructive behavior, the logical consequence is to repair, replace, or pay for the item.

Sandra, age seventeen, borrows her mom's cashmere sweater without permission and accidently tears it. Her mom intervenes.

"Sandra, you know you're not allowed to use my clothing without permission, and now you've damaged an expensive sweater," says her concerned mom.

"I'm sorry, Mom," says Sandra, contritely. "I didn't think it would hurt anything. I won't do it again."

"Thank you," replies her mom. "But you're going to have to pay for the damaged sweater with your allowance money and more jobs around the house." Sandra will likely think twice before borrowing her mom's clothes without permission again.

Adjusting Logical Consequences for Teens

The basic guidelines for applying consequences for children in early and middle childhood also apply to teens with one exception: teens often require consequences of longer duration. Longer-term consequences make sense to teens and have instructive value.

Does this mean all of your logical consequences for teens should be longer? Certainly not. Briefer is generally better because it permits more time for training, but your consequences should be long enough to be instructive. How long is that? There are no guidelines here. You're going to have to make a lot of judgment calls, like Dean's dad in the following example.

Fifteen-year-old Dean knows he's not supposed to ride his father's dirt bike unless they go together on weekends. But Dean really wants to show his friend that he knows how to ride. His parents aren't home.

Nobody is going to know, Dean thinks to himself. What's a little spin around the block going to hurt? He tells his buddy to get on and off they go.

That evening, a neighbor comes over to borrow some olive oil. She talks to Dean's parent briefly and comments, "Dean must be really happy to finally get his license. He sure looked pleased riding off with his friend today." When she leaves, his dad calls Dean downstairs.

"Dean, what's the rule about using the dirt bike when I'm not home?"

"I know, Dad," says Dean, "but I didn't think a little trip around the block would hurt anything."

"I'm not worried that you would do anything reckless," says his dad, "but that bike is not meant for the street, and you're not licensed or insured. If anything happens, who would be responsible?"

"Yeah, I guess it wasn't such a good idea," Dean admits.

"I'm confident you'll think things through before anything like this happens again," says his dad. "The bike is off limits to you altogether for the next six weeks. May I have your key, please?"

Six weeks is a long time, but the consequence will certainly impress Dean with the seriousness of the rule he violated. Dean understands compliance is required, not optional.

Guidelines to Remember

Children want and need to understand the rules of their world. They want to know what's expected of them, who's really in control, how far they can go, and what happens when they go too far. They want to know where they stand with others, and they want to measure their increasing skills and capabilities as they grow. Limits provide this essential information and provide a context or path for healthy testing and exploration.

Limit setting is a dynamic process. It changes as children grow and mature. The challenge for parents is to continually adjust and expand their limit-setting practices to keep pace with their children's development and readiness for more freedom and control over their lives. To accomplish this balancing act, parents need to be firm in their limit setting but also willing to revise their limits as children mature. When your children or teens press you for increased freedom and privileges, just set up new limits as a research experiment and test them out. Their behavior will answer the question about their readiness. The process will not let you down. You know how to give a clear message with your words, and you know how to support your words with logical consequences when your children or teens decide to test. Use these tools as often as you need them; they're your ticket to cooperation and credibility, and your child's ticket to getting along in the real world.

raising resilient children and teens

BY KENNETH R. GINSBURG, MD, MSED, A PEDIATRICIAN SPECIALIZING
IN ADOLESCENT MEDICINE, A PROFESSOR OF PEDIATRICS, AND PARENT
OF TWO TEENAGE DAUGHTERS

*Lydia is a fourteen-year-old who has always been at the top of her class
and is quite talented on the soccer field as well. She comes home one day
beside herself, announcing to her mother that she has had "the worst day
EVER!!" She had a huge fight with her best friend, Sita, and she never
wants to speak to her again. She also got a C on her history report, which
was "totally unfair because I worked really hard on it, and now I'm not
going to be on honor roll, and Mr. Leroy is a terrible teacher who hates
kids." Should her mother call Sita's mother to get together for coffee and
brainstorm how to get the girls back together? Should she tell Lydia that
Sita was never good for her anyway and she should just move on? Should
she demand a conference with Mr. Leroy?*

*Rashan had a sleepover this weekend with about ten boys from his fourth-
grade class. He sleeps late on Sunday and remains too tired to complete his*

book report for Monday. His score drops a grade for every day the work is late. What should his father do?

Sixteen-year-old Ari stays out late one night and is brought home by the police because he was found in the park with a group of kids who were smoking marijuana. He has a court date and might receive a substantial fine and lose his driver's permit. What should his parents do?

Maya works so hard building her tower. Her father beams with pride as he watches his five-year-old daughter meticulously place each block. As she is building the final story, the tower falls into a pile of rubble. She runs over to her father with tears streaming down her cheeks and grabs onto his legs. She says that she really isn't very good at building things and asks him to build a really tall tower for her. What should he do?

Seventeen-year-old Ashleigh yells "bye" as she is running downstairs to be picked up by friends. Her parents look out the window and see that the kids in the backseat all have bottles of beer; one of them is pouring beer on the driver's head. He laughs, cocks his head back, and swallows the beer as it streams out of the bottle. What should her parents do?

Childhood and adolescence is the time to make, learn from, and recover from mistakes. In fact, if kids don't make their share of mistakes while under their parents' watchful eyes, they may be destined to make bigger ones later when left to their own devices. Our challenge as parents is to strike that balance between allowing our kids to learn the natural consequences of their actions and protecting them from circumstances that may cause irreparable harm or threaten their safety. For our children to be able to endure adversity and ultimately to thrive despite, and perhaps because of, challenges, we need to do more than protect them, we need to make them resilient.

Why Resilience Matters

Resilience is the capacity to rise above difficult circumstances, the trait that allows us to exist in this less-than-perfect world while moving forward with hope and confidence even in the midst of adversity. Resilience is what it takes to navigate life's bumps and bruises and to use them as opportunities for growth. If we want our children to experience the world as fully as possible—unfortunately with all its pain, and thankfully with all its joy—our goal is *resilience.*

Resilience is a mindset. Resilient people see challenges as opportunities. They do not seek problems, but understand that strength comes from facing them. Rather than engaging in self-doubt, catastrophic thinking, or a "Why me?" mindset of victimization, they seek solutions.

Resilience is uneven. A person might be highly resilient in one aspect of life and need much higher levels of support in another. Resilience is not invulnerability, not isolation from all risk. In fact, if we accept that compassion and empathy are desired traits, we need to consider how these essential characteristics are earned: it is often through our personal pain.

Finally, resilience is not a trait of "perfect" people. Perfectionists fear making mistakes. They perform well but don't take chances to perform at their very best. Resilient people are more successful because they push their limits and learn from their mistakes. Resilience may be a core factor in determining not only who will adapt, but also who will succeed.

Teaching Kids to Be Resilient

Resilience is not an inborn temperament trait. It is affected by the circumstances of a child's life and the supports that surround her through good and bad times. Research repeatedly finds that a supportive, nurturing connection with an adult is the key ingredient that determines how children fare through adversity.

This makes our parental role as resilience builders of pivotal importance. The good news is that what we must do to foster our children's resilience is not so complicated; it is about loving our children while simultaneously caring for ourselves. Three recurrent themes seem to be at the core of how adults affect children's resilience:

Unconditional love is the bedrock of resilience because it creates security;

Children live up or down to adult expectations, for better or worse;

And children watch what we do more than they listen to what we say.

Unconditional Love Is Key to Building Resilience

I am the last child and adolescent advocate you would expect to agree to write for a body of work called *toughLOVE*. I am emphatically in favor of unconditional love. If I thought this book was about tough parenting—"My way or the highway," "You'll do as I say. Why? Because I said so!" "Nobody in this house comes home with a B+"—I would have declined participation. But what it's about is balanced parenting; parenting that is loving and responsive and promotes the kind of monitoring that keeps kids safe.

Unconditional love gives children the deep-seated security that allows them to take chances when they need to adapt to new circumstances and the knowledge that they are safe. Unconditional love doesn't mean unconditional approval. Parents can reject certain behaviors and simultaneously love the child fully. The key is that love is never withdrawn or threatened to be withheld based on a behavior.

It is about your child knowing that you are not going anywhere, no matter what. It is about them knowing that we love them for who they are, not for how they perform or whether we will be proud of the bumper stickers we can place on our cars. There is nothing more powerful than comforting a child with a hug accompanied by the simple words, "I love you." Not "I love you because . . ." or "I love you when . . . ," just "I love you." Sometimes words aren't even necessary. Our undivided presence offers security like none other.

Kids Live Up—or Down—to Our Expectations

Our children live up or down to our expectations. If we expect the best, they tend to live up to our standards. High standards matter, but let me be clear: By high standards, I am not referring to academic or athletic achievements. I am speaking of being a good person—considerate, respectful, honest, fair, generous, responsible . . . those qualities you care most about. On the other hand, when parents expect children to be lazy, argumentative, thoughtless, selfish, or dependent, kids sense it. "Why," they figure, "should I try to be any different? I guess I'm stupid, troubled, mindless, or whatever." And "I have nothing to lose. My parents already think I'm [fill in an adjective], so why shouldn't I just [fill in an action]?"

Further, we must never forget that our children's job is to get all of the resources—time, love, attention—they can get from us. In short, they will do what they learn gets attention. When your child was two, you learned quickly how to elicit good behavior: "catch them being good, redirect them when they are not." The same essential principle applies throughout childhood and during adolescence. The problem is that we tend to increasingly focus on what our kids are doing wrong as our time with them becomes more limited. This peaks during adolescence when our children's academic and social lives and our own increasingly busy schedules give us less time with them. We must treat that time as even more precious, focusing on how to help our kids navigate their world, rather than on bad grades or misbehaviors.

Young people also absorb messages from outside the family and adjust their behavior to meet those expectations. Think about how small children become even more adorable when passersby notice their antics. In sharp contrast, our adolescents notice how others expect them to be moody, impulsive, or irresponsible. The pervasive low expectations of our teens can harm their self-images and drive them toward behaviors they learn are "normal." After all, one of the fundamental questions of adolescence is "Am I normal?" They hunt for clues of what "normal" is and then mimic those images. Sometimes these messages support the positive image that we want our children to have. Other times, we must shield our children from harmful, even toxic, portrayals of youth and the low expectations such portrayals convey.

Children Do as We Do, Not as We Say

As children's most powerful models, parents are in the best position to teach them about stress and resilience. Whether they're toddlers or teens, children observe us closely. If we show them negative ways of coping with our own stress, they will follow our example. If we scream at the driver who cuts us off in traffic, our kids will assume road rage is acceptable. If we drink after work each evening to relax, we're sending the message that alcohol is an acceptable stress reliever. On the other hand, if we go for a run, soak in a bath, or talk over dinner as we process our day, they learn healthy stress management. Our children want healthy parents. More than that, they learn from us what it means to be—or not to be—emotionally, physically, and spiritually healthy and balanced. Truly, the greatest gift we can give our children is to model what healthy thirty-five-, forty-, and fifty-year-olds look like.

Building Resilience: The Seven Cs

Rick Little, Richard Lerner, and their colleagues at the International Youth Foundation have given us five Cs of confidence, competence, connection, character, and contribution as the key ingredients needed to ensure what they call Positive Youth Development. The resilience movement is tightly linked to and largely overlaps the positive youth development philosophy, but it also focuses on the importance of recovery from and overcoming adversity. So, to those five Cs I add coping and control.

To build resilience in children, we need to consider, then, these seven integral, interrelated components: competence, confidence, connection, character, contribution, coping, and control. Ask yourselves the questions following each of the Cs early and often and you will be building resilience in your kids and putting yourself on the path to creating competent, confident, connected adults who are in control of themselves, cope well with adversity, contribute to society, and demonstrate true character.

COMPETENCE

Competence is the ability or know-how to handle situations effectively. It's not a vague feeling or hunch that "I can do this." It is gained through actual experience. Children can't become competent without first developing a set of skills that allows them to trust their judgment, make responsible choices, and face difficult situations. In thinking about your child's competence and how to fortify it, ask yourself:

- Do I help my child focus on his strengths and build on them?
- Do I notice what she does well, or do I focus on her mistakes?
- When I need to point out a mistake, am I clear and focused or do I communicate that I believe he always messes up?
- Do I help him recognize what he has going for himself?
- Do I communicate in a way that empowers my child to make her own decisions, or do I undermine her sense of competence by giving her information in ways she can't grasp? In other words, do I lecture her, or do I facilitate her thinking?
- Do I trust him as the expert in his own life?
- Do I let her make safe mistakes so she has the opportunity to right herself, or do I try to protect her from every trip and fall?
- As I try to protect him, does my interference mistakenly send the message "I don't think you can handle this"?
- Do I recognize the competencies of each child without comparison to siblings? To neighbors? To classmates?

CONFIDENCE

True confidence, the solid belief in one's own abilities, is rooted in competence. Children gain confidence by demonstrating their competence in real situations. Confidence is not built by falsely elevating self-esteem. Telling each kid that he or she is as special as a butterfly or unique as a snowflake only leaves them unprepared for those moments they feel less than special. Children who experience their own competence and know they are safe and protected develop a deep-seated security that gives them the confidence to face and cope with challenges. When parents support children in finding their own islands of competence and building on them, they prepare kids to gain enough confidence to try new ventures and to trust their abilities to make sound choices. In thinking about your child's degree of confidence, consider the following questions:

- Do I see the best in my child so that she can see the best in herself?
- Do I clearly express that I expect the best qualities (not achievements, but personal qualities such as fairness, integrity, persistence, and kindness) in him?
- Do I help her recognize what she has done right or well?
- Do I treat him as an incapable child or respect him as a young person learning to navigate his world?
- Do I praise her often enough? Do I praise her honestly about specific achievements, or do I give such diffuse praise that it doesn't seem authentic and might in fact undermine her performance and drive her toward perfectionism?
- Do I catch him being good when he is generous, helpful, and kind or when he does something without being asked or prodded?
- Do I encourage her to strive just a little bit further because I believe she can succeed? Do I hold realistically high expectations?
- Do I unintentionally push him to take on more than he can realistically handle, causing him to stumble and lose confidence?
- When I need to criticize or correct her, do I focus only on what she's doing wrong, or do I remind her that she is capable of doing well?
- Do I avoid instilling shame in my child?

CONNECTION

Children with close ties to family, friends, school, and community are more likely to have a solid sense of security that produces strong values and prevents them from seeking destructive alternatives. Family is the central force in any child's life, but connections to civic, educational, religious, and athletic groups can also increase a young person's sense of belonging to a wider world and being safe within it. Some questions to ponder when considering how connected your child is to family and the broader world include:

- Do we build a sense of physical safety and emotional security within our home?
- Does my child know that I am absolutely crazy in love with him?
- Do I understand that the challenges my child will put me through on her path toward independence are normal developmental phases, or will I take them so personally that our relationship will be harmed?
- Do I allow my child to have and express all types of emotions, or do I suppress unpleasant feelings? Is he learning that going to other people for emotional support during difficult times is productive or shameful?
- Do we do everything to address conflict within our family and work to resolve problems rather than let them fester?
- Do we have a television and entertainment center in almost every room, or do we create a common space where our family shares time together?
- Do we create family time, when we can listen to and support each other? Dinner, perhaps, but it could just as easily be breakfast or every Sunday or just before bed.
- Do I encourage my child to take pride in the various ethnic, religious, or cultural groups to which we belong?

- Do I jealously guard my child from developing close relationships with others, or do I foster healthy relationships that I know will reinforce my positive messages?
- Do I protect my friends' and neighbors' children, just as I hope they will protect mine?

CHARACTER

Children need a fundamental sense of right and wrong to ensure they are prepared to make wise choices, contribute to the world, and become stable adults. Children with character enjoy a strong sense of self-worth and confidence. They are more comfortable sticking to their own values and demonstrating a caring attitude toward others. Children with tenacity, or grit, who can delay gratification, will ultimately be more successful. Some basic questions to ask yourself include:

- Do I help my child understand how his behaviors affect other people in good and bad ways?
- Am I helping my child recognize herself as a caring person?
- Do I allow him to clarify his own values?
- Do I allow her to consider right versus wrong and look beyond immediate satisfaction or selfish needs?
- Do I value him so clearly that I model the importance of caring for others?
- Do I demonstrate the importance of community?
- Do I help her develop a sense of spirituality?
- Am I careful to avoid racist, ethnic, or hateful statements or stereotypes? Am I clear how I regard these thoughts and statements whenever and wherever my child is exposed to them?
- Do I express how I think of others' needs when I make decisions or take actions?

CONTRIBUTION

It is a powerful lesson when children realize that the world is a better place *because they are in it.* Children who understand the importance of personal contribution gain a sense of purpose that can motivate them. They will not only take actions and make choices that improve the world, but they will also enhance their own competence, character, and sense of connection. Next, teens who contribute to their communities will be surrounded by reinforcing thank-yous instead of the low expectations and condemnation so many teens endure. Finally, we must grasp that the ultimate act of resilience is to reach out to another human being and ask for support. What enables someone to be able to reach for help without shame or stigma? In part, it is the experience of giving service. When one serves, one learns how good it feels. One learns that they do so not out of pity, but for pleasure and a sense of purpose. At some point, everyone will need to receive support. You want your child to be able to receive without feeling as though he or she is being pitied. Giving prepares one to be able to take. To foster this sense of contribution, here are some things to consider:

- Do I communicate to my child (at appropriate age levels, of course) that many people in the world do not have as much human contact, money, freedom, and security as they need?
- Do I teach the important value of serving others? Do I model generosity with my time and money?
- Do I make clear to my child that I believe she can improve the world?
- Do I create opportunities for each child to contribute in some specific way?
- Do I search my child's circle for other adults who might serve as role models who contribute to their communities and the world? Do I use these adults as examples to encourage my child to be the best he can be?

COPING

Children who learn to cope effectively with stress are better prepared to overcome life's challenges. The best protection against unsafe, worrisome behaviors may be a wide repertoire of positive, adaptive coping strategies. As we teach children this repertoire of coping and stress-reduction skills, here are some basic questions to ask ourselves:

- Do I help her understand the difference between a real crisis and something that just feels like an emergency?
- Do I model positive coping strategies on a consistent basis?
- Do I allow my child enough time to use imaginative play? Do I recognize that fantasy and play are childhood's tools to solve problems?
- Do I guide my child to develop positive, effective coping strategies?
- Do I believe that telling him to "just stop" negative behaviors will do any good?
- Do I recognize that for many young people, risk behaviors are attempts to alleviate their stress and pain?
- If my child participates in negative behaviors, do I condemn her for it? Do I recognize that I may only increase her sense of shame and therefore drive her toward more negativity?
- Do I model problem solving step by step, or do I just react emotionally when I'm overwhelmed?
- Do I model the response that sometimes the best thing to do is conserve energy and let go of the belief that I can tackle all problems?
- Do I model the importance of caring for our bodies through exercise, good nutrition, and adequate sleep? Do I model relaxation techniques?

- Do I encourage creative expression?
- As I struggle to compose myself so I can make fair, wise decisions under pressure, do I model how I take control rather than respond impulsively or rashly to stressful situations?
- Do I create a family environment in which talking, listening, and sharing is safe, comfortable, and productive?

CONTROL

When children realize that *they* can control the outcomes of their decisions and actions, they're more likely to know that they have the ability to do what it takes to bounce back. On the other hand, if parents make all the decisions, children are denied opportunities to learn control. A child who feels "everything always happens to me" tends to become passive, pessimistic, or even depressed. He sees control as external—whatever he does really doesn't matter because he has no control of the outcome. But a resilient child knows that he has internal control. By his choices and actions, he determines the results. He knows that he can make a difference, which further promotes his competence and confidence. Some questions about control:

- Do I help my child understand that life's events are not purely random and most things happen as a direct result of someone's actions and choices?
- On the other hand, do I help my child understand that he isn't responsible for many of the bad circumstances in his life (such as parents' separation or divorce)?
- Do I help him think about the future, but take it one step at a time?
- Do I help him recognize even his small successes so he can experience the knowledge that he can succeed?
- Do I help him understand that no one can control all

circumstances, but everyone can shift the odds by choosing positive or protective behaviors?

- Do I understand that discipline is about teaching, not punishing or controlling? Do I use discipline as a means to help my child understand that his actions produce certain consequences?
- Do I reward demonstrated responsibility with increased privileges?

A Web of Seven Cs

The seven Cs are intricately interwoven. Children need to experience *competence* to gain *confidence*. They need *connections* with an adult to reinforce those points of *competence*. They need *character* to know what they should *contribute* to their families and the world, and *character* is forged through deep *connection* to others. *Contribution* builds *character* and further strengthens *connections*. Children who *contribute* to their communities gain *confidence* as they feel more and more *competent*. All of this leads them to recognize that they can make a difference and change their environments, and this gives them a heightened sense of *control*. Children with a sense of *control* believe in their ability to solve problems so they will more tenaciously attack a problem until they find a solution. This newfound area of *competence* then enhances their *confidence*, which will be used the next time they need to reinforce their beliefs in their ability to *control* their environment. When children know they can *control* their environment, they will more likely use healthy *coping* strategies because the need to deaden the senses or escape reality will be lessened. A key *coping* strategy is turning to people with whom you have strong *connections*. And so on.

So What Should Lydia, Rashan, Ari, Maya, and Ashleigh's Parents Do?

I've been asking you to consider questions, rather than giving you cut-and-dried solutions, because parents are the greatest experts on their children's lives—only they know how to achieve the right balance of support their children need at any moment. There is a real danger to any "expert" being definitive with advice. That makes parenting look too easy, and leaves parents who have to navigate the real world feeling incapable. Sometimes our kids need more support than at other moments, and the art of parenting is striking that balance.

As you consider when to dive in to protect your children, when to gently help them find their own solutions, and when to get out of the way and allow them to learn the consequences of their actions, ask yourself three questions (yes, more questions!).

First, "Does my child need a little extra support right now so she will be more confident moving forward?" If so, give support in the form of gentle guidance, allowing her to still navigate the waters; that way she will own the solution and the lesson will more likely be long-standing.

Next, ask yourself, "Do I so relish the feeling of being needed that I may be choosing to jump in because it makes me feel good myself or because I believe my child's appreciation will draw him closer to me?" If your reflection makes you understand that your intervention is driven to fill your own needs, then remind yourself that children remain closer over the long term with parents who have supported their independence and growth.

Finally, ask yourself, "Is this an issue of safety or morality?" If the answer is yes, your child is depending on you to create appropriate boundaries and you need to do that—immediately and firmly.

Every time we try to solve children's problems for them, we

undercut their growing sense of competence. If we solve all their problems, they will remain dependent on us, and while it may be an attractive prospect to have our children always need us, we know that our job is to create independent, capable individuals. When we support a child's problem-solving skills by getting out of his way or by offering gentle guidance only when necessary or when requested, we foster his growing sense of self-reliance, independence, and resilience. We need to let children fail so they can fully understand the natural consequences of their decisions and so they can learn how to recover. However, when a subject involves safety—well, we do not let them put their hands on the stove.

Lydia's mother should use this opportunity to help her consider how she might have written a clearer report, and to take advantage of the opportunity to learn why Mr. Leroy did not think her work met her usual standard. If, in fact, Lydia believes Mr. Leroy has been unfair, this is a wonderful opportunity to learn self-advocacy skills. Regarding her fight with Sita, her mother should stand back! She'll work it out herself and learn a lot about relationships in the process. She'll probably be best friends with Sita again next week. If her mother criticized Sita too strongly in an effort to empathize with her daughter, she'd never hear about their friendship (or maybe others) again and therefore have lost a real opportunity to stay connected with her daughter.

Rashan has a wonderful opportunity as a fourth grader to learn about the consequences of poor planning and the importance of sleep to productivity. A lower grade will help the lesson to sink in. His father might help his fourth-grade son learn to plan ahead and to develop his time management skills. He shouldn't condemn the sleepover, that wasn't the problem. Kids should learn that fun is an important part of life! In fact, fun, is, well, more fun when work is no longer on your mind.

Ari's parents should be thankful for the opportunity for him to learn a life lesson before a tragedy might occur. Critically, they need to consider whether Ari has a real drug problem or whether this was experimentation. They should ask an objective professional to help them sort this through. Then they need to allow Ari to learn the consequences of his actions.

Maya's father should console her and enjoy one of those irreplaceable parenting moments when we help our children work through their frustration. Then, he should encourage her to get back to the drawing board because he knows that she can build a wonderful tower. If he builds it for her, he'll only send the message loudly and clearly, "You're so right, you are not capable of doing this."

There is no nuanced discussion to be had about how Ashleigh's parents should manage the situation. Impaired driving is a matter of safety and morality, even of life and death. Ashleigh's parents need to lock the door.

Portions of this chapter are excerpted and adapted, with permission, from Kenneth R. Ginsburg and M. M. Jablow, *Building Resilience in Children and Teens: Giving Kids Roots and Wings* (Elks Grove Village, IL: American Academy of Pediatrics, 2011).

parenting the new millennium teen

BY MICHAEL BRADLEY, EDD, A PRACTICING PSYCHOLOGIST,
BESTSELLING AUTHOR, AND DAD OF TWO

If looks could kill, I thought when I first saw Brian twelve years ago, then we're about to have a drive-by. At the grizzled old age of fourteen his face was rippling with rage, his eyes peering through gunfighter slits. Mom sat too close on his one side, her trembling hand extended in space, frozen halfway toward touching him, while she softly and repeatedly whispered, "Please be nice, Brian, please..." Mom was sinking in the quicksand of appeasement. On Brian's other side, as far away as the couch would allow, Dad gazed out the window with the empty "thousand-yard stare" of exhausted war veterans. Like them, he had been astonished to learn that his once-omnipotent anger and rage were outgunned when engaged with someone who suddenly seemed happy to get even crazier than he. Dad had been disarmed and was now lost in a desert of detachment. I lobbed Brian an easy home-run pitch: "So," I asked, "what brings you here?" He smacked it out of the park: "A minivan," he sneered, "and two psychos."

I immediately liked Brian. Of course, that's very easy to do when the infuriating teen is not your own, but he was straight up about his feelings. Or at least about what his feelings were in that moment. He was a poster boy for the emotional dilemma of most teens, who actually love *and* hate their parents almost simultaneously. I felt sorry for his parents, the "two psychos," who were grieving the loss of their once sweet, compliant boy, reeling from his bewildering transformation into this snarling mass of anger. Mom and Dad were also spot-on representations of new millennium parents, who so often feel confused, incompetent, and just so terribly sad. Their confusion arises from being unable to assimilate two very different adolescent worlds: the one they recall experiencing as teens and this new scary one that seems to be kidnapping their children. The feeling of incompetence results from using outdated parenting strategies, tactics we watched our parents employ. These once were effective, but now they only blow up with our own kids. In military parlance, we are trying to fight this new parenting war with the lessons from the last. That trick never works.

What *does* work is to gather the "intelligence" (knowledge) and "tactics" (strategies) you will need not only to survive your kid's teen years, but to use them to prepare her for a successful launch into adulthood. The "intel" you need for your mission includes two parts. First, I'll help you to understand your child's neurologically challenged teen brain, a bubbling ball of gray matter undergoing profound changes that dramatically affect its owner. This "jump-to-adulthood" rewiring can explain many of his new behaviors (including punching those holes through your walls). Second, we'll look at the sanity-challenging culture surrounding your teen, an unprecedented one that pummels him 24-7 with powerful suggestions to do things that will hurt him. Finally, I'll give you some strategies to overcome those neurological and cultural challenges that will allow you not just to survive these years as a loving family, but also to equip your child with assets to keep her safe, productive, and happy for when you are no longer in charge of her. But first take a deep breath, close your eyes, and envision the time of cosmic payback when your teenage grandchildren will be making your child crazy all over again.

The New Millennium Teen Brain
(Yes, there is a brain in there; no, it is
not the one you had hoped for.)

Just before the dawn of our new millennium Jay Giedd of the National Institutes of Health announced some stunning research. He showed that teenage brains are very much works in progress, with chaos-causing rewiring in brain regions that manage capabilities, such as rational judgment, emotional processing, and impulse control. This neurological process very much mimics the experience of renovating your house: it is heaven when done, but it is hell getting there. These findings stunned mostly everyone except, of course, parents and teachers of teenagers. I recall one of Jay's "teens are impulsive and judgment-impaired" conferences being keynoted by none other than President William Jefferson Clinton. I later would come to see that event as proving not only that God exists, but that she has a terrific sense of irony. That conference kicked off years of debate and research concerning whether those brain differences were really so significant, and if they could explain the angst recorded over time immemorial concerning the bewildering behaviors of adolescents.

The science that followed has expanded upon the view of teenagers as being, well—a little *crazy*. Years ago when I used that term to title my first book (*Yes, Your Teen Is Crazy!*), a professional ruckus erupted with anger directed at folks such as me for disrespecting and denigrating teens, and not treating them as the young adults our culture largely sees them to be. Yet, as any middle school teacher will tell you, teens are much better defined as *large children* than as *small adults*. I offer this as a view not to disrespect them, but to save them—from us and from themselves.

The saving-from-us part refers to how the science can help us parents to not take teens' difficult behaviors so painfully personally and then angrily react as if they're doing these things to wound us. Four areas of recent adolescent brain research have helped me stay much calmer during my own personal and professional teen wars. They explain how much of what upsets us about our teens is actually quite normal and, thankfully, a temporary challenge that heals with time.

The first area of research explains the improbably large number of guilt- and empathy-free teen "psychopaths" who are dragged into my office by their frightened parents. Researchers at the University College London Institute of Cognitive Neuroscience found that young teens have "conscience wiring" issues, and are unable to employ adult levels of empathy and guilt in decision making. These are critical abilities that help us adults not to be so hurtful. Their research showed that the thought process behind teen decision making tends to stay more in the self-centered brain regions during times when adults exhibit more widespread use of their brain's wiring. As those researchers summarized: "We think that a teenager's judgment of what they would do in a given situation is driven by the simple question 'What would *I* do?' Adults, on the other hand, ask, 'What would I do, given how I would feel and given *how the people around me would feel as a result of my actions?*'" (emphasis added). While some empathy and guilt can be found in five-year-olds (and often goes AWOL in fifty-year-olds) those and many other hallmarks of humanity don't fully mature until the teen brain stops renovating, which the brain scans now say is (are you sitting down?) at age twenty-five. So chill on the "she's a psychopath" thing. She'll get there, and she'll get there more quickly if you don't make things worse by yelling about something she can't easily fix right now.

A second informative and therefore calming finding is what I call the "stroke" phenomenon of young teens, wherein they temporarily lose skills they previously held, another result of that teen brain rewiring. Another University College London project found that young teens experience a decrement in their ability to process emotions, such as recognizing and distinguishing facial and verbal emotional signs in others, particularly those of anger and sadness. Other research expands on this, finding that young teens can experience parental expressions of fear and concern as *judgment* and *criticism*, causing them to seem about as stable as a jar of nitroglycerin. When you've been amazingly calm in explaining how concerned and afraid you were for your teen's terrible decision, did the shriek of "STOP YELLING AT ME" ever ring in your ears? Our kids typically recover from these "strokes" by sixteen, but those first few teen years can be maddening.

My third choice of "Ah ha! Now I get it" teen research looks at the explosion in adolescent ADHD diagnoses ("Okay, kiddies. Which one of you *doesn't* have ADHD?"). Many studies now have us worrying about the ADHD-like impact of the tech-driven hyperstimulation of vulnerable young brains by electronics, such as computers, video games, and smartphones (ironic name, no?). In one example, researchers at the University of Pittsburgh found that most younger teens are really, *really* lousy at staying on task in the face of a distraction such as a flashing light in the corner of a computer screen (maybe a text is waiting?). When compared with adults, teens tended to make much less use of brain regions that monitor personal performance, organize task strategies, and keep us focused on an assignment. The good news is that kids get much better at these things as they age out a tad (fifteen to twenty). The better news is that when promised significant performance rewards (a bribe they really want), they improve remarkably, to the point where at twenty years old they can almost match full adult levels of task discipline (remember that "significant rewards" part for later on). These findings align well with anecdotal evidence of the huge number of smart kids who drift through high school on a sea of mediocrity only to fire up in community college and then take off from there like academic rockets.

The final new research area that helps with my personal and professional parenting work looks at whether you should blame your teen's gangster friends for all of his issues, that notorious "peer pressure" thing where peers take your angelic altar boy and pressure him into dealing heroin. While most researchers hold that the friends don't make the teen but that the teen seeks the good or bad friends he wants, the buddies *can* take the fall for making him take more risks. Folks at Temple University found that when left alone with a computerized driving game, teens handled driving risks pretty much as did adults, proving that they do have the wiring to properly understand risks and avoid being dangerously stupid. However, unlike adults, when the teen's friends came into the room, they suddenly morphed into Evel Knievels, stomping on the gas pedal at red lights and blowing away the speed limits. This suggests that adolescent risk-taking rises not so much from faulty thinking but *from a greater need for reward*, the payoff in this instance being peer admiration for acting "cool" (or crazy). "They didn't take more chances because they suddenly downgraded the risk," the researchers reported. "They did so because they gave more weight to the payoff." Interestingly, this data lines up perfectly with the statistics showing how crash risks for sixteen-year-old drivers increase *exponentially* with each additional passenger in the car. Again, hold that "payoff/reward" thought for when I tell you later on how to turn this reward need back on your kid to keep him safe.

If you've had your brain-sharpening coffee before reading this, you likely are thinking, "Wait a minute. Maybe we weren't watching brain scans light up centuries ago, but adolescent brain neurology has probably been the same since at least the dawn of history, so are teens really crazier now?" The answer is no—and yes. The no answer can be found in ancient Greek writing, where an apparently very annoyed parent named Hesiod (eighth century BC) describes teens essentially as being crazy, exhibiting bewildering teen behaviors thousands of years ago. Those exact behaviors exploded in my kitchen this morning. But the "Yes, today's teens are crazier" answer refers to sharp increases in certain risk behaviors inspired by the brave new world we've set up around our kids. When it comes to evil forces in our kids' world, you could say that we've given nuclear weapons to terrorists.

The New Millennium Teen World ("And now for something *really* crazy . . .")

When parents of adolescents seek help they often are worried about teen risk behaviors, typically the dangers of sex, drugs, and violence. While some surveys claim that some risk numbers may have recently leveled off or even declined after soaring in past decades, a closer look at the data shows two other contemporary trends that make the high numbers of kids doing these scary things even scarier. The first trend is the increased *concentration* or *frequency* of the behavior. The second is the *younger ages* at which they start. These are both largely the results of the incessant tech-delivered presentation of risk behaviors as being "cool," powerful electronic suggestions that can push vulnerable, reward-starved teen brains to seek payoffs from doing things *that they already know can hurt them*. Think electronics, and you'll see the weapons or delivery systems. Think contemporary lyrics, videos, and messaging, and you'll see the ammo in the delivery systems. Together these produce a 24-7 electronic barrage of cultural prompts ("ads") to do bad things, a huge change from what there was in your day. One colleague defines his daughter's iPod as her Intracranial Provocation Device, since she's begun to act out so much of what he knows she hears from it. His fears are borne out by research showing that what kids see and hear does have profound effects on their behaviors, even when we account for other causal factors. For example, one study found that teens who saw lots of screen images of cigarette smoking had a *threefold* increase in smoking over those who saw only a few. Another study showed a spike in early-onset, high-risk sexual behavior in girls who listened to lots of sexually explicit and misogynistic lyrics ("[use] her, beat her, throw her in the trunk...").

So can the interaction of challenged teen brains and their (our) crazy culture hurt them? A few numbers about adolescent risk taking (of, sadly, *many* I can offer) make the point in a very parent-worrisome way.

First, in the world of teen sex, one researcher found that during a time in which teens reported having less sex, at least every fourth high school girl in America harbored a sexually transmitted disease, a 30 percent increase over five years. Incidentally, this conflicting research finding (one of many) has us worrying that our old data-collection system (self-reporting) provides significant underestimates of these behaviors. Pornography has recently evolved from a harmless curiosity about sex to becoming a bizarre "drug" for teenagers, with potentially addictionlike consequences. A healthy twenty-three-year-old recently wept in my office because he couldn't make love to the girl he passionately loves since his "old, weird porn" always takes over his thoughts. I'll spare you the details of his Internet-provided, love-blocking videos, but trust me when I say that today's porn has zero to do with lovemaking and much to do with degradation, misogyny, perversion, and pain. We now are seeing higher numbers of young folks addicted to strange (and sometimes debilitating) sexual fetishes to which they were Internet-exposed as young children, a neurologically fragile time when bizarre sexual images can "imprint" upon young brains with dramatic power. And if you think I'm only talking about the males, females now make up perhaps 25 percent of porn addicts, a number that rises every year. This is very new, and very contrary to the way we thought women were hardwired. Check out the *Report of the American Psychological Association Task Force on the Sexualization of Girls* (www.apa.org/pi /wpo/sexualization.html) and you'll see from where this stuff is coming. Clue: As Walt Kelly's cartoon character Pogo once said, "I have met the enemy and he is us."

Drugs raise another frightening example of how teen brains and culture mix as safely as driving and Dewar's. Booze has washed over new millennium adolescents like a 150-proof tsunami. And yes, alcohol is not only *a* drug, it is *the* drug, as in the most deadly for teens. Researchers at the University of Florida make the convincing case that *alcohol* is the true teen gateway drug, leading to all of the others. Other researchers pose the disquieting notion that every tenth student walking your high school's hallway has a serious problem with alcohol. Thirty percent of our children admit to (brag about?) binge drinking in the past thirty days.

Marijuana (you know, that nonaddictive, nondamaging drug?) has now been shown to not only be very addictive for teens, but also to cause apparently permanent and substantial decreases in IQ and specific cognitive capabilities. One researcher found that adults who started smoking heavily as teens kept repeating the same mistakes on tests, unable to self-correct. Cheech and Chong were very funny— and tragically prescient. These weed findings set off alarm bells when viewed with other science proving that people who start *any* addictive substance/behavior at age fourteen have an exponentially higher risk of addiction (sometimes fivefold) than folks who start using in adulthood. Before you weed warriors start writing your hate mail arguing that no one gets addicted to weed, check out the distinctions between *physiological dependence* and *psychological addiction*. *Dependence* is a short-lived, onetime battle in which the *body* needs a drug to not feel crummy (withdraw). With coffee, cigarettes, and opiates, for example, the user can hate how they feel on the drug and will do anything they can to eliminate that physiological dependence. *Addiction* is a lifelong horror of a war in which the user loves how they feel on the drug and will do anything they can to get more. Teenage "work-in-progress" brains turn out to be very vulnerable to the addictive effects of things such as porn, drugs, and probably screen use, much more so than adult brains.

Finally, in looking at the teen risk factor of violence, the data show a curious dichotomy. Kids are generally much less violent when it comes to acts like murder and assault (aside from kids in gang areas) than were my peers back in the day. However, sexual violence (which is all about violence, not sex) has grown to a point where every fifth coed on an American college campus now acknowledges having been sexually assaulted, a horrific number that correlates amazingly well with the rise of misogynistic prompts (lyrics and videos) barraging our kids. The true killer violence statistic is suicide, which shows an escalation over the past half century to where last year every sixth teen in the lunchroom was seriously contemplating ending her life. This is *crazy*.

When I lecture I'm usually asked what could be causing so many more of our teens to become suicidal as compared to past generations. I know of no definitively researched answer, but I'll share my guess: we take a group of brain-challenged people (teenagers), put them in a culture that doesn't just ask, but *insists*, they make very sophisticated decisions at very early ages about things we adults don't handle very well (sex, drugs, and violence) while we bombard them with suggestions to decide poorly, which they often predictably do. Then we adults act all astonished and outraged that today's teens are so terrible, and we punish and rage at them for being *exactly the way each of us would have been had we been raised in their world.* I believe that contemporary teen life often becomes lonely, cheap, and painful, and just not worth living. This is also crazy—and terribly sad, since it doesn't have to happen if you don't do what so many of us parents do: *abandon our teenagers just when they need us the most.* We parents claim we pull back because our teens tell us that they want us out of their lives and they push us away at every chance. But the truth is that we mostly abandon them because they *stop taking care of us.*

Parental Grief: The Secret Pain

When my twenty-two-year-old son, Ross, was four, he was the poster child for huggy kids. I'd come home at night after a rough day and he'd run to jump into my arms. Remember those hugs from your now-teen when she was four? Boy, I sure do. That complete acceptance and unconditional love was incredibly healing for me. I'd pick him up and put him on my lap, and tickle him up. And I loved to sniff the top of his head. Remember how the little guys had this soft, sweet smell on their heads? Those were wonderful days for me. You too, I'll bet. Then, when Ross turned thirteen, he stopped running to find me. I'd have to go and find him and essentially beg for sixty seconds of his time, a request that always seemed to be an intrusion for him. I'd skulk away, appearing mad but actually sad (I'm a guy; we don't do sad). I was mad/sad because *he stopped taking care of me* by appearing to withdraw that love and acceptance. And therein lies the source of our grief. We think we take care of our kids when they're small, but it's quite the opposite: *they* give *us* wonderful things. They think we're smart, funny, athletic, even magical. We can make monsters disappear. Then, overnight, we seem to lose it all, as if we had a terrible stroke and never knew it. Suddenly we're stupid, annoying, embarrassing, and have nothing of value to say. Over time most of us stop reaching out as much to our teens, since the rejection and loss can feel so bad. Our kids have no idea why we've grown cold (they're just growing up) and then they feel rejected and pull further away, just like we do. And a vicious cycle is born, a self-reinforcing set of responses that soon turns into a terribly lonely spiral of relationship decline, in which everyone feels bad but no one says anything.

The irony is that your teen pushing away from you is *exactly what he should be doing*. Remember childbirth? Was that an easy, soft, and snuggly experience, or was there some pain, yelling, effort, exhaustion, even a little bloodshed involved? I was there, and it did not look easy and snuggly. It was scary and hard! It was also the most miraculous, incredible experience I'll ever have. Life never becomes more real than in moments such as those, right?

Well, here you go again, the rebirthing of your child, a second miracle of separation. This time she's pulling away from your beliefs, your values, your music, your lifestyle; everything seems to be open to questioning, testing, and ridicule. So what wise words of counsel would I offer you after your kid so soundly rejects you? "Congratulations! You've obviously done a great job." That's exactly what your young teen is supposed to be doing in order to make the leap into adulthood by defining her own beliefs, values, and so on. I know it's difficult, but this is a good thing. If he forever embraced your identity, he'd be living in your basement when he's forty! You do not want that. So try to reframe his pushing away from you as the second miracle of birth that is providing him a "fire in the belly," an energy to become his own person and to make his own path in the world. He's learned about what you have to offer; now he must decide who he is. This is the way of things.

So have a good cry over the old days of parenting, dry your tears, turn the page, and get ready to be a part of the greatest miracle and challenge of all: *helping your child become an adult*. When shrinks argue about the most critical years of parenting, you'll often hear a lot about those first five years. I argue that the last five of active parenting (thirteen through eighteen) are *at least* as important, for that is when the future adult is truly being shaped. Now is *not* the time to quit on your kid, so buckle up—we're goin' in.

Strategies for New Millennium Parents of Teenagers (the Special Ops folks of the adult world)

Mission one is to define your mission. Most parents think that our primary job is to control our kids, a parenting goal that most of our parents embraced, one that more or less worked back in that last war. But for the new millennium fight facing your kid, the research is very clear that simply controlling your kid *doesn't* work well anymore, and that data syncs perfectly with what the science tells us about teen brains. Controlling responses use fear as their main ingredient. These include yelling, hitting, arguing, repetitive lecturing, punishing, and forced (as opposed to collaborative) signings of I-won't-do-bad-things pledges. These strategies, which seem so parentally attractive, are at best useless efforts that usually make things worse. Remember that young teens (once properly taught) *do* get the risks, they *don't* always get the guilt/empathy, and they *do* go for the immediate rewards even when they understand the risks. So relecturing or attempting to frighten them won't get the job done. And yet when the teen craziness chips are down, most of us still react with fear-based strategies, as did most of our parents. My father did. In fact he was an expert.

THE DEVIL'S MUSIC: 1967 VS. 2003

In '67 me and my "gangster friends," as my father lovingly referred to them, were in *his* basement (as he would often remind us) listening to the devil's music, aka The Doors. Presciently concerned about the behavioral effects of cultural prompts on teen brains, the old man stormed down the steps, grabbed the album (remember albums?), and smashed it on the record player, killing it as well. After the vinyl exploded through the room like shrapnel, he towered over us, waiting for someone to be dumb enough to say something. Knowing that the neighborhood treaties clearly specified that anyone's parent could beat up anyone's kid, we all remained quiet as he turned and stormed back up the stairs, murmuring about the "god d---, s---for-brain kids today, have no god-d---respect, cursing all the god-d---time..." a soliloquy I silently recognized as irony. While admittedly a fear-based tactic, you could well argue the old man's intervention was effective given the old war context. First, in relative dollars, that album cost a fortune back then. I didn't realize it at the time but we were essentially poor, so there was no "discretionary income" among me and my gangster friends to replace it. Second, decency laws and policies prevented public access sources (radio and TV) from playing the crazy Doors album cuts, so that was the end of The Doors' influence over me and my gangster friends for quite some time. In the old war you could largely *police your kid's environment.* It sort of worked—then. But what about now? If tonight you "smash" your daughter's horrific digital download by berating her while erasing it, what will she do? Yes, not only download that one again but add three others that are worse as revenge for your rage (remember being fourteen?).

Safety in this new millennium fight requires that we use *respect-based* (versus fear-based) tactics such as those I employed when *my* son was in *my* basement listening to *his* devil's music with *his* gangster friends. When I went downstairs, the CD player fell silent as it was mysteriously apt to do whenever I squeaked the top step of the basement stairs. To some very red faces I asked that the CD be allowed to continue. "Mr. Bradley," one voice piped up, "you don't really want to hear this." I agreed that I likely didn't want to but that I needed to. I told the gang that I wasn't there to take the CD, and I didn't even want to know whose it was; however, the price we would pay is that we'd all enjoy it together.

I'll spare you the sexual information I learned in that next two minutes (never too old to learn), but the key piece was something that had eluded me in my studies about the psychology of women, namely that females like to be beaten up. I now knew this was true since this authority figure on the CD said that even though beaten women cry and plead, they feel loved if you slap them around, and then they'll do "anything to please."

"Gentleman," I asked the boys, "do you think women like to be beaten up?"

"Why are you asking us that?" one puzzled kid inquired.

"Well, you're seeing and hearing this kind of stuff everywhere around you and I wonder if it affects what you think or do."

"That's stupid!" a chorus responded. "What kids see or hear can't make them do stuff!"

"Really!?" I responded. "I'll be right back." I returned with two graphs I used for a class I taught. "Look at this, gentlemen. This first graph shows how the most effective way to get kids to smoke cigarettes is to expose them to lots of on-screen smoking. Pretty stunning, no?" The smart kid wasn't quitting the contest. "That's just for something stupid like cigarettes," he critiqued. "Nobody would beat up a girl just 'cause some music says so." I sealed the ambush. "Really? Well, this second graph shows how sexual violence against girls has risen almost exactly with the rise of these sorts of lyrics. Maybe you guys would never do that, but what about some kid with an anger issue—might this kind of give him permission to do that? And do you think that many girls are accepting this insanity more than ever before? Does the phrase *bitch slapping* ever get used in your world?"

Ross absolutely hated these sessions. Once he alternatively offered to have me punch him in the face and get it over with more quickly. "Gentlemen," I admitted to his gang, "I would love to punch

Ross in the face and get this over with. Being ex-military and raised Irish Catholic, that sounds great to me. And what would it do? It would enrage and humiliate my son in front of his friends, and make that crazy person on your CD player my son's new hero, pushing my son away from me and into that crazy bastard's arms. Gentlemen," I explained, "I cannot win the fight with your technologically powerful culture to keep it away from you. That enemy is through my wire, it's over my walls. If I took this CD I know this crap would be raining back down on you the minute I leave. Those tactics won't work any-more." I spoke very slowly now, "Gentlemen, I cannot control what you *see*, or what you *hear*. Instead I must engage with you about what you *think* about what you see and what you hear, to try and keep you safe. And on that note, I've invited Ross's mother down to enlighten us from a female perspective as to whether women like to get beaten up." That's when the eye rolling and fake "fingers down the throat" started. But they listened in stone silence as my wife spoke about violence against women she had witnessed.

We cannot win that fight with our culture. Do not waste your precious ammo (time and contact) there. Focus instead upon their *beliefs* about the craziness to which they are exposed. Change a belief (or value) and you change a person, and inoculate them with some protection for when you are not around to control them when some crazy cultural prompt urges them to do something stupid. The research proves that after our conversation, the phrase *bitch slapping* likely did not sound quite as funny to those boys.

So now that you understand the "why" we need to use respect-based tactics, you're ready for the "how." With apologies to the au-thor of the first Ten Commandments, here's a new Ten to help you through another set of challenges.

---

toughLOVE TIPS

The Ten Commandments of Parenting New Millennium Teens

I: THOU SHALT BE AS THE DISPASSIONATE COP UNTO THINE OWN CHILD. All teens are nuts to some extent (you never were, right?) so don't take their craziness personally. Angry cops inspire angry citizens to angrily focus only upon the intimidating cops, forgetting that the citizens were the ones who blew the stop signs. Like that dispassionate cop who politely gives you tickets (aka "consequences"), stay controlled during crises so that your kid thinks more about *her* crazy behavior than *your* anger. Put the power to control his future in his hands by calmly constructing related consequences (preagreed-upon outcomes of actions) versus screamed, rarely enforced punishments ("you're grounded 'til you're thirty-five"). Punishments are where you hurt him after he's made a choice, without knowing exactly what that choice would cost him. That makes him *pissed at you*, which is the antecedent to more bad choices. Consequences are where his poor choices end up letting him down. That makes him get *pissed at himself*, which is the antecedent of psychological change: "Son, we agreed that if you drank again at an away sleepover that you were telling us all that you are not mature enough to make those tough decisions, and that a second bad decision would mean no away sleepovers for six months, allowing you to mature a bit more. I'm sure by then you'll be better at this."

"What? You mean I can't do sleepovers?"

"Son, I'm not trying to hurt (punish) you. I'm trying to protect you. Of course you can have sleepovers—here."

"But the kids won't come here!"

"Gee, son. Why is that?"

II: THOU SHALT LISTEN EVEN AS THINE OWN CHILD SHOUTS. Kids often say too little and shout too much, but the shouting can often be another form of communication. Become tough enough to withstand nonabusive yelling and wait it out without interrupting and screaming back. If you can hang on, your kid will finally become calmer and say what really has him upset. Over time, he'll learn to speak with more control by watching you speak with more control. Be what you want to see. Use framing questions ("What good thing happened today? What sucked?") versus vague ones ("How was your day?").

III: THOU SHALT NOT SHOUT; SPEAK THOU WISELY. You know how crazy and out of control your kid looks when she's screaming? You, as the parent, look a lot worse. Losing emotional control means losing precious respect in the eyes of your child, something you can't afford. Speak calmly and quietly in short, nonrepetitive sentences, or don't talk until you've regained control. Your yelling back is destructive and only creates a costly diversion from the real issues. Screaming at a screaming child is like putting out small fires with gasoline. When the rage is bubbling up in your throat, call a time-out and leave. Nothing good is about to happen. You'll be a much smarter parent after you scream in your car for a bit. I usually am.

IV: THOU SHALT ADD FIFTEEN MINUTES TO EVERY INTERACTION INVOLVING THY TEEN. Your job is *not to control your kid*, but *to teach your kid how to control herself.* Locking yourself into rigid schedules whenever difficult kids are involved is asking for trouble, since you're likely to resort to fear tactics. Much of what they do can become complex, maddening, and schedule-defying. Provide bumpers or reaction/thinking time for yourself so that your responses are more controlled and you can be less controlling. Always look for ways to hand off decision-making power to your child. Remember, a bad decision made well (where she thinks it through and chooses) is much more valuable than a good decision made poorly (where you choose for her). We all learn much more from our failures.

V: THOU SHALT REMAIN LOVING AND CONNECTED . . . EVEN WHILE BEING "HATED" AND AVOIDED. Parenting a child is a loving *and* conflict-based relationship. It's your job to "ruin" his life at times. In the proper dose, rage-free conflict with parents *feels like love* to kids: "Sorry, sweetie. I've heard your opinions about beer being harmless, but I can't allow drinking at your party because of the science I've shared with you about teen drinking. Can we compromise by getting that crazy, lighted, punch-fountain-thingy? I'm afraid that I love you too much to allow you to hurt yourself with alcohol." You'd be surprised how often kids are hoping they'll be able to say, "My parents wouldn't let me." Don't let the "business" of parenting override the "nurture" of parenting. Find ways to lovingly connect with your kids each day, *especially* when times are tough. I once paid my son five bucks to tolerate getting a coffee with me. He thought it was funny to get me on my knees until he forgot that he "hated" me as he chatted away over a latte. Try lying next to your teen on her bed late at night to shoot the breeze with questions, not to lecture with morality sermons. Because adolescent brains are wired to stay up late at night when the world is closing down, they can be so desperate for late-night interaction that they'll even talk to *you.*

VI: THOU SHALT NOT KILL (THOU MAYEST ENTERTAIN THOUGHTS OF KILLING, BUT . . .). No hitting. Ever. Hitting children to make them behave not only teaches them that might makes right, but it makes you look weak to them and costs dearly in respect currency. Besides, whacking a child is like whacking a stick of dynamite. It might not explode right away. But when it finally does it will demolish everything nearby. Getting physical with a child is playing in their stadium—you're giving them the home field advantage of accepting rage as a way of solving problems. Don't go there. Dads often argue this by saying, "My father, my coach, and my drill sergeant all hit me at times, and I loved and respected those men, and I turned out fine. So what's wrong with hitting?"

"Tell me what you loved and admired about your father," I'll ask.

"He was a good man," they answer. "He worked two jobs to get us through school, he coached everything, he gave everything for everyone else, never even had a decent pair of shoes."

"What a wonderful story," I'll answer. "You just spoke of that man's values, his character. Sir, you never mentioned the hitting. You shrugged off his hitting, and you were blown away by his character."

VII: THOU SHALT APOLOGIZE AT EVERY OPPORTUNITY. To children, adult apology is strength, not weakness. It is a marvelous tool for teaching humility, self-control, responsibility, compassion, respect, and self-acceptance. It does all these things like a Trojan horse that disables your kid's built-in lecture deflector. If you preach at your child, he closes down. But he'll sit and listen carefully to messages hidden within the robes of your own admissions of failure. You'll never look bigger to your child than when you make yourself smaller. But an apology does not have the word *but* or the phrase *you gotta understand*. Those are not apologies but are explanations or rationalizations. Stay on your side of the fence: "There is no excuse for my slapping you. I am so sorry, and I will try to never let that happen again."

VIII: THOU SHALT HONOR THY CHILD'S IDENTITY (EVEN THOUGH IT MAKETH THOU ILL). Green hair, metallic tongues, and pants with crotches so low that they need skid plates are all windows into that wonderful, horrible, laughable, and frightening teenage struggle called identity exploration. She's just trying to figure out who the heck she is, which happens to be *the* most important thing she should do right now. Those strange exterior identity experiments coincide with a critical interior process where her values, beliefs, and character are being formed. Once her identity is set in place, she is finally ready to safely navigate the world. As a rule of thumb, the less you fight the silly external things, the shorter they last. The more you help her to think about the internal things by quietly chatting without judging (versus loudly arguing and challenging), the more positive and powerful they become: "I understand how crazy it seems that at eighteen you can die for a country that won't allow you to drink alcohol or smoke weed. However, the science seems pretty clear that it can hurt you." Pick your battles wisely and save your "that's not happening" ammo for the life-threatening explorations like sex, drugs, and violence. Try to remember how weird you looked to your parents, and how important that weirdness was to you. Honor that silliness on the outside of your own kid, and you'll get more access to the seriousness inside.

IX: TO THINE OWN SELF BE TRUE. Your kid has enough problems. The last thing he needs is "cool" parents. He needs you to be an unchangingly corny, unhip, and out-of-date dinosaur who holds fast to a strong set of values in a morally free-falling culture. Be like the constant beacon of the lighthouse that stands unchanged above the dangerous seas of the world to periodically guide your child home to safe waters after a bad time. Be a parent *first*, not a friend. He's got friends. He needs parents. Hold on to your values, calmly but firmly. Show and share them, but don't preach or pound them. Soup kitchen shifts speak much louder than lectures.

X: THIS TOO SHALL PASS. In the rough phases, parenting a teenager can be overwhelming and terrifying. When we're sailing through the middle of a maelstrom, it's easy to believe that it will last forever. Thinking that this will be the eternal nature of your relationship with your child can destroy your morale, something you can't afford to lose. But like raging summer storms, these bad chapters *do* end, and almost everyone survives just fine, particularly if you lose your anger and keep your cool. As General Colin Powell often reminded his junior commanders, "Perpetual optimism is a force multiplier." I found that to be very true in the military, and even truer as a parent.

Remember to keep your eye on the real goal here. Your job is not to raise an Ivy League freshman. This gig is about raising the *parent of your grandchildren, the grandparent of your great-grandchildren.* Parenting is as close as we get to touching the face of infinity, so consider carefully. What do you want to pass along forever? Anger, criticism, sadness, rejection, and isolation? How about support, approval, tolerance, acceptance, and patience *especially* in the face of provocation? That second list reveals the magical ingredients of the incomprehensibly powerful parenting tool called love. It turns out that the happiest and most successful adults are *not* the ones who were tortured as teens into getting As in AP classes, but those who had parents who focused first on the *heart* of their child, knowing that lifelong achievement and passion follow the identity formation of strong values, positive beliefs, and confidence of character.

Twelve years ago Brian's parents started doing just that (remember Brian—on my couch?), and they did it in the face of terrible battles of drug abuse, rage, and rebellion. They accomplished their miracle by moving from the ends of that "parenting couch" where they sat in that first session (permissive mother versus authoritarian father) to meet in the "magic middle" parenting position: a firm and loving connection to the heart of their child. They stood shoulder-to-shoulder against Brian's rages, finding the grit to calmly and powerfully help him define his identity amid his madness. One of the last times I saw them, I watched as the parents did the "pick your battles" drill perfectly: "Son, we love you. We cannot allow you to do drugs. We know you are much more than that. You must be drug free for us to support you. We will give everything to help you. We will give not a penny that helps you do things that can hurt you so terribly. We love you far too much for that."

Last week I heard from Mom that a drug-free Brian had not only finished his master's degree but was now doing "an incredibly high-pressured, high-stress job that he absolutely *loves*," transforming all of his previously explosive, destructive, and frenetic adolescent energy into an adult passion for challenge and performance. As Mom put it, "I guess my husband and I learned to focus on the important stuff." Indeed.

In trying to sort the wheat of the important heart stuff from the chaff of the silly with my own teens, I use a cheery exercise I call my "deathbed" technique. When I arrive home tonight exhausted from a speaking tour, the odds of the kitchen being spotless (as my ex-military ego loves) are about the same as my being abducted by aliens. My wife, you see, just left on a trip of her own, and my fifteen-year-old daughter is not the most orderly teen you'll ever meet (was that fair, sweetheart?). When my feet stick to the syrup on the floor, I'll want to explode. Instead, I'll retreat to the garage, picture myself on my deathbed, and ask, "*How will I feel then about what I'm about to do tonight?*" That sobers me up pretty quick, helping me see what's truly important as I reenter the kitchen: "SARAH! Give me a hug. I missed you *sooo* much! I'm so impressed by that Latin grade Mom told me you got! Way to go, girl! Are you proud of that?" I'll hug her as long as she can stand, and then quietly add, "And, if you don't mind, do you think you could help me police up the kitchen a tad?" as I've only asked ten thousand, nine hundred and ninety nine times before. But those last words are only for me to hear as I shake my head, sigh, and grin.

And I'll grin because I have once again triumphed by remembering that love is, indeed, the most powerful, most potent force in parenting.

Good luck out there. Keep your head down.

"gimme" kids: the toxic cocktail of entitlement, narcissism, and materialism

BY MADELINE LEVINE, PHD, A PRACTICING CLINICAL PSYCHOLOGIST, BESTSELLING AUTHOR, AND MOM TO THREE SONS

Meet Travis. He's a bright young man on the cusp of his sixteenth birthday. Like most teenagers, he's thrilled about turning in his driving permit for a real license. His parents, after considerable discussion, decide that they will turn over their well-used Volvo station wagon to him if he passes his driving test. Elaine, his mom, has had her eye on a new car for several years, and this seems like a perfect solution. A reliable set of wheels Travis doesn't have to pay for. A new car for Elaine. What a perfect solution, right? Unfortunately not. When Elaine presents the station wagon keys to her son after a successful test at the DMV, he shoots her a look of scorn and states flatly, "I'm not driving that thing. No kid around here drives a 'Mom' car."

While shocked by her son's lack of gratitude, Elaine does not suggest that her son's alternative is to walk. Concerned about maintaining her relationship with her son, and not being an ungenerous parent, Elaine goes with her husband and buys Travis a vehicle he deems "acceptable," a brand-new Ford Mustang. Elaine still drives the Volvo.

You may be shaking your head in disbelief and thinking, What a brat Travis is! or What wimps his folks are! But the truth is that this basic scenario, one in which the child's sense of entitlement trumps the parents' common sense, is far from unusual. Many thoughtful, well-meaning parents can relate to it. The desire to be a generous parent, to see one's child happy, to fit into the community is an impulse we all have. And in general Travis is a good kid—he works hard at school, listens to his parents, rarely gets into trouble. He certainly isn't a "bad" kid. Unfortunately, the sense of entitlement, even narcissism, that Travis exhibits has become unremarkable in children these days. Researchers find that narcissism, entitlement's kissing cousin, characterized by a conviction of being special and a lack of empathy, is at a historical high among young people in this country.[1]

From this single scenario we cannot predict what kind of young man Travis will turn out to be. A host of other factors in his upbringing may temper what appears in the example above to be a disturbing sense of entitlement and lack of empathy. So let's not label Travis an entitled kid or even a narcissist (which carries a disturbing long-term prognosis) just yet. For the moment we'll say that Travis has a bad case of the "gimmes," something that is seen regularly in kids who have little sense of the balance between their own needs and the needs of others; kids who have been given too much and from whom too little has been expected. In order to avoid the proliferation of Travises, we need to understand the damage that is being done when we parent from a place of indulgence, fear, and lack of conviction.

Let's look at what is meant by the "gimmes" and consider the real danger that this particular constellation of attitudes and behaviors poses to our children's development. We'll explore why we too often parent in ways that promote the "gimmes," and finally, what we can do to minimize this toxic parenting style and return to a healthier, more appropriate (and frankly, saner) way of parenting!

Entitlement, Narcissism, and Materialism

Let's start by getting our terms right and understanding the conditions that lead to kids like Travis, who are oblivious to the needs of their families and insist that their own needs be given highest priority. Is Travis just a slightly more notable example of the expectable self-centeredness of adolescence? Will his behavior at sixteen be likely to embarrass him in a few years? Both the research and my three decades of experience as a clinical psychologist argue against this hopeful interpretation. A grateful kid is what we all hope for. A disappointed, maybe even slightly sulky kid wouldn't be likely to raise any alarms. But a teenager who believes that he is "owed" a new car, in spite of the fact that he's done nothing to earn it, is showing a degree of entitlement that bodes poorly both for his own mental health and for his relationships with others. And Travis's sense of entitlement is unlikely to end with his attitude about a car. Entitled kids feel that it is their due to receive material goods, unwarranted admiration, and special favors in many arenas. For example, every entitled teenager in America knows that the fastest way out of household chores is to remind parents about the upcoming AP test. The logic tends to be, "I'm such a special, talented student that I deserve a pass on anything as ordinary as household chores." Besides, most kids know that Mom will pick up the slack in spite of the fact that she's worked a full day herself *and* gotten dinner on the table.

While it's hard to say when exactly entitlement slips into narcissism, it's the striking lack of empathy that is most notable in narcissism. Travis's unempathic response to his parents indicates both entitlement and narcissism. Entitlement may be a precursor to narcissism, and since narcissistic people generally cause a lot of misery for those around them, it's worth picking up early expressions of entitlement in order to ward off more serious deficits in our kids down the road. A regular teen says to his mom, "I know you worked hard, but I'm beat and I just don't want to walk the dog tonight. Can you do it for me?" An entitled teen says, "Maybe it was a tough day for you, but it was a tougher day for me. After I babysat last week I think you owe me a favor. Please walk the dog for me." But the narcissistic teen is unlikely to give his parents' reality a nod and arrogantly insist that for the night the dog walking is "someone else's problem."

It's safe to say that Travis is entitled, narcissistic, and also materialistic. This is a toxic cocktail of character traits that have become all too common among kids and teens, regardless of socioeconomic level. While middle-class and blue-collar kids may not be manipulating their parents into buying them new cars, they may instead be insisting on expensive haircuts, the latest electronics, or the coolest shoes. Materialism is a value system that emphasizes wealth, status, image, and material consumption. It's a measure of how much we rate material things over other aspects of our lives, such as friends, family, and work. Teens have conflicting needs—both to "fit in" and to discover their individuality. Teens are busy constructing an identity, a sense of self that hopefully lays the foundation for a lifetime of resilience and relationships. This should be first and foremost internal work. But materialism causes a teen to rely on external measures for a sense of self.

Materialism is not the same as having money. Having enough money to meet basic needs is clearly critical and has a documented effect on how satisfied we are with our lives. But our current preoccupation with material goods has become disturbing. Walking down Fifth Avenue in New York the other day, I passed a designer shoe store. In one of the windows there was nothing but a pedestal with an elaborate stiletto-heeled shoe reverently positioned on top and bathed in the kind of light typically reserved for museums or churches. Clearly this shoe was being presented as an icon and seemed emblematic to me of how we have replaced our traditional icons of religion, family, and culture with the icons of consumerism. This kind of deification of objects represents the shallowest of values and promotes a disturbing message to both parents and children. Why choose the hard work of relationships when we can choose the simple seduction of objects? Just to be clear, I like a great pair of shoes as much as the next woman. What I'm pointing to here is the marketing that encourages us to think, even for a moment, that real satisfaction comes from acquisition. When the need to acquire stuff trumps other goals, endeavors, and interests, then work, friendship, marriage, hobbies, parenting, spiritual development, and intellectual challenges can all fall by the wayside. Liking stuff isn't the problem; liking stuff *more* than other experiences, more than people, is.

We can—and I clearly have—attached all kinds of labels to Travis's bad behavior. I also noted that he was, in other arenas of his life, a pretty good kid. Fortunately, Travis is still a work in progress. So while we may hold off diagnosing him, what is clear is that Travis is empty at the very point of development (adolescence) when all kinds of internal work is supposed to be happening. He believes that who he is will be determined not by self-reflection and character, but by the way he presents himself to the world through objects. The right car becomes a matter of life and death to him. There's real peril if Travis continues to focus on acquisitions and appearances, and if his parents continue to tolerate, and sometimes even encourage, this worldview (think not just cars, but grades, traveling teams, popularity). He will be unable to do the hard work of crafting an internal sense of self that is not dependent on "presentation" or the admiration of others. If "stuff" made us happier, then the United States—the land of individualism, self-gratification, retail therapy, and keeping up with the Joneses—would be the happiest place on earth. It isn't. It is actually an increasingly *un*happy nation. Travis is just our canary in the coal mine.

Why We're Raising "Gimme" Kids

I think it's safe to say most of us agree that the kind of behavior we saw in Travis was ugly. No one sets out to raise an entitled, narcissistic, materialistic kid. We recognize it when we see it, and we don't want to encourage it in the people we love more than anyone else in the world. So how does it happen?

Before I delve into the parental psyche, I'd like to make the point that materialism is woven deeply into the fabric of our culture. Valuing things is the norm, and some parents (not all) consciously or unconsciously buy into this attitude and inadvertently foster it in their kids. We model for our children the values we think are most important. And regardless of how articulate we may be about "good values," our kids watch us closely to see how we behave. If you talk about service to others but don't participate in your community, your child notices. If you push honesty and integrity but talk about how to avoid paying taxes or get out of a speeding ticket, your child notices. Children are highly attuned to whether or not their parents are actually walking the talk and frequently report that there is a yawning gap between what parents say and what they do.

Adolescents, in particular, are fine-tuned to notice hypocrisy and have little tolerance for it. This all-too-frequent disconnect between what we espouse, how we live, and what we tolerate in our children doesn't happen because we are bad parents. It happens because we fear that without the "right stuff," without unblemished performance, and without perpetual attention to the needs of our children, they will somehow find themselves disadvantaged in a world we see as unforgivingly competitive. Here are some of the reasons I believe that we are driven to indulge our children in ways that work against their character development and ultimate well-being.

We don't want our children to be unhappy.

Often, we seed our children with "gimme-ism" for reasons that are both simple and visceral. We don't like to see our children unhappy. By far, the most overwhelming reason is love. As parents, our most basic impulse is to give children what (we think) they need, and what they tell us they want (and yes, it can be difficult to distinguish between the two, especially in a society where having the right kind of stuff is the cultural norm). Providing material objects is a quick fix for unhappiness, and when kids are happy, parents are happy.

Admittedly, mixed in with these pure motives is a bit of self-preservation. In a society where adults are so often stressed, overworked, and exhausted, it's clearly much easier to reduce a child's distress with the promise of a Saturday-afternoon shopping spree or a pass on household chores than to take on the time-consuming and considerably more difficult task of dealing with the underlying issue. Who has the time or the energy?

More specifically, we want our children to be happy with us.

In the case of some parents (certainly not all), their own self-esteem and self-worth are dependent on their children's approval and goodwill. But without the social network that historically buoyed us—a grandmother upstairs, cousins and siblings down the block, a priest or rabbi stopping by on the way home—it's easy to become overly dependent on kids. Many parents unconsciously look to their children for entertainment, approbation, and even nurturing. A husband (or wife) who is gone much of the time, preoccupied with business, and often unavailable can make our kids look like a better bet for emotional sustenance.

Relying on one's children to fill a social void and make us feel good about ourselves is a recipe for overindulgence. And even for parents who don't fall into this category, buying the latest iPhone for a child who wants one is a quick, easy way to become the good guy. However connected and fulfilled you may be, it *always* feels good to be the good guy!

We rely on our children's accomplishments to show the world what good parents we are.

Parenting doesn't come, never has, with a parenting manual. Mostly parents have managed because they have historically been part of a community that devotes resources to helping young parents. In our ultra-competitive society, these resources can be hard to find. Parents often express a kind of confusion about "how I'm doing." Without older moms and dads and extended family around for guidance, it's tough to know exactly where one stands as a parent. As a result, many parents have come to assess their skills by noting the achievements of their children. Witness the explosion of bumper stickers trumpeting what college a child goes to or what level of academic excellence a child performs at. This conflation of who we are and how well we are parenting with our children's achievements makes many parents vulnerable to confusing boundaries and even identities. And your child is not responsible for boosting her own self-esteem. As parenting has increasingly become a blood sport, parents are willing to use whatever validation enhances their standing. This should not include your children's accomplishments. They belong to your children.

We're trying to give our children a "better" life.

The American Dream of hard work ensuring a future for our children that is more prosperous than our own is part of our national narrative. We want our children to have the possessions we couldn't and the opportunities we wish we'd had. We *don't* want them to face the perceived difficulties we identify in our own pasts. And we all have had losses, disappointments, and even, unfortunately, tragedies.

I grew up in a working-class family, in a small house with one bathroom and a backyard the size of a postage stamp. My parents did not have the money to buy the Bass Weejuns loafers that were popular when I was a child, and as a result I was hyperaware of my less trendy shoes bought at the local discount store. When I became a parent, I always made sure that my three sons had the shoes "everyone else" was wearing so that they would never experience the embarrassment that I had felt as a kid. Not having experienced much deprivation, being boys, and secure in their social standing, my sons were mostly confused by the onslaught of shoes that found their way into our home. I may have thought I was trying to give them a "better" childhood, but in fact I was simply trying to heal my own early sense of not being "good enough." Often when we give our kids too much, when we find ourselves tolerating behavior that we shouldn't, it's because we have confused our own history and needs with our child's. My sons were neither deprived nor embarrassed about their shoes. I had been confusing my needs with theirs—an unfortunately rather regular parental pitfall that we all need to be vigilant about.

We succumb to parental peer pressure.

When discussing summer activities with his parents, Jason asks to attend an outdoor summer camp where he'll be able to hike, canoe, and play sports. But when his mother, Judith, mentions her son's desire to other parents, she gets virtually the same response each time: "What? Jason is so talented at chess. Don't you think you should send him to a chess camp? I hear that talents like that are really valued at top schools." Despite his protests, Jason spends his summer sitting at a chessboard instead of enjoying the great outdoors.

Like Judith and her husband, many parents are guilt-tripped

into doing things against their instincts because they don't want to look uncaring, not "with it," or ignorant of their children's unique talents. Believing that other parents will think better of us if our kids have the right clothes and follow a certain trajectory on the way to "success" is an odd mindset, considering that our advice to those very children is to resist peer pressure. "If everyone jumped off the bridge, would you?" For many parents, the answer, unfortunately, seems to be yes.

We use prizes as carrots to motivate our children.

Especially in comfortable families, money and material objects tend to become default motivators. A mother sits in my office and offers her son a new car if he will just stop taking drugs; another mother unabashedly offers her daughter a hundred dollars for every pound she loses. I often see bribery and the promise of reward occurring on smaller scales, too: "Each week you go with no detention, Mom and I will add twenty dollars to your allowance." "If you get straight As, you can go on a shopping spree at the mall."

Frankly, this is a terrible way to instill motivation in kids. Trying to buy them off with "stuff" or money may seem, or even be, effective in the short term, but on its own I have *never* seen this strategy produce long-term effective change. In fact, it tends to weaken parental power and fortify childish greed.

It's worth noting again that all of these contributors to gimme-ism—even parental peer pressure and using bribes as motivation—are born out of wanting the best for our children. However misguided, we believe that we're helping our kids by assuring their place in the social order or by pushing them to achieve other positive goals. That's why the onset and growth of entitled, narcissistic, and materialistic children is often difficult to identify. Parents are so focused on obtaining "the best" for their children that they fail to see and understand the insidious impact their efforts are having. There is a boatload of research on the conditions under which kids are most likely to thrive: parenting that is warm, supportive, and clear about discipline and consequences; praise that is specific; motivation that is cultivated internally; a reliable and stable family structure; and the opportunity for kids to take age-appropriate risks. Healthy children come from conditions that are known to cultivate a strong sense of self and a robust set of coping skills, not from a sense of entitlement or a preoccupation with material goods.

The Consequences of Gimme-ism

I doubt that many parents are under the illusion that the gimmes is a good thing. Still, large numbers of us *do* act as though it is unfortunate but nevertheless acceptable, so long as the time, effort, and personal resources we're pouring into our children ultimately reap a personal, intellectual, and financial bonanza for them. When asked, the vast majority of parents say that they just want their children to be happy.

So how's this going for our children? Drs. Ed Diener and David Myers, two of the nation's foremost researchers on money and happiness, have pooled data from more than a million people in forty-five countries. They found that the majority of people worldwide, regardless of age, race, or socioeconomic status, appear to be relatively happy as long as their basic needs are met. Happiness does not rise in direct proportion to the wealth of any particular country.[2] Even the very richest among us (the Forbes 100) enjoy only a marginally higher level of happiness than the average American.[3] As for our children: rates of depression have doubled in the past two decades,[4] anxiety disorders have become the most common teen psychiatric diagnosis,[5] preteen and teen suicide numbers have quadrupled,[6] 25 percent of college students are substance abusers, and both eating disorders and self-mutilation are on the rise.[7] The conclusion is that, in spite of all we believe we are giving our children, they are not happy campers. Far from it. Is it really the triumvirate of entitlement, narcissism, and materialism that is promoting a generation of kids who are not simply bratty but impaired as well? And if so, why?

The gimmes promotes a reliance on extrinsic motivation.

One of the most important tasks of growing up is developing self-efficacy, the feeling that you are in charge of your own life and have the power to accomplish what you want. We *all* need to feel that we have a major hand in what happens to us. Normally, self-efficacy is developed when kids see the benefit of behaviors *for themselves*. You study hard, you get good grades. You focus on being friendly and polite, people like you. You eat less junk food, you lose weight. You practice the violin, your skill improves.

Internal motivation of this sort is not tied to rewards; it is the catalyst that gets kids to engage in activities that are satisfying *for their own sake*. Think of the little boy who spends hours constructing elaborate Lego buildings from scratch, or the adolescent girl who pours her feelings into writing short stories night after night. Carol Dweck's research illustrates the value of not being the motivator for our children. Kids are given puzzles to solve and then are divided into two groups: one group is simply allowed to play and experiment with the puzzles; the other group is "encouraged" to do well by being told how special and talented they are. Counterintuitive as it may seem, the kids in the group that is told nothing, that is allowed to play, experiment, and make mistakes, ultimately are not only better puzzle solvers but are much more likely to enjoy puzzles. After all, they're working for the pleasure of it, not in order to gain someone else's approval.[8]

Unfortunately, a lifetime of being consoled, pacified, and motivated by material rewards or by the admiration of others has created a legion of kids whose primary motivation comes from outside themselves. This is one reason that more affluent youngsters are especially at risk of contracting the gimmes—they are able to easily change their circumstances through external means. However, this is a bad bargain because it cultivates shallow values and allows kids to neglect or skip altogether the development of internal motivation. Parents would do well to create a little necessity in the lives of their children. No passes from loading the dishwasher because there is an AP exam the next day. Kids should know that they are needed members of a community (and your home is their first community!) and that they are expected to consider the needs of others besides themselves. Kids who feel capable of handling everyday tasks feel good about themselves, and this fosters an internal sense of competence and helps to drive internal motivation.

Materialistic, externally motivated kids often feel a diminished sense of control because the things they need magically appear regardless of their actions or inactions. They tend to confuse performance, which is accompanied by rewards, with true learning. As a result, they have lower grades, lower achievement scores, less interest in learning, less ability to think creatively, and greater psychological impairment than children who are internally motivated.[9]

The gimmes squashes resourcefulness.

Motivation and resourcefulness go hand in hand. When faced with a problem, an internally motivated child takes on the responsibility of finding a solution. An internally motivated kid tends to relish the challenge of "doing it on my own." Whatever the circumstances, he is likely to develop new ways of thinking, doing, and behaving—in other words, resourcefulness. As he learns more and performs better, his ability to problem-solve, compromise, and make things happen grows, thus preparing him to take on increasingly difficult challenges.

Take, for instance, an internally motivated child who wants a new bike. If she's resourceful, she will figure out ways to earn some money, perhaps by doing yard work for neighbors, babysitting, or tutoring younger kids. She may even work out a "matching grant" program with her parents. In addition to earning a new bike, she has also learned that using the resources at her disposal will help her get what she wants. This lesson will ultimately make her a good friend, worker, spouse, etc.

On the other hand, an externally motivated child comes to see the outside world, especially the stuff that can be bought there, as a dependable (if temporary) source of relief and satisfaction. It's likely that his parents simply buy him a new bike right away when he asks for one, teaching him that the world is there to meet his desires and that he doesn't need to work to make things happen. When real life eventually steps in, he will be severely disappointed by its disinclination to accommodate him, and he will lack the tools to meet challenges and move forward. The adult equivalent of a bike will remain out of his reach.

Resourcefulness also extends to alleviating emotional distress. One of the important tasks of childhood and adolescence is learning how to handle difficult feelings. Kids must learn to reduce emotional distress, manage anxiety, cope with uncomfortable feelings, and so forth. In many cases, they will use another person such as a parent, friend, or mentor to help solve the problem.

Materialism supplants using people to solve problems and nurture oneself. Sixteen-year-old Allison is representative of this new breed of materialistic teenager. Overall a bright and charming girl, she doesn't exhibit any overt problems. When she seems low, she is easily perked up by shopping sprees with her mother. Afterward, many of her acquisitions hang unworn in her closet. However, her parents are only mildly concerned, reasoning that these unused purchases are a small price to pay for the temporary lift she gets from buying things.

Allison isn't unusual in needing to be perked up every now and then; we all go through low periods. The problem is that her parents have taught her that external things should be her main means of relieving emotional distress. They have prevented her from developing internal resources, such as resilience and a strong sense of self, that might carry her through tough times. What Allison really needs is help learning how to understand and cope with uncomfortable feelings, whether that means taking a run, deep breathing, talking to friends, writing out her feelings, using humor, or being curious about what's bothering her—*not* unlimited access to Mom and Dad's credit cards.

The gimmes interferes with the ability to work well with others.

Children need work experiences to develop a sense that success is a function of their own efforts. Some of this development happens in school; some happens at home when kids participate in family chores. But when children are given too much, they are less likely to develop a work ethic. Why put forth effort and engage in mental or physical exertion when you already have everything you need or want?

I am reminded of a story told by Dr. Donna Mehregany, a child and adolescent psychiatrist and clinical faculty member at Case Western Reserve in Cleveland, Ohio, whose practice of adolescents is drawn largely from affluent suburbs. While babysitting the nine-year-old son and five-year-old daughter of a neighborhood friend, Dr. Mehregany asked her own nine-year-old son and her friend's son if they would watch his sister briefly while she attended to some work, and offered the boys two dollars each as an incentive. Her friend's son was taken aback and then contemptuous. "I have two million dollars in my trust fund. Why would I work for two dollars?"

This attitude on *any* scale is unhealthy. Not only does a disinclination to step into the world of work because of preexisting resources alienate others; it also prevents kids from learning how many other aspects there are to life besides a bank statement.

The gimmes also encourages unhealthy competition. This is particularly worrisome at a time when all business executives are stressing the workplace need for kids who are collaborative. Materialism, entitlement, and competition encourage the belief that resources are scarce and divides people into the haves and have-nots. Materialistic kids, therefore, are much more likely to pit themselves against their peers. In an important study that looks at who chooses to cooperate with friends and who chooses to "get ahead," researchers find that college students who rate high on materialism are far more likely to choose "getting ahead" over "cooperating with their friends."[10] This does not bode well for kids who are on the verge of looking for work in a difficult economy.

Listen for a moment to the voices of those who are doing the hiring at the kinds of institutions many of us hope will employ our kids. Dr. Murzy Jhabvala, one of the chief engineers at NASA's Goddard Space Flight Center, is struck by "the sense of entitlement some new employees often have—a 'what will the agency/company do for *me?*' attitude. The 'get the job done—whatever it takes' mindset that was part of my training seems to have gone by the wayside."

Likewise, Tim Koogle, the founding CEO of Yahoo!, is concerned that kids aren't developing the set of leadership skills they'll need in the global economy—skills not focused on being the company "hero" but on *creating conditions* for collaboration, integrations, and group solving of complex problems.

While the concerns that Jhabvala, Koogle, and many other business leaders have can't entirely be laid at the feet of overindulgent parents (and an outdated educational system), it seems clear that our current parenting approach tilts toward producing the kinds of kids who are unlikely to fare well either personally or in the flat economy that they will inherit.

Materialism creates an unhealthy attachment to things.

Again, the problem with materialism isn't that people value stuff; it's that they value stuff more than family, friends, work, etc. As a young and inexperienced therapist, I was part of a team that counseled a very wealthy couple going through a divorce. The wife spent hours in my office lamenting the loss of her lifestyle. She fixated most on her sheets, which were the finest Egyptian cotton, scented and carefully ironed by the laundress. As a financially struggling twenty-eight-year-old intern, I couldn't understand why this woman was so attached to her sheets. After all, she stood to lose so much more. Now I know that, for her, luxuries had become necessities. She had become attached to the material benefits that accompanied her marriage, and she anticipated feeling deprived without them. Her sheets represented her entire material lifestyle.

The same thing can happen with children. If for any reason family circumstances change and their "stuff" is more limited, children can be miserable. And, as I've already established, they are likely to lack the emotional resources and resilience to effectively move forward. In fact, materialistic kids have higher rates of depression and substance abuse than nonmaterialistic kids.[11] Substance abuse is a natural outcome for kids who are accustomed to looking outside themselves for solace and relief.

How Parents Can Discourage the Gimmes

It's likely that all Americans are materialistic to some degree. After all, we are constantly surrounded by indirect and direct messages telling us that various material items will make us happier, better looking, more desirable, higher in status, etc. However, materialism as a primary value system (and the sense of entitlement that often accompanies it) is not inevitable. As parents we're in an ideal position to make sure that our children do not grow up believing that *things* are what matter most in life.

Transmitting values is one of the most important parenting jobs we have. It is our responsibility to steer the subculture of materialism and entitlement back in the right direction. Here's how you can start.

TAKE AN HONEST LOOK AT THE SIGNALS YOU'RE SENDING. Vicki brought her teenage daughter Natalia into my office, worried that Natalia was too materialistic. Eyeing the Balanciaga bag that Natalia nonchalantly dumped beside her chair, I was inclined to agree. But it wasn't long into the session when Natalia asked to use my computer. She logged into her mother's Hermès account and showed me that Vicki had purchased six Birkin bags, stating, "You've got the wrong person in your office." Like Vicki (whose case is admittedly extreme), we can find it can be easy to ignore our own materialistic habits while being concerned about those same tendencies in our children.

"Do as I say, not as I do" is a terribly ineffective parenting strategy. Kids, who are both observant and absorbent, will consciously and unconsciously model the behaviors and attitudes they see *you* displaying. When parents value financial success more than affiliation, community, or self-acceptance, they are likely to have children who share those values.[12] Take a close look at your own actions and comments. Do you say things like "Well, I guess Bill has finally made it—he's driving a Benz," or wonder aloud why friends had to sell their plane/condo/exotic car." Do you go on (and on and on) about the expensive birthday gift your son received from his grandparents? Do you speak with the same respect to the worker in the local grocery store as you do to your financial advisor?

Obsessing over your child's grades—or harping on your own desire to make more money—can also push the gimmes and teach your child to value achievement over satisfying work. It's not that there's anything wrong with an occasional observation about finances, but your kids are paying strict attention to what you pay attention to. This lets them know what matters to you. Make sure that you talk about commitment, integrity, acts of service, philanthrophy, and generosity. Kids need to know that these are the conditions of life that are on your radar. Dinnertime, something families should strive to enjoy together on a regular basis, is a perfect time to talk about moral choices and explain why you made them. This can be as simple as how you chose to send fifty dollars to one charity over another or whether cheating is ever justified. It wasn't so long ago that kids, teens in particular, were interested in discussing moral issues in depth and with vigor. Try to stoke that natural interest of teens as they find themselves more able to think deeply about complex issues.

ASK YOURSELF IF YOU'RE CAVING IN TO PARENTAL PEER PRESSURE. Why did you buy your child that trendy new backpack at the beginning of the academic year? After all, the one he used last year isn't torn, stained, or too small. Did you believe he "needed" an upgrade—or did some part of you not want to be the parent of the out-of-style kid? Likewise, are other parents' opinions factoring into your decision to put your daughter in an intensive gymnastics program, or to hire an SAT prep tutor for your high school freshman?

It's very important to delve into what motivates your parenting decisions. A need for meaning and approval in your own life can translate into decisions that may not have your child's best interests at heart. If your primary identity derives from being a parent and your identity as an individual has pretty much disappeared (that's a *very* important distinction, fine as it can be sometimes), you need to get a life, as the saying goes. Take a class. Explore a new—or old—

hobby. Clear time in your schedule for friends. In other words, do something that you find interesting, meaningful, or fulfilling that does *not* involve your children.

STOP GIVING "THINGS" AS REWARDS. Especially when done on a constant or near-constant basis, using material items to reward and motivate children inhibits the development of internal motivation and reinforces materialistic values. When possible, substitute meaningful experiences for things, and tie those experiences to your child's budding strengths and interests. Not only will you be showing support, you'll be strengthening the parent-child bond in a positive way. For example, instead of promising a new iPad (or even a new car) for graduation, tell your outdoorsy teenager that your family will go on a weekend camping trip at a state park. You might also take a younger child showing an interest in paleontology to a natural history museum instead of giving her a gaming system after she brings home a much-improved report card.

MAKE KIDS PAY FOR THEIR OWN "EXTRAS," AT LEAST SOME OF THE TIME. Some of the wisest, and most successful wealthy parents I know are extremely careful about how much money their children have. These parents have their kids participate in family chores and neighborhood jobs and do not discuss family wealth with their kids—after all, none of it was earned by the child! No matter the nature of your family finances (*especially* if they theoretically allow you to provide everything your child needs and wants), this is a good model to follow.

In addition, encourage your children to earn money at age-appropriate jobs. You may not want them to work much (or at all) during the school year—actually, there *is* something to the notion that kids should be focusing on their studies, as long as it isn't taken overboard—but they can work during summer vacations. Require them to use the money they earn, as well as monetary gifts they may have received for birthday or holiday gifts, to purchase desired items.

Tell your son that he must contribute a certain percentage toward that new Xbox. Establish ahead of time with your daughter that you'll provide a certain amount of clothing "staples" each season; any other fashion must-haves are up to her to acquire. This isn't being "mean"; it's certainly not depriving or hurting your children. Instead it's teaching them the value of work, sustainable financial practices, and the satisfaction that comes from accomplishing a goal on one's own.

One of the best things I ever did to contribute to my kids' educations was sitting down with them when they turned thirteen and constructing a budget that would cover all of their needs. At the time the amount of money seemed high, but it was designed to cover everything from athletic shoes to pizza after soccer games. Once my son saw the chunk that was gone when he bought the Air Jordans he was used to getting from me, he had a revelation. Shoes came in all different price ranges, as did many of his purchased items. He opted to give up Air Jordans (while discovering Payless) and keep the saved money for the social activities he valued. To this day he is careful about money, often replacing full-price items with discounted ones. I did this with each of my three sons, and frankly it saved me money and helped them develop a sensible and sustainable attitude toward the role of money and stuff in their lives. It gave them a sense of control about finances, which they have maintained into adulthood. While they seemed like hefty sums at the time, once we figured in all their needs and some of their wants, it was, in fact, a great bargain!

ASSIGN CHORES. Family is a child's first community and serves as a template for how to live and work in a community for the rest of one's life. Required chores transmit the idea that contribution and collaboration are necessary to maintain the common good. Also, children will learn that taking on less-than-enjoyable tasks is a necessary part of life. Their work ethic will be strengthened, they will be more likely to take future responsibilities seriously, and entitlement will be less likely to take root in them.

EMPHASIZE RELATIONSHIPS. Most psychologists agree on the fundamental needs of humans. On a basic biological level, we need food, shelter, and clothing. But we also have so-called higher-order needs, which include authentic self-expression, intimate relationships, and contributions to the community.[13] In other words, positive social relationships with people who know you deeply lead to happiness. When you emphasize the importance of relationships to your children, you contribute to their well-being in a fundamental way, and you also increase the chances that they will value people more highly than material items and that they will develop a sense of empathy and responsibility toward others. After all, if we're subscribing to the long-term view of parenting (which we should!), then we are more interested in what kind of friend, spouse, and parent our child will eventually be and less concerned about their GPA at the end of every quarter.

ENCOURAGE GIVING BACK AND ACTS OF KINDNESS. This is another way to encourage relationship building, contributions to the larger community, and the development of a perspective that goes beyond shoes, clothing, toys, gadgets, and cars. One of the most effective ways to help your children develop generosity and empathy is to get involved *with them* in some sort of community activity. It's a two-birds-with-one-stone scenario: your children will see that there's meaning and joy in selflessness and they'll also spend time connecting with you, their parents.

People with religious and/or spiritual affiliations tend to be happier. Involvement in this way helps develop rituals in families, which are often good insurance for continued family involvement down the line. Furthermore, having an active spiritual or religious life combats materialism by reminding kids that there are greater forces in the world, and that they have a responsibility to be of service. I am reminded of the Hebrew phrase *tikkun olam*, meaning "healing the world." It is the antithesis of entitlement, narcissism, and materialism.

Practicing some of the tactics I've laid out here may not be easy. For many parents, they surely won't be. If you have fallen into a pattern of lavishing kids with stuff (for whatever reason), modeling materialism, allowing (or even encouraging) selfish, entitled behavior, you may find it a struggle to change your ways. Your challenge is not unlike that of a severely overweight, sedentary person deciding to lose one hundred pounds and train for a marathon. You're going to feel deprived at times and long-unused muscles are going to protest loudly. But the payoff is surely worth making the effort.

Why? Because the payoff is a happy, well-adjusted, authentically successful child. The Travises of the world, grasping for the trappings of teenage status and perpetually indulged by parents who can't say no, are not just bratty. They are crippled and deeply unhappy. They may not know it now, but they will when they hit the real world, unarmed with the tools they need to navigate it. No parent I know wants that outcome for the child they love.

Do a careful inventory of the values that you intend to promote and those you actually do promote, and judge how well they are aligned with your parenting practices. In my book *Teach Your Children Well*, there is a series of exercises that can help you see whether what you believe is really what you are communicating. I have been a clinical psychologist for close to thirty years. No parent has ever come into my office seeking advice on how to damage their children or turn them into self-centered, emotionally stunted adults. While we all hope that our children do well in school, we hope with even greater fervor that they will do well in life. Our job is to help them to know and appreciate themselves deeply, to be resilient in the face of adversity, to approach the world with zest, to find work that is satisfying, friends and spouses who are loving and loyal, and to hold a deep belief that they have something meaningful to contribute to the world. This is how we turn out good kids who become good adults. This is how we avoid raising self-centered, materialistic kids and instead parent for authentic success. This doesn't ensure an easy life for our children. Nothing can do that. But it does ensure that our children will find joy and meaning in their lives and that they will be well equipped to meet the inevitable challenges of life.

1. J. M. Twenge, *Generation Me: Why Today's Young Americans Are More Confident, Assertive, Entitled—and More Miserable Than Ever Before* (New York: Free Press, 2006), 69–71.

2. D. Myers and E. Diener, "The Pursuit of Happiness," *Scientific American* 274 (5) 1996, 70–72.

3. E. Diener, J. Horwitz, and R. A. Emmons, "Happiness of the Very Wealthy," *Social Indicators Research* 16 (1985), 263–74.

4. S. Collishaw, et al., "Time Trends in Adolescent Mental Health," *Journal of Child Psychology and Psychiatry*, 45 (8) 2004, 1350–62.

5. *Ibid.*

6. CDC, http://www.cdc.gov/violenceprevention/pub/youth_suicide.html.

7. YoungMinds, (2011) *100,000 Children and Young People Could Be Hospitalised Due to Self-Harm by 2020 Warns YoungMinds* (London: YoungMinds, 2011).

8. C. Dweck, *Mindset* (New York: Ballantine Books, 2007).

9. W. S. Grolnick, *The Psychology of Parental Control: How Well-Meant Parenting Backfires* (Mahwah, NJ: Lawrence Erlbaum Associates, 2003). See also A. Kohn, *Punished by Rewards* (Boston: Houghton Mifflin, 1999).

10. K. M. Sheldon, M. S. Sheldon, and R. Osbaldiston, "Prosocial Values and Group Assortation in an N-Person Prisoner's Dilemma," *Human Nature* 11 (2000), 387–404.

11. T. Kasser and R. M. Ryan, "A Dark Side of the American Dream: Correlates of Financial Success as a Central Life Aspiration," *Journal of Personality and Social Psychology* 65 (1993), 410–22.

12. T. Kasser, R. M. Ryan, and M. Zax, "The Relations of Maternal and Social Environments to Late Adolescents' Materialistic and Prosocial Values," *Developmental Psychology* 31 (6) 1995, 907–14.

13. A. H. Maslow, *Motivation and Personality*, 2nd ed. (New York: Harper & Row, 1970).

why empathy matters and how to raise kids who will be empathic adults

BY FRAN WALFISH, PSYD, FORMER SCHOOL PSYCHOLOGIST, CURRENT CHILD AND FAMILY PSYCHOTHERAPIST, AND EXTREMELY PROUD AUNT

Maya was a beautiful nine-year-old girl with long shiny dark hair who was referred to me several years ago. At face value you might believe she was a nice little girl, because she gave a first impression of politeness and smiles, but according to her parents and teachers Maya lied, bullied her classmates, and was angry and defiant every single day.

My young friend also had an alarming lack of concern for others. As an example, when Maya's maternal grandfather died, her parents were devastated and grieved deeply. Maya, however, showed no concern for either her parents or her grandfather, and instead threw a series of temper tantrums because the family postponed a big vacation so they could attend the funeral.

Despite all this, Maya's parents loved and adored her (and her younger sister). But they were unwitting contributors to their daughter's problems. Maya's mother overprotected her daughters, could not hold a disciplinary boundary if her life depended on it, and intermittently collapsed when Maya was defiant. For example, when Maya wanted an iPhone and her mother said no, Maya threw huge tantrums and demanded it so consistently and relentlessly that her mother finally caved and bought her the phone.

Her father wavered between appropriate discipline and explosive bursts of anger followed by consequences that were often far too harsh. When it came to the phone, he first appropriately said, "No, you can't have it because nine is too young." When Maya didn't listen, the third time he explained his decision he exploded into a rage and told her she could not have playdates during the next three weeks. This lengthy punishment, of course, gave Maya legitimate reason to be angry and kept the cycle of defiance going.

Neither of these opposite parenting styles allowed for empathic understanding of Maya's feelings or emotions. Nor did they allow Maya to deal with her own feelings or understand that her parents acknowledged, validated, or accepted her, flaws and all. All of this combined to produce a lack of empathy in Maya that led to her inappropriate behavior.

When I first began seeing her, Maya was at a critical crossroad and needed help. Just after my first session with her, Maya had a defining incident at home. She was from an upper-middle-class family, but her family was financially and socially below that of most of her classmates. One day Maya came home and demanded that she be given an expensive pair of designer jeans. Many of the girls at school had them, and Maya insisted that she have a pair too. When her parents explained they could not afford the jeans, Maya went ballistic. Her longing for something she could not have turned into greed, and her inability to understand her parents' position showed a profound lack of empathy.

Empathy is a crucial personality trait in a child's character development. It is the capacity to imagine one's self in another person's skin, to feel what they feel in a given circumstance; and it is learned experientially. We learn to be empathic by being empathized with, especially during infancy and toddlerhood. When a baby cries, he hopes there is a consistent, warm, empathic response from a steady primary attachment figure, such as his mother.

If this does not happen, as the baby matures into childhood and adolescence, disruptive behaviors can occur. When a teen who has no empathy continually talks out of turn in class, he will show no remorse about his disruptive behavior when his teacher asks him to stop. Rather than comply, he might point a finger at the teacher and mock her, or say, "She's so *mean*." The teen has no capacity to understand his behavior from the perspective of others, including his teacher and fellow classmates.

Empathy Is Crucial to Humanity

Many studies show that a lack of empathy can cause people to display behaviors that range from self-absorption to cruelty. A 2010 study at the University of Michigan Institute for Social Research found that today's college students are 40 percent less empathetic than students were in 1979. According to the findings, today's students are less likely to describe themselves as "soft-hearted" or to have "tender, concerned feelings" for others. They are more likely, meanwhile, to admit that "other people's misfortunes" usually don't disturb them.[1]

Cambridge University professor Simon Baron-Cohen discusses similar findings in his book *The Science of Evil*, where he explains that an erosion of empathy can explain why some people commit cruel acts.[2]

Empathy is also an essential part of being human. Without it, most relationships risk collapse. It is human nature to want to be seen, validated, understood, and accepted, but without empathy none of this can occur. Most people received empathy from others when they were very young, but whether or not a person shows empathy when she is older depends on a combination of how much empathy she has innately and how much she was given.

A 2011 study in *Child Development* looked at research that involved 270,000 students and compared those who participated in empathic learning programs with those who had not. The findings showed that students who received empathic training not only had increased social and emotional skills, but also had an eleven-point increase in standardized achievement test scores.[3] Yes, empathy is important.

The good news is that spending quality time with an empathetic grandparent, aunt, or nanny can give babies and young children what mom or dad might not be able to. For an older child, a warm, nurturing teacher who also balances limits and boundaries can be helpful. When an important authority figure such as a teacher, coach, counselor, pastor, or rabbi relates with empathy to a child, it goes into the child like quick-healing penicilin. It truly can affect a young person in an enormously positive way—if the child admires, respects, and aspires to be like the figure. Providing steady empathy to a child can definitely navigate the future direction the child will take. When empathy is given to children, they learn to be empathetic.

Empathy is a prime issue in my practice. I teach parents to respond to their child's struggles in a consistent manner over a long period of time—sometimes over many years—by using empathetic narration. With an older child, words to the effect of "Right now you are mad at me and hate me. I understand that," combined with clear and definite boundaries, can be very effective.

When you are using empathic narration, it is essential that your tone of voice be compassionate and empathetic. With your tone, words, and body language, you must show that you truly understand what your child is feeling. Only in that way will your child learn to reciprocate to you and to others. You might say to your daughter, "It's time to turn off the TV, take a bath, and get ready for bed." If her response is, "No, I don't want to," you can come back in a kind, compassionate, empathetic voice and say, "I know how hard it is to stop when you want more." If your tone is not filled with empathy, however, your daughter may react with anger.

If, despite all your efforts, you do not see empathy in your son or daughter by age six or seven, you should contact a child psychologist for an evaluation.

The Dire Consequences of Lacking Empathy

I wish I could have given this information to Maya's parents when she was that age. At nine, she had already developed serious narcissistic traits in her personality. Maya truly did not care about other people, caused her parents stress, did not feel bad in class when she continually refused to comply with her teacher's requests, did not care when she interrupted her teachers' lessons and distracted other kids, was angry and disrespectful, and showed no guilt when she took things from her sister.

This personality results in major self-absorption and includes a pattern of grandiosity, a huge need for admiration, a lack of empathy for others, and no self-reflection or accountability. I hoped narcissism was all Maya had developed, because everything I knew about her led me to believe that if she continued down her current road, she could develop into a sociopath.

A sociopath is a person who disregards the rights of others, fails to conform to social norms, disrespects lawful behaviors, lies repeatedly, is impulsive and fails to plan ahead, is aggressive, shows reckless disregard for the safety of himself and others, is indifferent, and shows a lack of remorse. The onset is almost always before the age of fifteen, but typically has not been diagnosed as such until after a child turns eighteen.

The sociopath diagnosis, by the way, is more common than you might think. Harvard psychologist Dr. Martha Stout, author of *The Sociopath Next Door*, reveals that up to 4 percent of people—or one in twenty-five—possess no conscience, feel no guilt, and are, therefore, sociopaths. One of the main ingredients in having a conscience is empathy, so you can see why I felt a genuine concern for Maya.

Early on, Maya tried to shine me on with false sweetness in an effort to worm her way out of therapy. If you have ever watched the old sitcom *Leave It to Beaver*, you might be familiar with the manipulative Eddie Haskell character. Maya had the same type of overly "good" mannerisms with me that Eddie showed to the parents of his friends.

When Maya realized her Miss Goody Two-Shoes approach was not going to work with me, she then put me through the wringer. She refused to speak. She pouted. She would not look at me. She stomped her foot. She crossed her arms. She was the poster child of resistance. But after a while she found that, unlike her mother, I did not collapse when faced with her behavior. Instead, I talked to her with empathic narration week after week after week.

I also taught her parents the appropriate words to say, so she would hear lots of empathic narration at home. And I showed her dad that instead of being angry at her behavior with regard to the designer jeans that she wanted, the better choice was a metaphoric arm of support. The words I gave him to use were: "I see how badly you want the designer jeans, so you can have what other girls have and feel part of the group. Right now we do not have the money to pay for them, but we will set up a structure for a period of time so you can earn the money by doing household chores to buy the things you want. Your mom and I will also pitch in and pay a portion."

Upon hearing that news, Maya had the inevitable temper tantrum. But, I taught her mom to say, with compassion: "I understand your anger, but we cannot have that kind of noise in our house. If you need to yell, you must go into your bedroom and close the door. When you are ready to come out and use an indoor voice, we really want you to join the rest of us."

Maya's mom and dad each had to learn to balance nurturing and love, while still holding the line. That was the hardest part of Maya's treatment because it was terrifying for her mom to hold the line, and it took a while for her dad to appreciate the importance of a softer, empathic approach with his daughter. To make progress, I served myself up as a "parent" to Maya's mom and dad. I was warm and empathic to them when they did well, but I busted them with straight talk when they needed to make a change.

As for Maya, I initially gave her quality individual time to develop warmth as a foundation for the boundaries that were to come. Then I presented a clear structure where I told Maya that specific negative behaviors would now lead to specific consequences. I developed the consequences with her parents, as I knew they had to sting harshly for a short amount of time to keep Maya motivated and trying. Then I held fast when Maya raged at me. But, instead of raging back, I said with compassion things such as, "I bet it feels great to blast a grown-up," and "I know how angry you feel."

As with many people who have a lack of empathy, underneath Maya's entitlement and grandiosity was a huge well of rage and anger, and beyond that was an invisible bottomless pit of nothingness. Maya needed to rage at her mom and dad, but they could not handle that emotionally. Her parents had to learn to tolerate and bear being the target of their child's powerful feelings. What is not acceptable is disrespect and rage. Rather than be defensive, attack back, or collapse, I gave Maya's mom and dad the following words to say: "I hear you. I understand you are mad and I want to hear more so we can work it out, but you cannot use disrespectful words."

Over two or three years, Maya gradually allowed herself to become closer to me and her parents. She still tested us constantly, but we kept in mind that she ranted because she needed to know that we could still be trusted. Slowly, ever so slowly, Maya's rants became less frequent and more empathetic. Instead of them being all about her, her feelings gradually began to include others. When she said, "Do you hate me?" I knew we had rounded a corner because her words indicated that she cared how I felt about her. Maya was coming out of the red danger zone.

I continued therapy with Maya on a reduced scale throughout her adolescence to help her through the natural separation process from her parents. Today Maya is doing well in college and has many friends. She even recently took time to care for her mother after her mom had minor surgery. The person Maya was when she first came to me could never have done that.

But behind the sullen anger and rage was a little girl who was crying out for help. Kudos to Maya's parents for recognizing that—and also for staying the course for so long with her treatment.

Of course, most kids never reach the point of needing such serious treatment. But all kids, and many adults, could use help in this area. Here's a short list of things you can do at home every day that will increase your empathy and help instill empathy in your children.

---

toughLOVE TIPS
How to instill empathy

---

1. Choose one thing about your child that you can express appreciation to them about. "I love how gentle you are with the kitty cat," or "You did a nice thing when you helped your brother make his bed."

2. Ask yourself, "What is my child feeling?" especially during difficult moments. Imagine yourself as a ten-year-old boy who has no one to sit with during lunch at school. How would you feel? Then use those feelings to empathize with your son.

3. Follow through on every promise to your children. Consistency is a key element in establishing both boundaries and empathy, and your children need to know they can always depend on you for both.

4. Understand the huge impact that you have on your kids. For better or worse, your children model your behavior. If you smoke, drink, stay out late, and party, then do not be surprised if your teenage children do the same thing.

5. When they are old enough, involve your children in a volunteer or service project that helps others. When kids see the result of a good deed, it instills the importance of it in their minds. It also becomes personal and helps empathy to grow.

6. Learn to listen by reflecting your child's thoughts and feelings back to him or her. Be sure they are your son or daughter's feelings, and not your feelings, though. Listen.

7. Ask questions such as: "What can I do to help?" and "What do you need?" Sometimes kids do not know how to

express their wants and needs, and it takes a series of gentle questions to find out what is going on.

8. Observe how your kids express their feelings, and take special note of their body language and other nonverbal communication. A child who says "Hi" with a bright face, smile, and a skip in his walk is in a different place emotionally than a child who says "Hi" with his eyes downcast and his shoulders slumped.

9. Maintain a home environment that is emotionally safe, friendly, and facilitates open communication. Your children need to know that whatever the situation is, they can come to you without being raged at.

Empathic narration is key to establishing empathy, and the family dinner table is a great place to practice it. Family dinners are also wonderful opportunities to learn about taking turns in talking and listening. This is important because listening is a big component of empathy. If you do not listen, truly listen, you will never know what someone else thinks and feels. If you do not know another's thoughts and feelings, you cannot narrate them back.

Kids and adults alike often become excited about their own ideas, and chime in or interrupt while someone else is speaking. The dinner table offers a golden opportunity for parents to referee the flow of conversation, and make sure each person's turn to talk is not interrupted. This is also a chance for your kids to grow in empathy in front of your very eyes. If you praise them for every incremental step toward respectful listening behavior, for every empathic comment toward another, you will be well on your way toward developing empathy in your children.

In closing, it is important that you do five things to ensure that your child develops empathy. The earlier you can start this, the better, but even if you have an older child, a teen, or even an adult child, these five steps will help your son or daughter become more empathetic.

---

toughLOVE TIPS
Ensuring empathetic development

---

1. **See your child for who he or she is, warts and all.** Say to her, "No one is perfect," then own up to your own errors when you make them. This will help your child accept herself, flaws and all.

2. **Empathize out loud to narrate your child's struggle in the moment.** You could say, "It's really hard when you try your best and do not make it on the team," in a kind, compassionate, empathetic tone.

3. **Be kind to your child while balancing empathic nurturing with firm boundaries.** Even when you have to say no and your child fights you, stay kind and respectful. Never lose your cool and attack back.

4. **Feel empathy for yourself, so that you can feel empathy for your child.** Accept the fact that you will make mistakes. We are all on a learning curve, but the key is to acknowledge your mistakes, own up to them, and start over. "Oops, there I go again," said gently as you own up to your own misstep, can go a long way. In this way you are modeling empathy for your own imperfections.

5. **Recognize your own level of empathy, even though this is easier said than done.** Lack of empathy is a classic sign of self-absorption. Is it in you to automatically think about the impact of your words and behavior on other people? If not, use empathic narration on yourself. Over time you will begin to see yourself in the shoes of others, and can instill this very important personality trait in your children.

. . .

We need to remember that empathy will not develop overnight. Nor will a lack of empathy show up all at once. Parents need to pay attention, be engaged, and be patient. Good humans take time.

1. Keith O'Brien, "The Empathy Deficit," October 17, 2010. http://www.boston.com/bostonglobe/ideas/articles/2010/10/17/the_empathy_deficit/.

2. "Could a Lack of Empathy Explain Cruelty?" *Talk of the Nation*, Ira Flatow, host, September 30, 2011. http://www.npr.org/2011/09/30/140954023/could-a-lack-of-empathy-explain-cruelty.

3. Joseph A. Durlak, Roger P. Weissberg, Allison B. Dymnicki, Rebecca D. Taylor, and, Kriston B. Schellinger, "The Impact of Enhancing Students' Social and Emotional Learning: A Meta-Analysis of School-Based Universal Interventions," *Child Development*, February 3, 2011. http://onlinelibrary.wiley.com/doi/10.1111/j.1467-8624.2010.01564.x/full.

engaging with your kids: what is family time these days and how can we make the most of it?

BY ELLEN GALINSKY, MS, PRESIDENT AND COFOUNDER OF
FAMILIES AND WORK INSTITUTE (FWI) AND MOM OF TWO

If I were to ask you to think about a word that describes life today, what would your word be?

In recent years, speaking about my book *Mind in the Making*, I've asked this question of many audiences. If you are anything like them, you would answer with words like *busy, stressful, hectic, complicated, information overload, multitasking.* The words used by parents across this country—from bustling cities on the coasts to the seemingly quieter communities on the plains, from the Deep South to the far North—almost always reflect a sense of feeling pulled in too many directions without enough time to respond. As one mother said: "I have these endless to-do lists and of course there is no way that I can *ever* get everything done."

Time has become a very precious commodity.

The percentage of employees who feel deprived of time continues to spiral up and up, according to the ongoing nationally representative research of the U.S. workforce that my organization, Families and Work Institute (FWI), conducts. Three in four of us don't feel we have enough time with our children, while about three in five of us don't have enough with our spouses or partners and for ourselves. The time-saving devices that were supposed to give us more time seem to give us less. The every-time, every-place technology and the pressured pace of life all contribute to the feeling of living in a time famine.[1]

As people feel more deprived of time, time has become progressively more precious—a new currency. In one study, almost half of young employees (45 percent) said they would trade a higher salary for more flexibility about where and when they work.[2] In our research, we asked employees what would be important to them if they were thinking about taking a new job, and 87 percent—men and women alike—said that flexibility would be essential or very important.[3]

Figure 1: Time famine: 1992–2008

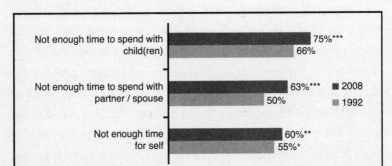

** p < .01; *** p < .001.

Sources: Families and Work Institute, National Study of the Changing Workforce, 1992, 2005, and 2008.

Today's parents spend *as much* or *more* time with children than those of previous generations.

Although 75 percent of employed parents don't feel they have enough time with their children, numerous studies show that parents actually spend *as much or more* time with their kids than in the past few decades. When we compare employed mothers in 1977 with those in 2008, FWI's National Study of the Changing Workforce found—perhaps surprisingly—that the amount of time mothers reported spending with children under thirteen has *not* gone down, despite the fact that employed mothers were working longer hours in 2008 than in 1977.[4]

The American Time Use Survey uses time diaries to drill down into how people spend their time. Individuals are asked to tell an interviewer about a twenty-four-hour period: what they were doing, for how long, with whom, and where they were at the time of each activity. In comparing findings over the years, the researchers found that mothers' time in caring for their children under eighteen dipped between 1965 and 1975 (when baby-boom households gave way to households with fewer children) but time with children has been rising ever since.[5] Although at-home mothers spend more time with their children than mothers who are employed, both groups continue to increase their time with their children. Suzanne Bianchi, a lead researcher on this study, wrote, "A comparison of mothers' diaries shows that employed mothers were recording as much time doing primary child care in 2000 as nonemployed mothers did in 1975."[6]

Where do mothers, especially those who are employed, find this time? They do less housework. There is more dust in all of our houses! And fathers? Numerous studies show that their time with children has steadily increased over the years.[7] Our National Study of the Changing Workforce found that on workdays, fathers' time

Figure 2: Mothers' and fathers' average time (in hours) spent with their children under 13 years old on workdays (1977–2008)

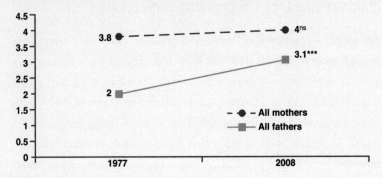

ns = not significant; *** = p < .001

Statistically significant differences between fathers and mothers: 1977; 2008 (1977 n = 455; 2008 n = 512)

Source: U.S. Department of Labor, Quality of Employment Survey, 1977; Families and Work Institute, National Study of the Changing Workforce, 2008.

Figure 3: Young mothers' and fathers' (under 29) average time (in hours) spent with their children under 13 years old on workdays (1977–2008)

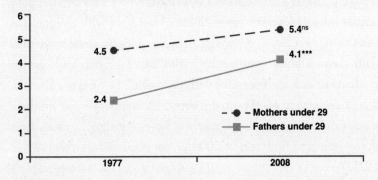

ns = not significant; *** = p < .001

Statistically significant differences between young fathers and mothers. 1977 ***; 2008 ns (1977 n = 124; 2008 n = 95)

Source: U.S. Department of Labor, Quality of Employment Survey, 1977; Families and Work Institute, National Study of the Changing Workforce, 2008.

with their children under thirteen increased by more than one hour over the past three decades.

For younger fathers—Millennials—the change was even more dramatic, an increase of 1.7 hours![8]

Family time has become more scattered, scheduled, and higher-stakes.

If the time that families are spending with children has increased, why do we feel more deprived of time than ever? From our research, there are a number of reasons. First, the time we have with our kids is more scattered: it happens in fits and starts, not in long stretches. And it is more prone to interruptions. We hear our iPhones or BlackBerrys ping while we are helping the kids with their homework. We jump between tasks on our never-ending to-do lists.[9] Children are also more scheduled than in the past.[10] Technology, the escalating demands of work, and family life today all contribute to our feeling that we don't have enough time.

Many parents also feel that the stakes are higher. Many of us have read the research on the importance of family dinners and family time together. We have heard about the research on the brain development of young children. We want to be involved parents in a world that makes it difficult.

Children want their parents to be less stressed and tired.

In this chapter on family time, I am going to take an unusual approach. I am going to look at what *children—not just adults*—say matters most, sharing suggestions about how we can make the most of the family time we have. My data come from two nationally representative studies I conducted, one of children in the third through the twelfth grades and one of parents with children from birth through eighteen years. Together, these studies are called and were published as *Ask the Children*.[11] I also use data from our other studies and from my book *Mind in the Making*.[12]

In *Ask the Children*, I asked children "one wish" questions about their parents who are employed—a mother, a father, or the person who is like a mother or father to them: *"If you were granted one wish that would change the way that your mother's/your father's work affects your life, what would that wish be?"*

In the separate survey of parents, I asked them to guess what their children would wish. Most parents (56 percent) guessed that their children would wish for more time together.

Perhaps surprisingly, more time was *not* at the top of children's wish lists when given just *one* wish. Only 10 percent of children made that wish about their mothers and 15.5 percent made that wish about their fathers. Most children wished that their mothers (34 percent) and their fathers (27.5 percent) would be less stressed and tired. By contrast, only 2 percent of parents guessed that their children would wish for less tired and stressed parents.

Does this finding mean that children don't care about family time? No, not at all! Children wouldn't care about parents being less stressed and tired if they didn't care about the time they spend together as a family.

However, most people who hear about this finding conclude, "It's quality time, not quantity time that matters most." For me, this interpretation signals we are stuck in the wrong debates. We tend to think in either/or terms, such as, it's quality *or* quantity time. Even the word *balance* that's used indicates an either/or mentality. If you give to one side of your life, then you are taking away from the other. But our data and the data of other researchers don't fit these either/or frameworks.

Below I share eight findings and their implications for family time. I begin with the roadblocks to family time—guilt and stress—

because they can cloud the time families have together, no matter how much time it is and no matter how often it occurs.

Parents *need* to destress.

Parental stress can be a roadblock to family time. The Ask the Children study found that about one third of children (32 percent) worried about their parents often or very often. If the children who said they sometimes worried about their parents were included, the percentage went up to two-thirds of children. One of the major reasons that children worried about their parents was because of the stress in their lives. Worry and stress can spill over into family time!

THINK ABOUT WHAT ASPECT OF YOUR LIFE IS CAUSING YOU THE MOST STRESS AND CHANGE WHAT YOU CAN CHANGE. Ask yourself the "one wish" question: "If you were granted one wish that would change the stresses that negatively affect your family time, what would that wish be?" Continue thinking about what is causing you the most stress until you come upon something you can change right now—to get a small win. For example, it may be something at home: the laundry piling up or having to make school lunches. Get help if you can.

It may be something about work. Our research indicates that employees are in much better mental and physical health when they have jobs that provide (1) job autonomy, or having some say about how to do their jobs; (2) learning opportunities that challenge and stretch them; (3) a culture of respect and trust; (4) economic security—satisfaction with pay, benefits, and opportunities for advancing; (5) supervisor support for succeeding on the job; and (6) work-life fit as well as access to workplace flexibility.[13] When you think about these factors, is there something you want to and can change?

One parent speaks of learning to take more control of when she says yes and when she says no: "I've learned only this past month to say to people. 'I can't do that on that day. I'm not available.' And when they say, 'Oh, well, what are you doing? Maybe you can switch your plans,' I just say, 'No, I wish I could help, but I really can't.' I used to say, 'Maybe I can,' and I used to tell them what I was doing, as if it was their responsibility to determine what I should do."

DEVELOP TECHNIQUES FOR MANAGING STRESS, ESPECIALLY TRANSITIONS IN THE MORNINGS AND THE EVENINGS. Do mornings turn into "rush hour" in your home? Find ways to plan ahead, such as setting out clothes the night before or making lunches. One mother said: "I trained myself in fifteen-minute increments to get up one hour earlier. Now I have time for a leisurely shower, coffee, and time with a good book before the morning madness begins. I firmly resist the temptation to do work or chores during this time. My rule is 'What can I do that is fun?'"

If evenings are the problem, find ways to turn off work or whatever you have been doing before family time. As a girl, age sixteen, put it: "Leave your work at work, and put on your parenting suit at home."

Techniques for leaving work at work can include meditating before leaving, listening to music, or changing clothes when you get home. My son made me a very cheerful tape to listen to in the car for my commute home. He called it "Prozac for driving" because he knew that it was such happy music that I would come home happy.

CREATE HELLO TRADITIONS WITH YOUR CHILDREN. Understand that the end of the day can be "arsenic hour"—you are not sure whether you want to take it or give it to the children. Children save up their concerns for the people that they feel the safest with—their parents. So have a homecoming routine—perhaps stopping what you are doing and just spending family time together. Don't forget to include food. Give them a healthy snack and have one yourself.

IF YOU HAVE HAD A STRESSFUL DAY, DEAL WITH IT DIRECTLY. Children, even the youngest children, are very attuned to our stress. One child said: "You can tell [if your parent is in a bad mood] because you get a short and simple answer." Another said his parents keep away from him if they have had a bad day: "If they had a bad day, they won't talk. Or they will just go off by themselves." Other kids steer clear of their parents: "If they have had a bad day, I just leave them alone. I just give them time to cool down." Or: "When [my mother] is really angry, we stay away. I don't want to get my head bitten off. So I just back down . . . go out of the room."

Children told me they also play detective to figure out what is wrong. One child told me of sitting out of sight, listening to her mother talk on the phone to a friend to find out what was really going on. Still others told me of sending their youngest sibling into the room where their parents were speaking in harsh tones. They had learned that the parents didn't think that the youngest child understood so they continued to talk. When that child returned to his siblings, he repeated the words he had heard.

There are several repercussions of how children respond to our stress:

- Children tend to think that what is going on is their fault. So assure them that it isn't their fault. Explain what has happened clearly in ways that are age appropriate: "I had a bad day today, just like you sometimes have a bad day at school. I will be fine soon. I just need to cool down."
- Children may hear only the negative side of the story, not the positive side. For example, parents tend to complain

about the bad things that happen at work but don't report on the good things. Perhaps as a result, most children don't think their parents like their work. The Ask the Children study found that while three in five parents liked their jobs a lot, only two in five children thought that their parents liked their jobs a lot.[14] Make sure you tell them both sides of the story—what you like and what you don't like about what you do in addition to parenting. As one fifteen-year-old boy stated: "You have to work and teach your children how to work. Also, let them know to do something they'll enjoy."

• In addition to focusing on your stress because it worries them, children are looking to you as a role model to learn how to handle stressful situations themselves. So remember to tell them how to resolve a difficult situation in appropriate ways so that they can learn from how you take on challenges. Taking on challenges is an important skill for you and for your children!

Parents need to understand and manage feelings of guilt.

Parents often feel guilty about the time they spend away from their children, especially mothers who are employed. These feelings are reinforced by the national conversation we've been having about employed mothers, in which being an employed mother is typically seen as *either* good for children (puts food on the table and a roof over their heads, and serves as a role model) *or* bad for children (takes parents away).

The volume on this conversation has been turned down by the recent recession, especially because the majority of mothers—70.9 percent with children under 18 and 64.2 percent with children under six—are in the labor force[15] and because mothers are a significant source of economic stability for their children. Mothers contribute 45 percent of family income.[16] Despite the fact that this is the new normal, employed mothers and at-home mothers alike—as well as fathers—can feel guilty and torn about the time they spend away from their children.

Looking at how employment affects children offers insight into the research realities behind these feelings. The way that the Ask the Children study probed how having a working mother—and working father—affected children was to ask the children themselves! For example, the study asked children in the third through the twelfth grades to rate their parents on twelve parenting skills that research indicates are linked to children's healthy development and school success. These included "raising me with good values"; "being someone I can go to when I am upset"; "appreciates me for who I am"; "encourages me to want to learn and to enjoy learning"; "is involved with my school or child care"; and so forth.

When we compared the children's ratings for mothers who were employed to ratings for at-home mothers, we found no differences! Note that many of these items relate to family time, such as "spends time talking with me," "is there for me when I am sick," "provides family traditions and rituals," and "knows what is really going on in my life."

While these results may be surprising to some, they shouldn't be. They confirm several decades of research that indicates that you can't tell very much about how a child will turn out *simply* because his or her mother works. As Lois Hoffman and her colleagues at the University of Michigan point out on the basis of a longitudinal study they conducted, maternal employment per se doesn't affect children. It is the context in which maternal employment takes place that matters.[17] Likewise, the National Institute of Child Health and Human Development (NICHD) study, which has been following approximately 1,200 children from ten communities from birth through their teen years, has found that mothers' employment does not, in and of itself, harm the bond between mother and child.[18]

Children understand that parents have to work. In the Ask the Children study, only 2 percent of the children wanted their mother to stay home. A twelve-year-old boy said: "If parents wish to provide some of the better things in life, both parents need to work and share the home and children responsibilities." A twelve-year-old girl wanted mothers to know: *Work if you want to work!* And a fifteen-year-old girl echoed decades of studies on the impact of maternal employment on children when she stated: "It's okay to work. The kid is going to turn out the same way if you work or if you don't work."

Overall, the research shows that what matters most is how children are parented by their mothers and fathers: what values their parents have, how parents connect to their children, and whether the children are priorities in their parents' lives. And again the large majority of children know this. A boy, age thirteen, said: "Keep on working and supporting your children."

But the kids admonished parents to put their children first, as in the words of an eleven-year-old boy and a ten-year-old girl, respectively: "Unless you are dying of starvation or are strongly in the need of money, *put your family before the work*." And "Your children are the most important part of your life—love them more than work."

Guilt can cloud our feelings, no matter what our lives involve, and stand in the way of what children are calling for. It can also lead us to try to make up our perceived wrongdoings to children, whatever the source of guilt. So let's look at how guilt functions, something I explored deeply in *The Six Stages of Parenthood*.[19]

UNDERSTAND HOW GUILT FUNCTIONS. Contrary to those who want to erase guilt, I think that guilt is, in fact, a useful emotion when it first appears because it tells us that there is a discrepancy between what we expect and what is happening. It's like a fever that tells us that something is wrong with our body. But—and this is an essential "but"—like a fever, guilt can become destructive *if* it rages untreated.

USE GUILT AS A PROMPT TO FIGURE OUT WHERE THE DISCREPANCY LIES BETWEEN WHAT YOU EXPECT AND WHAT IS HAPPENING, AND CHANGE EITHER YOUR EXPECTATIONS OR BEHAVIOR. Let's say you may expect family time to be cheerful and happy and you feel guilty when it's not. That's a good example of having an opportunity to change your expectations to be more realistic. It is unlikely that family time will always be cheerful because time with those about whom we care the most will inevitably have its ups and downs. So use that insight to change your expectation to be more realistic, accepting that there will be cheerful family times and times that are contentious.

A next step is figuring out how to deal with the issues that make family time disruptive. Often, having a meeting to uncover the problems and involving family members in brainstorming solutions and then trying them out is an effective way to deal with this challenge.

You may *not* want to yell at your children when family time turns into turmoil. You may decide that this is a realistic expectation and you want to change your behavior to live up to this expectation, so you find techniques to control your own feelings, such as a time-out for *you* to collect yourself before you say things you don't want to say or before you yell.

I have found that parental growth comes from this very process—recognizing when there is a discrepancy between expectations and reality and changing either your expectation or changing your behavior.[20]

MANAGE GUILT—DON'T LET IT MANAGE YOU. A mother recounts how it took her a long time to learn this but once she did, her life improved. She said, "Now I'm finally able to say I need this job, I like this job, but my kids come first. I'm finally able to shove the guilt of needing to be at work. And it's just too bad that it took me twelve years to do it. I wish I had been able to learn this a lot sooner, when the girls were younger."

As I said, I compare guilt to a fever—useful for figuring out the discrepancy between what we expect and what is happening, but destructive if it continues unaddressed.

One of the best examples of letting guilt get the better of us is that we give in to our children's every wish and whim to make up for something, such as our time away from our kids. When we do this, their wishes and whims become like bottomless pits that we can never fill. We may know this deep inside but it seems easier to have the family time go well rather than say no or "you can't" and end up with an angry or sad child.

But the short-term pain of saying no yields a longer-term gain. Don't fall into the guilt trap!!

Kids want more time with Dad.

Let's now look at how children feel about the time they do have with their parents. The national conversation that we've been having about work and family life focuses on mothers. Yet in finding after finding in my Ask the Children study, the importance of fathers to children is striking. For example, children were asked if they had too little, enough, or too much time with their mothers and fathers. Children were more likely to say that they had too little time with their fathers (35 percent) than their mothers (28 percent). Remember that 75 percent of parents say they don't have enough time with their kids—so parents feel more deprived of time than children do, yet about one in three children want more time, especially with dads!

One twelve-year-old girl whose father took frequent business trips said, "I miss him. He's gone for short times. He calls from where he is. I'd rather have him at home during that time, but I know he has to do it because it's part of his job." Another girl whose father worked very hard, including on weekends, said, "I can't spend much time with him because he's working. Sometimes I go with him to work on the weekends. But I just wish that he wouldn't work so much."

This finding illustrates why it is so important to ask the children rather than to rely on our own assumptions.

FAMILY TIME IS FOR MOTHERS AND FATHERS. It can be all-together time or time alone with one parent or another. If you are a single parent or a dual-mom or -dad family, this finding of course applies to whoever is important in your children's lives—the partners, grandparents, aunts, uncles, or close friends—male and female.

LEARN TO AGREE TO AGREE AND AGREE TO DISAGREE. Any time there are two people involved in caring for children—whether a mother and father or a parent and grandparent or parent and child-care provider—there will be disagreements. It's best to assume that will be the case and figure out what your most important values are as a parent and ask the others with whom you share the care of your child to support you on your key values, and you will likewise support him or her. Here you are *agreeing to agree.*

On the less important issues, agree that it is okay to do things differently. In fact, children prosper when they learn that different adults in their lives (from their families to their teachers) have different expectations. Here you are *agreeing to disagree.*

An example of this from my own parenting is that my husband comes from a family of teasers and he began teasing our children when they were little. I didn't like that and asked him to please support me by not teasing our kids. Likewise, eating food with zero additives was more important to him than to me, but I supported him on making sure that our children ate well (for which I am grateful today). We agreed to agree on these ways of being with our children. But we also agreed to disagree about things that were less important to both of us, like their having chewing gum (as long as it was healthy chewing gum).

Teens not only need time with their parents, they *want* it.

Teenagers are more likely than younger children to want more time with their parents. Thirty-nine percent of children thirteen through eighteen years old felt they had too little time with their fathers compared with 29 percent of children eight through twelve years old. Similarly, 30 percent of children thirteen through eighteen felt they had too little time with their mothers, compared with 24.5 percent of the younger children.

Although the image of the bravado teenager, wanting to push away—even to get away from—his or her parents is well rooted in our culture and experience, these data paint a very different picture and one that we need to listen to. Some reasons for this are logical. We spend more time with younger children than older children and that's partially because teens are busy with their own lives.

When I asked teens to explain why they thought older children were more likely to want time with their parents than younger children, they said it had to do with the dawning realization that someday—in fact someday in the not-too-distant future—they would be on their own, which made them yearn for time with their families now. But as one teenage boy stated, we have been so busy pushing our parents away that it is hard to reach back to ask for time. One boy, age fourteen, expressed it well as advice to the parents of teens, "Don't be afraid to talk to your kids. They may act like they don't want you talking to them, but actually it's very important you do. Talking to your kids is great and they want you to whether you think they do or not."

FAMILY TIME CAN HAPPEN DURING IN-BETWEEN TIMES, ESPECIALLY WITH TEENS. With older children, some of the best opportunities to be together and talk occur when you don't have to make eye contact, such as in the car or at bedtime when the lights are dimmed. In fact, one mother of teenagers would ask her children to go on night walks with her: "I would take them, one by one, for walks in the dark, because they'll tell you anything in the dark—they have that cover. They're safe. I wouldn't say, 'We need to talk because something's bothering you.' I'd say, 'I really need you to go walk with me tonight.' 'Sure, Mom.' He's helping me. So he would go with me and we'd walk around the block. We might walk for an hour and I'd hear everything that's going on in his mind and heart. That's how I knew my kids—because we walked in the dark."

Time in the car can be a great time to talk as well. As a mother says: "Get them in the car, turn the music on low, and talk. They'll talk to you there." A girl, age fourteen, noted how important family time is: "Children need to be talked to and listened to. Our problems are just as big as yours."

IF YOU WANT TO FIND OUT WHAT IS GOING ON, ASK SPECIFIC QUESTIONS, NOT GENERAL ONES. Children are less likely to answer general questions like "How was school today?" than concrete ones: "What did your teacher think about the paper you wrote?"

BUILD ON THEIR INTERESTS, WHETHER THEY'RE YOUR INTERESTS OR NOT. During her teen years, shopping was my daughter's "sport of choice." So we went shopping together. It was not my favorite thing to do but the time with her more than made up for it (and she had a strict clothes allowance so she was figuring out how to be frugal and save her money as well). Our son loved music and movies and was always eager to do that with us.

CREATE GIVING-BACK TIMES. You can also create things that you do together as a family to give back. One family with teens, for example, volunteered to cook together for an organization with the mission of preparing and delivering nutritious, high-quality meals to people who are ill and unable to provide or prepare meals for themselves. It made the entire family feel good about giving back, but it also gave them purposeful time together.

Forget quality time *or* quantity time. Think focused time *and* hang-around time.

In the debates about family time, people argue about which is most important: quality time or quantity time. The assumption seems to be that simply spending more time is *the* answer to all of our problems. In our collective minds, we tend to dissect—to separate almost surgically—the amount of time parents and children spend together from what they do in that time. But *both* the amount of time and what happens in that time should go together. They can't really be separated when it comes to the impact on children.

My studies, like those of others, have found that the amount of time children spend with their parents matters. In the Ask the Children study, I looked at how much time children reported spending with their parents as well as what happened in that time—the activities that parents and children did together, whether the time was rushed or calm, and whether children felt that their parents could really focus on them when they were together. I found that *all* were important to how children assessed their parents' parenting skills and how successful they felt their parents were in managing work and family life.[21]

Another reason that the quality time versus quantity time notion is an outmoded one is because the word *quality* has been so romanticized, talked about with such reverence, that it connotes perfection. Nothing ever goes wrong in quality time. No children ever throw food at each other across the dining room table. No children are ever surly with us. No children are ever too busy to be with us. There are no disagreements, no arguments, no fights, no icy silences. But that's not reality in my house, nor probably in yours.

There is a need for a new language to talk about family time with children. When I asked children and parents about "what works," the words used to describe the best family times were *focused time* and *hang-around time*.

SPEND TIME WITH YOUR CHILDREN. Children whose parents spend more time with them view their parents' competence more positively and are more likely to see them as role models. Is there a magic amount of time? No, but it should feel (more or less) like enough time to both you and your children. As one boy, age twelve, in the Ask the Children study, put it: "The more time you spend with your kids, the stronger the bond between you. If you can't find time, make time."

SPEND HANG-AROUND TIME WITH YOUR CHILDREN. What is hang-around time? First of all, it is time when you don't feel rushed and frantic. Two in five children somewhat or strongly agreed that their time with their mothers and fathers was rushed. When children had less rushed time with their parents, they tended to see them more positively. There are, of course, moments when we do have to rush, but it is important for children to also experience some moments when everyone is off the treadmill.

Hang-around time can be time when you are not necessarily interacting, but just being nearby. You are doing something and so are they. Parents can also set aside "special times" when they are hanging out. They stay in their pajamas on Saturday morning. They putter around the house while the kids are doing their own thing. When my children were teens, I often found that the best conversations started when we were hanging out. My son, for example, would become like a hovercraft. If I turned around and started a conversation about something—anything—then he would begin to talk about what was really on his mind.

SPEND FOCUSED TIME WITH YOUR CHILDREN. What does focus mean? It means being attuned to the child's cues and clues, paying attention. It means being responsive. It includes listening to a child when the child wants to talk. It includes comforting a child who is unhappy, whether that child is a preschooler or a teenager. It also includes caring about the child's learning and extending it, whether this is a young child who is excited about the world around him or her or an older child studying about science or math. In the words of parents, focused time is:

> "Reading to my children."

> "Finding some little thing I can do with each of [my children] separately . . . whether it is just going to the drugstore and getting to where we're going in the car for ten, fifteen minutes."

> "Planning with my thirteen-year-old how he can earn the money to purchase the pair of tennis shoes he wants."

> "Making sure the channels of communication are open."

> "Being a good listener if there are problems."

Focused time is building in children the trust that you are there for them.

When asked for her message to parents in America in the Ask the Children study, a girl, age fourteen, wrote: "When your child is asking for attention, give it to them. Don't keep working and not talk to your child. Go to games when they are in sports. Don't promise them something you can't keep. It will hurt them."

Know that the small, everyday moments really matter to your kids.

In the qualitative study I conducted with children and parents all over the country before designing the quantitative studies for *Ask the Children*, one of my questions was: "What do you think you (your children) will remember most from this time in your (their) lives?"

I was struck yet again by the differences in parents' and children's responses. Parents tended to talk about the big moments—the all-star extravaganza events, like the trip to a theme park or the unusual birthday party or special gift. While these were, of course, memorable to your children too, it was the small, everyday moments they told me about. In one family, it was always singing in the car. In another family, it was a bedtime story they told every night about a cow, a pig, and a chicken. The children would say a sentence to start the story and the mother would make up the rest. In still another family, it was each child talking about his or her day during dinnertime. In still another family, it was making pancakes together on Sunday mornings.

KNOW THAT SMALL MOMENTS MAKE A BIG DIFFERENCE. Just knowing this should help you think about and plan family time.

CREATE FAMILY TRADITIONS AND SUSTAIN THEM. What are the everyday moments that could become traditions in your family? In ours, it has been making biscuits together. We always make biscuits as a family for special breakfasts and when my children were younger, they would make them into funny shapes—Easter bunnies at Easter time, Valentines for Valentine's Day, aliens and crazy animals for regular Sundays. They would guess what each other's biscuits were. Then we would gather at the kitchen table, feast on the biscuits, and tell funny stories.

Just recently, my grown daughter, who just had her own child, wanted to make biscuits and as I told her the recipe, she made them. I know that this tradition will go forward in her family, as will the tradition of telling funny stories.

We have stories from my kids growing up that always send all of us into total hysterics. There was the time when I was trying to order lemon sorbet in a French restaurant and I ordered a car (I said Citroën when I should have said *citron*). Or there was the time when Uncle Bill had an electronic device (nicknamed Oscar) at home that was programmed to call him at work if there was a problem (say, the pipes freezing). One day when Bill was out to lunch, Oscar got transferred to the switchboard at Bill's company, calling repeatedly, talking in a weird electronic voice about the temperature and water pressure, and coming close to triggering a company-wide security alert. These and other stories still make us laugh, no matter what else is going on. Studies by Robin Fivush of Emory University reinforce the importance of family stories during family time. She and her colleagues have found that knowing about your family history helps children thrive.[22]

INCLUDE A PREDICTABLE AND REGULAR "SPECIAL TIME" AS ONE OF YOUR FAMILY TRADITIONS. There has been a lot of discussion about the importance of dinnertime to children's positive development.[23] But it isn't just having dinner together that is the magic bullet—it is the regular time together, a point Bruce Feiler makes in *The Secret of Happy Families* when he says, "it's not about the dinner, it's about the family."[24] It may be dinnertime or it could just as well be breakfast.

(See Jill Castle's take on this topic in "The Art of Mealtime" on page 202.) Or it could be the time just before your children go to sleep, when you read or tell stories or sing together.

Children in our study reinforced the importance of regular family time when they asked parents to "Please plan one to two nights for only family." During that time, they asked parents to . . .

"Play games, solve problems, etc."

"Ask your kids how their day was."

"Listen to our problems—our problems are just as big as yours."

"Ask them how they feel about your work."

The key to making this time a good family time is making it predictable and having the focus be on the people present. It is best to turn off the TV, cell phones, and tablets and be together. Having traditions around these special times is important.

Family time can be a time to promote crucial life skills.

We tend to think of family time as a time just to *be* together, but many of the most important lessons for life—life skills—can be nurtured and thrive during this time. In *Mind in the Making*, I identify seven life skills that all involve the executive functions of the brain that research has shown help children thrive now and in the future.

What are executive functions of the brain? They are the brain functions we use to manage our attention, our emotions, and our behavior in pursuit of our goals. Adele Diamond of the University of British Columbia states that executive functions predict children's life success as well as—if not better than—IQ tests, as she explains:

Typical traditional IQ tests measure what's called crystallized intelligence, which is mostly your recall of what you've already learned—like what's the meaning of this word, or what's the capital of that country? What executive functions tap is your ability to use what you already know—to be creative with it, to problem-solve with it—so it's very related to fluid intelligence, because that requires reasoning and using information.[25]

Executive functions emerge during the early years and mature in adulthood, so it is never too late to nurture them. They have a strong bearing on school success, too. Diamond says:

If you look at what predicts how well children will do later in school, more and more evidence is showing that executive functions—working memory and inhibition—actually predict success better than IQ tests.

---

toughLOVE TIPS

Here are some suggestions for how to promote the most important executive-function life skills during family time.

PROMOTE FOCUS AND SELF-CONTROL BY PLAYING GAMES. Children need the skill of Focus and Self-Control to achieve their goals, especially in a world that is filled with distractions and information overload. Family time provides a great time to promote this skill by playing games, such as Do the Opposite. In this game, children (beginning at about four years old) have to do the opposite of what you say. If you say "Touch your toes," they should touch their heads. Or if you say "Touch your head," they should touch their toes. For older children, you can add Simon Says into the mix so that children can only "do the opposite" when you say "Simon says." This game has been found to predict school readiness and school success in studies by Megan McClelland and her colleagues at Oregon State University.[26]

These games can be played at any time and are especially good at the times when you might otherwise be waiting or getting ready to do something else. A father who dropped his preschool children off at child care before heading for work said:

> We would have terrible struggles in the morning until I set up a game we do every morning. We play Simon Says: Simon Says get your coat. Simon Says get your lunch. Go out the door. Whoops—I caught you because I didn't say Simon Says so you can't go out the door until I say Simon Says.

Other games that promote Focus and Self-Control are Red Light-Green Light and Freeze Tag. Note that family time is not only time to *be together or talk to each other*, it is time to *do* things—to be active together.

PROMOTE PERSPECTIVE TAKING BY PLAYING "WHAT WERE THEY THINKING?" Children need the skill of Perspective Taking to understand the complex social world of today. Perspective Taking goes beyond empathy; it involves figuring out what others think and feel. Studies reveal that children with Perspective Taking skills are more likely to be ready for and to succeed in school, to understand literature, and to get into fewer conflicts.[27] You can promote this skill by playing the game What Were They Thinking? Whether you are reading a book or talking about what's going on with your children's friends, you can ask your kids: "What do you think this person was thinking and feeling?" Family time is a time for kids to learn to make sense of the social landscape in which they live.

PROMOTE COMMUNICATING BY TELLING STORIES. Communicating is more than understanding language, speaking, reading, and writing. It is the skill of determining what one wants to communicate and realizing how that communication will be heard. Write down your children's earliest stories and share them with the family so they can get feedback on what they communicate. As they get older, build a story time into family time so that children get practice in listening to and sharing stories.

PROMOTE MAKING CONNECTIONS BY LOOKING AT HOW THINGS GO TOGETHER. Making Connections is at the heart of learning, figuring out how things go together—what's the same, what's different—and sorting things into categories. Making Connections underlies symbolic relationships: that numbers stand for a set quantity of things or that letters stand for sounds and for words. Use family time for looking at how things go together, doing puzzles or playing games that involve matching, such as dominoes.

Help children make unusual connections, which are the basis of creativity and innovation. You can ask, "How do these three objects go together in one way? Now how do they go together in a different way?" That helps them learn to think outside the box.

PROMOTE CRITICAL THINKING BY HELPING CHILDREN THINK LIKE SCIENTISTS. Critical Thinking is the ongoing search for valid and reliable knowledge to guide beliefs, decisions, and actions. At its core, it is helping children think like scientists. You can promote Critical Thinking by asking children to critique the ads they see on television or in the media. Ask them, "How do you know what they are saying about this product is real? What is this company trying to sell you? Does it make you want to buy it? Why or why not?"

You can also promote Critical Thinking by helping children seek and find answers to their what, why, and how questions. Rather than answering these questions too quickly, see if you can find the answers together or set up an experiment to provide answers. For example, if your children ask why the water in the fish tank goes down, ask them to put out bowls of water and measure the water levels over time. These activities are great for family time and the bonus is they promote Critical Thinking.[28]

PROMOTE TAKING ON CHALLENGES BY SOLVING FAMILY PROBLEMS. Many of us fantasize that family time will be happy-ever-after time, but that's neither possible nor productive. Life is full of stresses and challenges. The children who learn to take on challenges (instead of avoiding or simply coping with them) do better in school and life.[29] So turn the family fights into productive family time by having children take increasing responsibility for resolving these disputes.

An example from my parenting was settling the fights that used to take place in the backseat of the car when I drove my kids to school. When they became an everyday occurrence, we called a family meeting and told the children: "We are not interested in who starts the fights. We are interested in who has good ideas for stopping them."

We always followed a steplike process for solving problems. Each child was asked to: (1) think of a few suggestions for how to address the problem; (2) discuss how each suggestion would work for everyone in the family; and (3) as a group, select one of the suggestions to try, but before doing so, the kids would also set consequences if the solution didn't work. In the case of the car fights, our kids came up with the idea of each child bringing along a car kit—a bag filled with toys he or she liked to play with in the car. When that stopped working, another family meeting was called. Their next solution was to create a pretend radio show where they would interview each other. The process continued until they outgrew fighting in the back-seat of the car!

PROMOTE SELF-DIRECTED ENGAGED LEARNING BY HELPING CHILDREN SET GOALS. Remember that executive functions are always driven by goals—not only setting them, but then following through. An example is figuring out what to do when children come to you complaining that they are bored. Rather than try to entertain them, you can help them make a list of "10 Things to Do When I'm Bored." The list can be as long as "100 Things." When your children come to you saying they have nothing to do, have them go to the list, select something, and then carry out that activity. In doing so, you are helping them establish and enact goals, but more important, you are encouraging them to be self-directed engaged learners.

You will have better family time if you make some time for yourself.

Research that the Families and Work Institute has conducted finds that people who take time for themselves are the least stressed.[30] Children get it. When asked about their messages for parents in the Ask the Children study, a sixteen-year-old boy wrote of the need for parents to "calm down": "In Spain, they take a two- to three-hour nap in the middle of the day. We need that here. Parents need to be able to sit down, relax, and enjoy what they're doing." An eleven-year-old boy echoed this sentiment: "I know all of you are trying to help your children, but if you have to, take a rest."

In 2012, the FWI conducted a study of a national sample of women to find out how they spent their free time for *Real Simple* magazine.[31] We found that about a third (31 percent) of women often or very often felt guilty when they chose to spend time on themselves. So instead of taking me-time, they spent the moments they had on household chores or tasks that brought them little pleasure. For example, three of the activities that at least 62 percent of women engaged in during what they described as their free time (cleaning, doing laundry, organizing/decluttering) were three of the least enjoyed activities. In addition, many of the women (58 percent) felt that they had to finish all of their chores before they could enjoy time for themselves.

On the other hand, when women actually spent time doing something for themselves, they were more likely to be satisfied with their lives.[32] Yes, the laundry is there, but so are we! You may be tired of hearing it, but the airplane adage is true: you really do need to put on your own oxygen mask first before helping your child put on his. When you give yourself time, you are more likely to create the kind of family time you really want.

My one wish

I have spent many years as a researcher asking others "one wish" questions. If you were to turn my question back at me, you might ask: "If you were granted one wish that would change family time for parents and children, what would that wish be?"

Here's my answer. My wish would be that parents' eyes would light up when they see their children. Children look at our eyes. They can tell whether we want to be with them or not. It is all there, reflected in our eyes. A girl, age eighteen, sums up this point. She advises parents to "Take time to show love for your children, because we *are* the future of America."

All of the tips about spending family time together mean nothing unless our eyes show that we *want* to be together! That's why this is "my one wish" for family time.

1. E. Galinsky, K. Aumann, and J. T. Bond, *Times Are Changing: Gender and Generation at Work and at Home* (New York: Families and Work Institute, 2011).
2. Cisco, The Cisco connected world report: Employee expectations, demands and behavior—accessing networks, applications and information anywhere, anytime and with any device (2010). Retrieved from http://newsroom.cisco.com/dlls/2010/ekits/cwr_final.pdf.
3. Families and Work Institute, *2011 Guide to Bold New Ideas for Making Work Work* (New York: Families and Work Institute and Society for Human Resource Management, 2011).
4. Galinsky, Aumann, and Bond, *Times Are Changing.*
5. S. Bianchi, "Changing Families, Changing Workplaces," *Future of Children*, 21(2) 2011, 15–36.
6. Ibid.
7. S. Bianchi, "Family change and time allocation in American families," program paper from Focus on Workplace Flexibility (Washington, DC, November 29–30, 2010). Bianchi, "Changing families, changing workplaces," 15–36. Galinsky, Aumann, and Bond, *Times Are Changing.*
8. K. Aumann, E. Galinsky, and K. Matos, *The New Male Mystique* (New York: Families and Work Institute, 2012).
9. Galinsky, Aumann, and Bond, *Times Are Changing.*
10. S. Hofferth, "Changes in American Children's Time, 1997–2003," *International Journal of Time Use Research* 6(1) 2009, 26–47.
11. E. Galinsky, *Ask the Children: The Breakthrough Study That Reveals How to Succeed at Work and Parenting* (New York: Quill, 2000).
12. E. Galinsky, *Mind in the Making: The Seven Essential Skills Every Child Needs* (New York: HarperCollins, 2010).
13. K. Aumann and E. Galinsky, *The State of Health in the American Workforce: Does Having an Effective Workplace Matter?* (New York: Families and Work Institute, 2011).
14. E. Galinsky, *Ask the Children.*
15. U.S. Bureau of Labor Statistics, 1975–2011 Annual Social and Economic Supplements, Current Population Survey (2011). Retrieved from http://www.bls.gov/cps/wlf-databook-2012.pdf.
16. Galinsky, Aumann, and Bond, *Times Are Changing.*
17. L. W. Hoffman and L. M. Youngblade, *Mothers at Work: Effects on Children's Well-being* (New York: Cambridge University Press, 1999).

18. D. L. Vandell, J. Belsky, M. Burchinal, L. Steinberg, and N. Vandergrift, NICHD Early Child Care Research Network, "Do Effects of Early Child Care Extend to Age 15 Years?" results from the NICHD study of early child care and youth development, *Child Development* 81(3) 2010, 737–56.

19. E. Galinsky, *The Six Stages of Parenthood* (New York: Addison-Wesley, 1987).

20. Ibid.

21. Galinsky, *Ask the Children*.

22. R. Fivush and F. A. Fromhoff, "Style and Structure in Mother-Child Conversations about the Past," *Discourse Processes* 11(3) 1988, 337–55.

23. National Center on Addiction and Substance Abuse at Columbia University, *The Importance of Family Dinners VII* (New York: Columbia University, 2011).

24. B. Feiler, *The Secrets of Happy Families* (New York: William Morrow, 2013).

25. Galinsky, *Mind in the Making*.

26. M. M. McClelland, A. C. Acock, A. Piccinin, S. A. Rhea, and M. C. Stallings, "Relations Between Preschool Attention Span-Persistence and Age 25 Educational Outcomes," *Early Childhood Research Quarterly* 28(2) 2012, 314–24. M. M. McClelland, and C. E. Cameron, "Self-Regulation in Early Childhood: Improving Conceptual Clarity and Developing Ecologically Valid Measures," *Child Development Perspectives* 6(2) 2012, 136–42. M. M. McClelland, C. E. Cameron, C. M. Connor, C. L. Farris, A. M. Jewkes, and F. J. Morrison, "Links Between Behavioral Regulation and Preschoolers' Literacy, Vocabulary and Math Skills," *Developmental Psychology* 43(4) 2007, 947–59. M. M. McClelland, e-mail to E. Galinsky, August 9, 2009. M. M. McClelland, A. C. Acock, and F. J. Morrison, "The Impact of Kindergarten Learning-Related Skills on Academic Trajectories at the End of Elementary School," *Early Childhood Research Quarterly* 21(4) 2006, 471–90. S. L. Tominey and M. M. McClelland, "Red Light, Purple Light: Findings from a Randomized Trial Using Circle Time Games to Improve Behavioral Self-Regulation in Preschool," *Early Education and Development* 22(3) 2011, 489–519.

27. J. L. Aber, S. M. Jones, J. L. Brown, N. Chaudry, and F. Samples, "Resolving Conflict Creatively: Evaluating the Developmental Effects of a School-Based Violence Prevention Program in Neighborhood and Classroom Context," *Development and Psychopathology* 10(2) 1998, 187–213. J. L. Aber, interview with E. Galinsky, August 2, 2006. A. Gopnik, interview with E. Galinsky, November 29, 2001. A. Gopnik, *The Philosophical Baby: What Children's Minds Tell Us about Truth, Love, and the Meaning of Life* (New

York: Farrar, Straus, & Giroux, 2009). A. Gopnik and L. E. Schulz, "Mechanisms of Theory Formation in Young Children," *Trends in Cognitive Science* 8(8) 2004, 371–77. A. Gopnik and V. Slaughter, "Young Children's Understanding of Changes in Their Mental States," *Child Development* 62(1) 1991, 98–110. L. L. Ontai and R. A. Thompson, "Patterns of Attachment and Maternal Discourse Effects on Children's Emotional Understanding from 3 to 5 Years of Age," *Social Development* 11(4) 2002, 433–50. B. M. Repacholi and A. Gopnik, "Early Reasoning about Desires: Evidence from 14- and 18-Month-Olds," *Developmental Psychology* 33(1) 1997, 12–21. R. Thompson, interview with E. Galinsky, September 28, 2001.

28. F. C. Keil, *Concepts, Kinds, and Cognitive Development* (Cambridge, MA: MIT Press, 1989), p. 184. D. Klahr and M. Nigam, "The Equivalence of Learning Paths in Early Science Instruction: Effects of Direct Instruction and Discovery Learning," *Psychological Science,* 15(10) 2004, 661–67. L. E. Schulz and E. B. Bonawitz, "Serious Fun: Preschoolers Engage in More Exploratory Play When Evidence Is Confounded," *Developmental Psychology* 43(4) 2007, 1045–50.

29. C. S. Dweck, *Mindset: The New Psychology of Success* (New York: Ballantine Books, 2008). M. R. Gunnar, L. Brodersen, K. Krueger, and J. Rigatuso, "Dampening of Adrenocortical Responses During Infancy: Normative Changes and Individual Differences," *Child Development* 67(3) 1996, 887–89.

30. E. Galinsky, K. Salmond, J. T. Bond, M. Brumit Kropf, M. Moore, and B. Harrington, *Leaders in a Global Economy: A Study of Executive Women and Men* (New York: Families and Work Institute, Catalyst, and Boston College Center for Work & Family, 2002).

31. E. Galinsky, "Free Time: Why Women's Views of It Are Out of Sync with Reality," *Huffington Post*, March 7, 2012. Retrieved from http://www.huffing tonpost.com/ellen-galinsky/free-time_b_132490 0.html.

32. L. S. Blackwell, K. H. Trzesniewski, and C. S. Dweck, "Implicit Theories of Intelligence Predict Achievement Across an Adolescent Transition: A Longitudinal Study and an Intervention," *Child Development* 78(1) 2007, 246–63. M. S. Cary and D. Klahr, "Developing Elementary Science Skills: Instructional Effectiveness and Path Independence," *Cognitive Development* 23(4) 2008, 488–511. Z. Chen and D. Klahr, "All Other Things Being Equal: Acquisition and Transfer of the Control of Variables Strategy," *Child Development* 70(5) 1999, 1098–120. S. M. Jones, J. L. Brown, and J. L. Aber, "Classroom Settings as Targets of Intervention and Research," in M. Shinn

and H. Yoshikawa, eds., *Toward Positive Youth Development: Transforming Schools and Community Programs* (New York: Oxford University Press, 2008), pp. 58–77. D. J. Laible and R. A. Thompson, "Mother-Child Discourse, Attachment Security, Shared Positive Affect, and Early Conscience Development," *Child Development* 7(5) 2000, 1424–40. C. C. Ponitz, M. M. McClelland, J. S. Matthews, and F. J. Morrison, "A Structured Observation of Behavior Self-Regulation and Its Contribution to Kindergarten Outcomes," *Developmental Psychology* 45(3) 2009, 605–19.

part two

PUTTING EVERYTHING INTO ACTION

deciding what your family values

BY ANN CORWIN, PHD, MED, AN AUTHORITY IN THE FIELD OF CHILD
DEVELOPMENT, A PARENTING CONSULTANT, AND MOM OF TWO

Have you ever seen another parent struggling with a child who's having a tantrum and felt compelled to stop and say, "How can I help? I was in this same situation with my child yesterday, so I know just how you feel." But instead, you try not to make eye contact and walk on by.

The reason it's so incredibly difficult for most of us to stop to help is because of our *values*—our set of beliefs and ideals that drives our thinking, causing thoughts like the following to pop into our heads: "I probably wouldn't be able to really help anyway," or "She probably doesn't want my help," and "Everyone would probably think I'm just a know-it-all" or "Maybe we have different values and she'd be offended."

What Are Family Values?

What do we value as individuals, as parents? How do we go about creating our family values? Typically, values are either subconsciously passed down from generation to generation or decided on by family problem solving when issues come up with children or in their community.

Decision making, a skill that is learned by weighing and measuring various options, is the foundation of establishing family values. Sometimes problem solving includes discussion among all family members, even extended family. Other times, it's just the parents making decisions together without the children.

I'd like to share an e-mail I recently received that illustrates a typical values-based dilemma one family was facing:

Hi, Dr. Ann,

My daughter, age eight, has been taking dance lessons for three years. She is at a high level of dancing and we have invested a lot of time and money into this sport. She now wants to stop dancing and wants to take an after-school class with her friend. I am torn because she is so talented and has put so much into dancing over the past years. But I also want her to have fun with her friends and try new things. (She told me that dancing is stressful and that she just doesn't like it anymore.) Am I sending the wrong message if I let her quit?

How you respond to a situation like this depends on your family values:

How much do you *value* never quitting?

How much do you *value* your child's opinion?

Is one of your *values* the successful accomplishments of your daughter?

Identifying Your Family Values

I've found a five-step approach that guides families in establishing values that will help them work through issues from quitting dance to extending curfew to buying a motorcycle and beyond.

STEP ONE: CREATE A FRIENDLY BRAINSTORMING ENVIRONMENT

Making decisions can be tough, so the friendlier the environment, the easier it will be for your family to build your values together. Start to get everyone on board by using the word *decisions*, which means that everyone gets a say in what happens. This is done best by having family meetings or gatherings to talk, ask questions, and problem-solve if necessary. A safe environment allows for open discussion so no one feels threatened by sharing their individual opinions. A playful environment helps with relaxation, and this is how families learn to not take themselves too seriously while they make a serious family plan. Food is a must. Games are good, too.

For instance, you could play a form of musical chairs, placing chairs in a circle with enough chairs for everyone minus one. One person begins by standing in the center of the circle and stating a value that he or she has, like playing games once a week with the family. Everyone who agrees with that value has to get up and move to another chair (note: you cannot just move to the chair on either side of you) and the last person with nowhere to sit heads to the center of the circle to state their value. If no one agrees with the stated value by the person in the center, then that person just says another value until someone agrees with it and has to get up and move to another chair. Someone should be designated as a note taker to write down all of the shared values and individual values (with each person's name listed beside his or her stated value) on a large sheet of paper so everyone can see them (or, if you prefer, on a computer or tablet). This way you end up with a list of identified values.

STEP TWO: DISPLAY YOUR FAMILY VALUES

It's one thing to say that you value something, but sometimes quite another to practice what you value. In order to get your kids to buy into your family values, you need to give them something tangible to touch and see in order to remember them. This will also help your kids to follow them. After all, children are no different from parents in the sense that if we feel ownership of our decisions about anything, we buy into them more and that translates into practicing values we've created.

One idea I've used for years to help families do this is to have a child lie down on top of a piece of butcher paper that covers the length and width of his body. With a large black magic marker, draw the outline of his body. Then have him get up and write his name inside the outline anywhere he wants. Next, transfer the values you all identified in your brainstorming or musical chairs game into the inside of the traced body. Last, pin this up in a prominent place in your home, like the family living area or your child's room if he prefers (you know he might take even further ownership of these values if they are posted in his own space). Now this piece of art automatically becomes a talking point and a place where values are kept in your home. No one has to guess, or be reminded, what their values are as they are there to see, discuss, and be used to keep the family on track.

To help tweens and teens with this same concept, just watch for where your child is practicing your family values without even thinking about it—and point out the values they are automatically practicing. For example, make note when a child is respectful of adults and property, kind and thoughtful to peers, or working hard to accomplish goals. Tell your teens you watched as they knew "just what to do" to practice the values that your family has established. Then finally surprise your tween or teen with something you know they've been wanting to do or have, such as money for the movies or to buy music or trusting them to go somewhere by themselves.

STEP THREE: ENCOURAGE ALL FAMILY MEMBERS TO CONTINUE CONTRIBUTING TO THE VALUES

In addition to brainstorming family values together, you can contribute to them individually or have your kids establish values for themselves. Play the musical chairs game every so often, or just add to the list as values arise. For open communication, and so your children know they have a say in your family values, you might also place a values suggestion box or jar in a prominent spot in the house, where every member of the family can put in slips of paper stating their ideas or beliefs, with their name attached or included anonymously to be read during your ongoing family meetings.

Another idea for contributing to your family values is for parents to make a "values date night." Before you go out for an evening without the children, each parent writes down their nonnegotiable values. Then, while you are out alone and without interruption, each of you reads your values to the other. The ones you agree on are then presented to your children as "parent values."

STEP FOUR: OVERCOME DISAGREEMENTS ABOUT VALUES

Disagreements about values are why you need a problem-solving formula in your family. One of your values may be religious beliefs, including going to church or synagogue, or praying. What if, at some point, your child either does not believe what you believe in or wants to participate in religious activities outside of your chosen religion? You need to decide on a plan about what you will do if that happens, otherwise you might experience oppositional behavior by your child.

I've always believed that prevention is the best medicine. So what's a parent to do to prevent too much tension, or defiance of established family values? When your kids oppose the value that you've established, for whatever reason, keep in mind that their aggression is usually masking a feeling of being confused by something. The first thing you should do is go back and clarify why you have the value, otherwise a cycle of aggression will begin. It usually goes something like this: your child is confused by something (in this case, whether she needs to follow your established values about religion). If that confusion does not get clarified, she will become scared, and the number one defense mechanism for confusion is aggression. If she is confused or scared, it is normal for her to act aggressively until someone, usually the parent, clarifies the confusion for her. In other words, instead of focusing on your child's defiance, focus on restating your values and showing your child how to follow them in a way that is comfortable for you both.

STEP FIVE: PUT FAMILY VALUES INTO ACTION

We recently conducted a survey of parents asking them to share values they would like to put into practice. Here are some examples of those values and how we suggested they could put them into action.

One of the family values that a parent listed was "Help others in need." This is definitely one of those easier-said-than-done values. As well-meaning parents, we might put a Goodwill bag on the driveway for pickup, or take our kids to drop off old stuff at the local church or community center, but remember that the only thing your kids see is the actual drop-off, not where or to whom their old stuff goes.

For the past decade, I have been teaching parents about my Get-to-Give Rule: for everything your children get, they need to find something of theirs to personally give to another child in need. If your child requests a toy at the store, and it's something you would like to get them, your immediate response might be "What could we give of yours to some other child in need?" This not only keeps your closet clean, but it keeps the arguing and whining to a minimum every time your child wants something. It not only shows your kids appreciation for what they have, but gets them thinking of others the minute they think of themselves. Have them identify an appropriate charity or institution that could use the donation and then have them deliver it in person.

Another family in our survey wanted "Share your day at the dinner table" to be a family value. Again, it's one thing to say you're going to do this and quite another to actually do it, especially if your child refuses to talk. Most of us parents have experienced a time or two when we ask our children how their day was and they say one word ("Okay" or "Fine"), and then we ask if anything exciting happened and they proceed to say "Nothing." So where do parents go from there?

Here's an idea about what you can do to enhance conversation at the dinner table, if that is a value you have decided on for your family. Cut out two small, round pieces of felt and glue them on the bottom of a cotton ball to make feet, so it sits upright on its own. This becomes a "talking head" symbol. Whoever has the talking head in front of their plate gets to begin a conversation. Parents can decide who starts it each night, or you can draw straws to decide who's next (or use any other method that works for your family). The person who has the ball can say anything they want to about their day, uninterrupted by anyone else, as the talking head signifies that it's that designated person's turn to talk. When they are done with one or two topics, they get to throw the talking head to someone else for it to be their turn. Kids tend to love this because they get to throw things at the table.

The process of setting and keeping family values will define who your family is and what you're all about, since you'll own these values. Anybody who's spent time with our family knows that the Corwins really value saying thank you, and they love to have fun, dance together, and give to others in need. What will your family be known for?

Sample Family Values

(parent responses from a survey on theparentingdoctor.com)

Always say thank you.

Take responsibility for what you do and say.

Be kind and forgiving, even when others are not.

Be a blessing to others.

Have an attitude of gratitude.

Be a friend to the friendless.

Share your day at the dinner table (toss cotton ball).

Pray before bed.

Tell your kids how proud you are of them every day.

Lift each other up, don't bring each other down.

Laugh at yourself.

Choose wisely; each choice has a consequence.

Help others in need (Get-to-Give Rule).

Practice what you teach your children.

Ask for something for your birthday that you can donate to someone else in need.

Teach by doing.

Always be kind.

Treat others the way you would like them to treat you.

Try to understand where others are coming from; it creates compassion.

Teach others how to treat you.

Have zero tolerance for disrespect and bullies.

Wherever you go and whatever you do, go and do it with all of your heart.

Treat yourself with respect.

Love and you will be loved.

Smile and forgive.

Use your talents well.

Eat dinner as a family.

Take time to talk to learn how your kids feel and what they think.

Establish a family game night/movie night and stick to it.

Always talk to strangers, but never go anywhere with them.

Remember that spending time is much more valuable than spending money.

Accept others as they are and accept yourself as you are.

Know that you can do anything you put your mind to.

Acknowledge that success is important for self-respect and confidence.

Watch what you say and what you do—your reputation matters.

Cherish people for their heart, not just their exterior.

routine zen: teaching independence and gaining sanity

BY LYNNE KENNEY, PSYD, A PRACTICING PEDIATRIC PSYCHOLOGIST AND MOTHER OF TWO

It's 6:00 a.m. and your automatic coffeepot is sending you an early-morning wake-up call with wafting hazelnut aromas. Your partner is out of the shower and out of the door, leaving you to bask in the sunlight of your Zen-style spa. A quick cleanup and you're dressed in today's finest, feeling fresh as a lark. You walk downstairs to find your eight-year-old finishing up her homework and your ten-year-old making roast beef and caramelized onion sandwiches for everyone. You smile as you sit down to read the "Online Parenting Daily," as you think, "I've got it made."

SCREECH . . . Whoa! This isn't what the morning looks like in your home? Well, it could! No, really. Okay, maybe peanut butter and jelly would replace roast beef, but it's certainly possible that your kids could put away their laundry and make their lunches, and you could have ten guilt-free minutes with your morning planner. *What does it take? Planning, preparation, and accountability.* In other words, creating realistic routines.

In this era of smartphones, algebra in third grade, and working from home, most of us are too busy and overwhelmed to take the time to generate family schedules, teach our kids the twenty life skills they need to know before college, and build reliable family routines. But if we wish to reside in peaceful homes and raise independent, competent kids, we've got to start planning. It is never too late to improve your task management, implement healthy routines, get back to family dinner, and live in a more joy-filled home.

What is a routine anyway? We often think of routines as a series of tasks or activities done consistently in a similar order each time. So when you go to the gym, you warm up, stretch, run on the elliptical machine, lift weights, then cool down. That's a routine. When you prepare for bed, pull down your covers, make sure your book is by your bedside, turn off your iPad, and climb into bed, that's a routine. But routines can do more than just provide structure. They can be a means to family harmony.

In this chapter we'll explore how routines help children develop, why families need routines, and how to create routines that enhance family relationships. Your goal as a parent is to maintain attachment and connectedness with your children as you guide them toward becoming capable, skillful adults. When you develop routines collaboratively, your children participate more fully in your family rhythm, leading to a more peaceful home.

How Can Routines Help My Family?

ROUTINES HELP CREATE A PREDICTABLE ENVIRONMENT IN WHICH CHILDREN CAN LEARN, GROW, AND THRIVE

Children feel safe when they know what's coming next. Think of how often your children ask, "Then what will we do?" or "What will we do next, Mom?" Routines enhance a sense of personal mastery, and they allow children to develop independence by knowing what is expected. When children live with safe, predictable routines, they feel empowered, confident, and competent. Even teens need routines. Routines keep everyone safe.

ROUTINES ENHANCE COLLABORATION AND COOPERATION WITHIN YOUR FAMILY

When you take the time to talk with children about what they will do when, in what order, and in what time frame, they have the opportunity to become better thinkers, problem solvers, and decision makers. By teaching your kids habits and routines, you are also setting them up for success as college students and independent adults by helping them develop the executive function skills to plan ahead.

ROUTINES DECREASE POWER STRUGGLES

When children participate in the development of daily routines, they feel like an integral part of the family "team," which leads to better behavioral compliance and makes them feel more competent and independent.

When children know "the routine," they rely on you less to tell them what is expected and they learn to rely more on themselves. If the evening hygiene routine is take a bath, wash your hair, brush your teeth, and put on your pajamas, there is no bossing your kids around, getting upset, feeling irritated, or being frustrated. The routine is just what they do, the same way, pretty much all the time.

When your teens wish to shift the rules, bargain, and negotiate, routines help you to say, "I hear you, but in our family we are home for dinner by 6:00 p.m."

Routines can be more efficient than rules, because they allow you to collaborate with your children on what is expected in your family, which causes less opposition down the line. When your little ones grow up to be tweens and teens, they are used to the fact that your family has routines for expected behavior and they are to live in accordance with your expectations. For example, your "borrow the car" routine really comes in handy when your teen says, "Dad, can I keep the car until 11:00 p.m.?" when he knows very well curfew is 10:00 p.m. It's easy then to say, "We've discussed this and agreed the car comes home at 10:00 p.m., same routine, every time you borrow the car. Love you, son."

ROUTINES FOSTER TASK COMPLETION

Children are generally productive and like being busy and doing things. That's why they're always asking you, "Can we go to the park?" or "Can we play outside?" When routines are well established, it's easy to respond, "We sure can go outside, after we finish clearing the table, washing the dishes, and putting them in the dishwasher like we do every night."

ROUTINES FOSTER INDEPENDENCE

When routines are consistent, children are able to successfully complete expected tasks and activities without prompts, cues, or warnings. This enhances children's confidence and self-esteem. If you have a family routine of turning off devices forty-five minutes before bedtime to let melatonin rise and the brain calm, you will see how well these routines are internalized and then exhibited without prompting when your daughter has a midweek sleepover and tells her friend,

"We have a test tomorrow, let's turn off our phones so we can relax before we go to sleep."

"Not in my house," you say? Give it a try. You'll see.

ROUTINES HELP CHILDREN STAY ON TASK

Some children are distracted easily and focus on compelling stimuli, such as television, computers, and technology, which lead them off task. Routines, on the other hand, tell a child's brain, first we do this, then we do that, which enhances a child's ability to begin, execute, and complete the tasks of everyday living.

Collaboration Is Key to Creating Successful Routines

While creating routines makes things run smoothly, collaborating with your child gives your family's routines their meaning. When you collaborate with your children, your behavior says to them:

You have a valuable viewpoint.

I am interested in what you think about this.

Together we can solve problems.

When we put our heads together we develop better ideas.

We are a family, not an autocracy.

Here are four simple steps to get you started collaborating as you begin to create your family's routines.

Listen with a nonjudgmental ear. When you ask for your child's opinion, listen openly without correcting or amending his response. Providing your child the space to talk, discuss, explore, and problem-solve is good for your relationship.

Ask open-ended questions that enhance exploration. "I see that ..." "I hear that ..." I wonder if ..." "What do you think about ..." "What makes that happen?" "What could we do differently?"

Try it their way. "Okay, so I hear you saying you'd like to try doing homework after dinner." "What would that look like?" "How much time do you think you'd have?" "Do you think you'll be too tired?" "Let's give it a try and see how it works." "I'm open."

Notice what is going well. When your child participates in exploring, talking, and working things out, compliment his or her effort. Tell your child how proud you are that you are working together to build a happier family.

Let's look at how your family can get some of your own routines started.

Developing a Successful Morning Routine

It is really useful for you as a parent to identify the four or five times a day it would help you, your children, and your family to have routines. Morning, homework, and bedtime routines are a good start. Once you've established times, collaborate with your kids to figure out routines that everybody's happy with. Since many parents express frustration over early-morning routines, let's begin there. The first thing you can do is to get a marker board (I would get a marker board for each child), sit down at your kitchen table, and ask the children what are five things they do every morning and in what order.

It sounds like this: "It will be much more fun in our family if, when you get up, we all know exactly what we're expected to do, in what order, because that makes our mornings more relaxing. So let's think about it. In the morning we tend to get up and go to the bathroom, take off our pajamas, put them in the hamper, put on our new clothes, come downstairs, eat our breakfast, brush our teeth, brush our hair, put on our shoes, and gather our backpacks. Let's figure out how much time each of these tasks should take, and whatever time you have left over, you'll be able to play."

Have your children write down their preferred routine, and leave check boxes next to each step so they can keep track of what they've done and what they have yet to do. Most kids enjoy doing this.

While morning routines vary in every family, most children need about forty-five minutes to complete their early-morning routine. Rushing increases the production of stress hormones, so we like a routine that is calm, slow, and well organized. Here are a few ideas for creating happy wake-up and get-out-the-door routines. You should of course personalize and change these—and all the routines in this chapter—so that they best apply to your own children and family.

Create a "soft entry" into the morning. Give your kids a gentle verbal reminder or a little touch on the shoulder that says, "We're getting up in ten minutes."

Have all your own tasks completed before you get the kids up. They need a parent to gently guide them through the early-morning routine, not be frazzled with his or her own.

Have a hearty breakfast ready. Prepare as much as possible the night before, and save the complicated meals for the weekends. Include kids in the process and make that part of the routine, too: pouring cereal, buttering toast, putting juice on the table, clearing their plates.

Be prepared. Make lunches, put out tomorrow's outfit, and leave packed backpacks at the door the night before.

Model being an adult. Teach your tweens and teens how to use checklists, smartphones, and tech tools to manage the complexities of their academics, sports, and travel.

One cool thing about marker boards is that you can give every child a different color, and let them mark off which tasks they've accomplished. You can do this with afternoon and evening routines, too. Your older children may wish to keep their routines, tasks, and goals on their smartphones or other technology. That all works. The important thing is that you match schedule management, task accomplishment, and project planning to the communication styles of your children. The more they write it, draw it, and even transfer it to another medium, such as a white board, the more their brains will get into the habit of being organized.

Developing a Successful Homework Routine

Jessica has a five-year-old, a seven-year-old, and a sixteen-year-old at home. She told me recently that before she had children she had wonderful routines and systems; she prepared and planned for everything. She says, "You know what I was like—a future executive on a mission for success. But now that I have children, they all have individual need sets. I feel like all day long I'm juggling balls and I'm living in chaos."

The easiest way to help Jessica learn how to plan and prepare successfully for everyday life events in her family was to go through just one example in detail. I asked her, of all of the everyday tasks—making breakfast, cleaning up after breakfast, getting the kids ready for school, getting them out the door on time, picking the kids up after sports or activities, and driving the teenagers around later on—what made her feel most stuck? She said homework time.

So we took a step-by-step approach to creating routines that would make homework more successful, looking at the who, what, when, where, and how of creating a successful homework routine.

Jessica's three children are old enough that they are assigned homework mostly on a daily basis. In fact, her sixteen-year-old is quite accomplished. He is used to completing homework on his own. The role he has not played to date is helping the younger children understand the value of routines by mentoring and coaching them.

The entire family needed systems. Systems help meet the needs of children of all ages, based on their levels of independence and competency. We explored system options and decided on this one:

1. **Get home.** The children will come home, drop their backpacks at the back door, run upstairs, take off their school clothes, put their school clothes in the hamper, put their play clothes on, and come downstairs for a snack.

   Jessica's teenager, Jason, goes to soccer practice right after school. When he arrives home at 4:00 p.m. he will drop his backpack, shower, and then mentor the younger children by asking them how their homework is going and offer any needed help. Children love attention from their older siblings, and Jason feels valued when he can help his siblings. When everyone has a clear role in the family, homework time runs smoothly.

   Okay, back to the elementary-agers.

2. **Get ready for homework.** The children will all sit at the kitchen table while they eat their snack. Mom will bring the backpacks to the table so that each child may unpack their backpack, take out their planner, review the homework that needs to be completed today, and then on a separate piece of paper write down exactly how they're going to approach their homework.

   What subject are they going to do first?
   What homework are they going to do in that subject?
   What materials are they going to need?

3. **Gather supplies.** Jessica has been creating a home for everything (and teaching her children to put everything back in its assigned home). She even has a portable homework kit. It is a box filled with Dixie cups of all of the items that

may be needed to successfully complete homework: colored pencils, pens, regular pencils, erasers, tape, scissors, glue, plain paper, lined paper, and so on.

4. **Help your kids focus.** Jessica turns on the timer and for the next twenty minutes the children each initiate their specific homework task while she sits at the table monitoring, helping, and engaging so that the children can successfully attend to the task, stay focused on their homework, and get each step of the homework process completed successfully.

5. **Manage time frames for success.** For her little one, who squirms and worms and fidgets and dawdles, Jessica's job is to say the child's name and remind him, "For the next twenty minutes we're doing this piece of homework." After those twenty minutes the little one is allowed to get up and take a break. The seven-year-old is usually able to go on for another twenty minutes, and within forty minutes of thoughtful, consistent homework participation, Jessica's kids are able to complete their homework tasks, feel good about what they've done, and then go on to other fun activities.

After establishing the system with Jessica and, of course, collaborating with her children on how they'd like it to go (because that is the most important part), Jessica said, "You know what, I kind of did this but I wasn't consistent enough. One child would get up, they would need to go to the bathroom, they would need a drink, somebody would have forgotten a book. Now that we're all approaching homework as a family in a forty-minute time frame, it feels like one piece of daily work that we all do together." She continued, "When we're successful at homework, we're happy, we're relieved, and then we can go on to family fun."

After dinner as Jessica is cleaning up with the help of the rest of the family, she can turn more of her attention to Jason and ask, "Are you needing any support around your homework tonight?" Jason would rather FaceTime his friend and that's just fine. He knows his mom and dad are there if he needs them.

Think of routines in chunks, not in timelines. Routines are bits of focused activities that one needs to accomplish during different parts of each day. Jessica's homework routine was successful, everyone knew what was expected, and they used a system for homework completion.

Developing a Successful Bedtime Routine

Similar to you, your children need consistent sleep-wake routines, a cozy sleep setting, and a consistent presleep (getting ready for bed) routine. Here are some tips to help your child get to sleep with ease.

Make sure your child is tired and ready for sleep at the appropriate time. Generally, after a nap that lasts sixty minutes or longer, children, teens, and adults will not be ready to sleep again for at least six hours. If your teen snoozes for an hour before dinner, anticipate finding him wide awake until midnight or so. While these are general guidelines and everyone varies, it's helpful to think that short naps are great, and longer naps may shift a child's sleep cycle.

Write down the bedtime routine and post it up, or use marker boards as with the morning routine. Again, collaborate with your children on the plan. You might ask:

- What would they like to do in what order? (Shower, bathe, use the bathroom, brush their teeth, kiss the other parent or care provider good night, say good night to siblings, put on pajamas, etc.)
- How many books do they want you to read with them per evening, or how much time do they want to spend reading?

- What will the plan be if they can't fall asleep? (Listen to soothing music, think about something that made them happy that day, take calming breaths, make up a story, etc.)
- Your teen may enjoy playing on his phone or tablet until he falls asleep. Make a plan to have him turn off his device forty-five minutes before he plans to sleep. It's a good idea to get in the habit of plugging devices in outside of bedrooms as the backlighting keeps the brain awake.

These days, teens need to get up quite early (in my opinion way too early) to go to school. Helping your teen get prepared the night before allows him the gift of calm as he runs out the door in the morning. Part of your own routine may be dropping off his sports or music equipment at practice so that he doesn't have to carry a hockey bag or cello to school.

Talk your child through the routine each and every night until she can talk you through the routine. And adapt routines as your children get older. Tweens and teens need routines as well. Collaborate with your older children to make sure that they are doing what is important, not just what is fun. This will help them to internalize routines and rhythm (the tempo and timing of routines), and even project management or goal setting as they prepare for college.

Chores, aka Family Contributions

Let's wrap things up by talking about how you can enhance mastery and independence for your children by adding age-appropriate tasks to their everyday routines. Teaching kids the skills of everyday living is an important aspect of changing and redesigning routines as your kids get older.

In general terms, these tasks are called chores, I actually like to call them *family contributions*. At different ages and stages, you can add small tasks to the child's routine that really are opportunities to graduate to the next age level. So instead of saying to your child "Your chore is to make your bed," "Your chore is to fold the laundry," or "You forgot to feed the dog," I feel it is much more successful when teaching routines and tasks that lead to independence, mastery, and accountability to phrase it more this way: "It's very exciting because now it's spring and you're seven and lots of seven-year-olds are able to . . ." Or simply remind a teen that "I think the dog is hungry."

Once you present a new activity to a younger child, you can go on to add, "So let's actually practice. Let's write down the three school lunches you like the most, and let's take the time today to practice making them."

This works, for one, because children love spending time with you. And kids like to be productive and they want to be masterful. Instead of expecting your kids to be able to do things that may seem daunting to them, you'll feel comfortable knowing that they're set up for success.

---

toughLOVE TIPS

Here's a list of skills that many school-age kids are capable of doing at various ages. You can begin to thread these skill sets into your kids' daily routines to make them more successful as they get older. Add to and personalize these lists as you go along.

Ages four to five:

Carry in and put away nonbreakable groceries.

Dust surfaces on their own.

Get dressed (most four- to five-year-olds can get dressed on their own except for tying their shoes).

Get snacks when they're at eye level in the refrigerator.

Go with Mommy or Daddy to the mailbox and carry the mail
inside.

Help in food preparation with Mommy or Daddy's assistance.

Help Mommy and Daddy make the bed.

Put clean plastic dishes away in the kids' cupboards.

Put toys and books in their homes.

Put dirty clothing in the hamper.

Put trash in bags to help Mommy and Daddy throw away the
trash.

Set the table with safe tableware.

Ages six to eight:

Bathe their bodies on their own.

Brush their teeth on their own.

Help Mommy or Daddy with outdoor yard work.

Help pick up clothing and trash from the car.

Help put groceries away.

Make their own beds.

Help sort the laundry into whites, colors, and darks.

Help wash the car.

Keep rooms cleaned up and picked up.

Mop, sweep, and dust.

Put their own laundry that's been folded away in the proper
drawers.

Take pets outside for a walk in the backyard.

Ages nine to twelve:

Do outside chores like raking the leaves, on their own or with
Mom and Dad.

Help prepare simple meals with safe cutlery.

Help prepare grocery lists.

Learn how to hand-wash the dishes.

Learn how to separate laundry, put it in the washer, add soap
and fabric softener, and transfer clothing to the dryer.

Sew on buttons that have fallen off.

Take items out of the refrigerator and wipe down the
refrigerator.

Vacuum the car.

Walk, brush, and bathe pets.

Wash and dry the car.

Wipe down the bathroom.

Wipe kitchen counters.

Wipe windows with a window cleaner and a cotton cloth.

Ages thirteen to sixteen:

Babysit siblings.

Bring dishes to the sink, clean dishes, put them in the
dishwasher, and run the dishwasher.

Clean the bathrooms.

Garden and manage the yard.

Help siblings learn daily tasks.

Organize closets.

Organize the garage.

Organize the pantry.

Plan and make meals.

Play with younger siblings so that Mom and Dad can get tasks
or work done.

Provide folded laundry for the younger siblings to put in their
proper homes.

Separate, clean, and fold laundry.

Serve meals at the breakfast, lunch, or dinner table.

Wash, dry, and vacuum the car.

Mission Accomplished!

The value of preparing and planning each day's events and incorporating routines into your daily life cannot be underestimated. Many of us have specific behaviors in mind that we would like our children to exhibit. As an example, we'd like our children to get up, take off their nightclothes, put them in the hamper, go to the bathroom, brush their teeth, come back and get dressed, come downstairs and eat breakfast, do their hair, brush their teeth again, grab their backpacks, and be out the door for a successful day.

The challenge is that we need to teach our children how to exhibit these behaviors in a step-by-step manner. Now, you might be that lucky parent who has a child who does this all on his own, but most children really need to be taught the individual steps in every routine in order to be successful.

When we begin the conversation with our children and we ask them how they'd like to do it, we engage them in the process of preparation and planning, leading to peaceful days and successful outcomes in families.

the art of mealtime

BY JILL CASTLE, MS, RDN, PEDIATRIC NUTRITION EXPERT AND MOM OF FOUR

Karima is a seasoned mom. With five children ranging from college to school age, she is a master at juggling homework, after-school activities, school breaks, pets, household demands, and a husband who travels for work. But mealtimes are her roadblock. "My biggest challenge is dealing with the ever-changing and growing information about what is healthy to eat and what isn't," she says. "I don't want food to become an obsession or a fear. What is good for one person isn't necessarily good for all. Allergies, family history, misinformation, too much information . . . sometimes it's all too stressful! All this effort and I still don't know if I am doing the right thing."

Karima isn't alone. Many parents struggle with family mealtime and the nagging worry that they could be doing things better. They worry about whether the food they offer is healthy enough, or they stress about the amounts their children eat (too much or too little). They worry about not getting enough family meals together during the week due to crazy schedules, and that good nutrition takes a backseat to the activity du jour. "Finding the time to make a homemade meal after working and fitting in the kids' schedules is my biggest challenge," says Paula, a mom of three. We parents feel such pressure to get healthy meals on the table fast. And, once we do get it on the table, we hope and pray our teens show up!

Even parents who have mastered the art of nutritious, timely meals can't always get their kids to eat what they serve. Some parents, like Whitney, mom of two teens and one middle-schooler, end up making separate meals. "No one likes the same thing, ever! Multimeal making at 6:00 p.m. stinks!" exclaims Whitney. Other parents may be dealing with ongoing picky eating issues carried over from toddlerhood or the appetite fluctuations that go hand in hand with childhood. For Colleen, mom of a teenager, the daily challenge lies in managing her teen's hunger. "She eats me out of house and home after school and then won't eat her dinner," she says with a sigh.

No wonder mealtime makes even the most accomplished, knowledgeable parent begin to sweat! It's no secret that the family meal in America has become more of a chore than a fulfilling part of parenthood. A fading family tradition riddled with growing conflict, doubt, and guilt. But what if there were a way to bring harmony and peace to the table, and make preparing family meals easier (without hiring a personal chef) at the same time? A way to bring the joy and nutrition back to the table and take the guilt and worry away?

It *is* possible to make family mealtime nutritious, pleasant, and rewarding for everyone. You just need the right information, approach, and perspective. While I can't create more time for you or coach you into becoming a master chef, I *can* give you the nutrition knowledge you need, an approach to mealtime that works, and an understanding of your child's developmental stage as it relates to eating behavior. What you have come to know in this book as toughLOVE, is what Maryann Jacobsen and I call "Fearless Feeding" in our book by the same name.

You Are the Nutrition Guide

First, you need to understand an important role you acquired when you had children: your role as the nutrition guide. As the nutrition guide, you are in charge of cultivating your child's palate by introducing him to a variety of foods, even in the face of picky eating. You, not your child, are in charge of the content, timing, and location of all meals and snacks, even throughout adolescence. While teens will gain independence in this area, you'll still be at the helm, providing guidance when needed or helping them get back on track.

You are responsible for your child's nutrition education and nutrition attitudes, because school won't do the job you can, and the world will teach her to fear some foods, overvalue others, and even dislike her body. You are in charge of setting limits with less-than-healthy foods and showing your child a model of healthy eating and activity. You will help him interpret his own hunger and fullness signals, and respect them, taking care to avoid nagging him to eat more or taking food away when he is still hungry. The biggest job you have, and perhaps the most challenging, is teaching your children how to make the right food choices for their health and wellness, and helping them *want* to do this for themselves.

THE NUTRITIONAL GATEKEEPER

Brian Wansink, PhD, tells us about the nutritional gatekeeper in his book *Mindless Eating*. He identifies parents as the nutritional gatekeepers of the family. The family gatekeeper is responsible for the food items that enter the home, as well as most of what gets chosen and eaten outside of the home. In fact, in this role parents influence more than 70 percent of what children eat.[1] Boiled down, this means that if you buy cheesy chips at the store, your child will eat cheesy chips. If you don't set limits on convenience food items at school or outside activities, he will feel unlimited in these venues. Research also suggests that children who eat the same meals as their parents eat healthier overall, which makes choosing food for the family meals extra important.[2] The bottom line is: you have quite a bit of say in what your children eat. Make sure you have a representation of what you want them eating in the home and set limits for outside eating. It's much easier to say yes to nutritious food than to worry about and patrol unhealthy snacks. By the time your child reaches adolescence, she will have a better sense of healthy choices when out and about.

Jody wishes she had taken this simple step earlier. "I can't tell you the number of times I've said no to chips, soda, and cookies," she says. "By not having them in the house, the role of food police nearly disappears!"

HOW YOU HANDLE MEALTIME

Your approach to mealtime is also important. Charlie, father of four, hates spinach. He attributes this strong feeling to his childhood, when his mother would make him "clean his plate," including the despised spinach, before he could leave the table. Forcing children to clean their plates, rewarding them with dessert for eating meat or veggies, and limiting extra helpings to curb calorie intake are just a few tactics that can backfire on even the most well-intentioned parent. These practices almost never work to produce the desired outcome: liking a food, a healthy intake, and mindfulness with eating.

You're the Star

In spite of what you may feel, you truly hold the most influence over your child's nutrition and eating, no matter what her age.[3] But the path to healthy eating is rocky and winding. I will tell you, there is no straight shot at the goal: a healthy adult. You will face undeniable competition. From the time your child leaves for kindergarten to the time he's headed for college, there will be outside influences molding his nutrition behaviors. School, friends, and media all have the power to influence your child's perception of nutrition, what she eats, whether she diets or not, and how she feels about herself.[4] You will deal with changing developments that encompass mental, emotional, and social aspects of your child, as well as physical ones, which will also impact eating. You will face food preferences and eating habits that are difficult to navigate.

KEEP YOUR EYE ON THE PRIZE

Often, parents are caught up in getting their child to eat today, and they forget how long it can take for children to develop healthy eating habits—eighteen years or an entire childhood! While the day-in, day-out food choices *do* matter, sometimes parents freak out when a single choice isn't healthy or a child skips a meal. The reality is, it's not about what is eaten or not eaten today. Rather, it's about the big (nutrition) picture. Does eating match hunger, growth, and activity levels? What does the food variety look like? What habits are forming?

The learning curve for nutritious eating (how to do it, what to eat, and how to balance all foods) is steep, and the progression to a healthy adulthood occurs one meal at a time. A bad eating day won't turn your child into a junk-food junkie, nor will a nutritious day turn her into the best eater on the block. Keep your eye on the future. Just like learning to ride a bike as a child, or drive a car as a teen, we intuitively know these endeavors will take time and practice. We patiently allow for mistakes and do-overs, while having the wherewithal to wait until mastery is achieved. We need this same attitude and patience when feeding our children. Be patient, be positive, and guide your child with the end goal in mind.

Nutrition: A Piece of the Feeding Puzzle

Like Karima, you may feel overwhelmed by the abundance of nutrition information, conflicting advice about what (and what not) to eat, and worry you're getting it all wrong. First, rest assured that food, while important in raising healthy children, is not what it's all about. There's more to the story, which we'll dig into later. In fact, don't get caught up in perfect food—because there isn't any. And there's no perfect meal, either. The best meals are the meals that your family will eat and that will contribute to their health and well-being.

GROWTH DICTATES NUTRITION

First, you need to understand that children's growth is varied at different stages. School-age children experience steady growth, which means their appetites are relatively stable as well. You can expect your school-age child to gain about four pounds each year and grow about two to three inches. That is, until they hit puberty and growth accelerates. At this time, expect to see weight gain and linear growth at their greatest, next to that of infancy. In fact, teenagers gain about twenty to thirty pounds during the course of adolescence and grow three to four inches annually (females and males, respectively).[5] As a result, appetite increases and so does eating, matching the expanding calorie needs associated with this growth spurt. Male teens have the highest caloric requirements of any age and gender, topping out at 3,200 a day for an active fourteen- to eighteen-year-old boy, which will surprise no one who's seen a member of that species eat an entire box of cereal at one sitting. No wonder parents of adolescent boys have a hard time keeping the pantry and refrigerator stocked! In contrast, the calorie needs of an active eight-year-old girl top out at 1,800 a day.

I'M HUNGRY!

Your best approach during these growth years is to stay ahead of hunger by planning nutritious and satisfying meals and snacks for every three to five hours, depending on your child's age. Younger children eat every three to four hours and teens every four to five hours. This timing will help prevent kids from becoming overly hungry, which can lead to overeating. And it doesn't mean you have to prepare food that often—just have it available.

Lori complained that her fifteen-year-old son, Dan, was imbalanced in his eating. "He skips breakfast because he wakes up late and is starving when he gets home after school. He ends up eating constantly until dinnertime," she says. What Lori didn't understand was that Dan had higher energy needs due to his stage of growth, and he was not eating enough at the start of his day, which intensified his hunger after school. He was making the mistake many teens make, something I call "back loading" (meeting calorie needs during the last half of the day). His constant eating after school was a sign that he was playing "calorie catch-up," eating the needed calories he missed at the beginning of the day. I suggested Lori get a structure going with meals and snacks timed every three to five hours. She could wake Dan up early so he'd have time for a nutritious and substantial breakfast before school (aka "front loading").

Dan also needed to make sure he included a good source of protein at lunch, such as deli meat, cheese, yogurt or milk, and a high-fiber item like whole-grain bread, fresh fruit, salad, or beans. These two nutrients, protein and fiber, along with some fat, would help him stay satisfied after eating and quell his hunger until snack time. Snacks, too, should be healthy, satisfying, and nutritious. In fact, put a little magic in snacks by adding protein, which can boost satisfaction and result in eating less overall.[6] When Lori and Dan mapped out the meal structure, improved the food quality, and front-loaded with

Satisfying Snack Ideas

Dry cereal and dried cherries

Oat O's, peanuts, and carob chips

Shredded-wheat cereal, low-fat milk, and blueberries

Layered yogurt, granola, and strawberries

Skewered cantaloupe and cheddar cheese cubes

Apple and cheese slices

Banana dipped in peanut butter

Strawberries dipped in strawberry cream cheese

Clementine and cheese stick

Applesauce cup and graham crackers

Hummus and flat pretzels

Hummus and baby carrots

Tomato and cottage cheese

Oatmeal cookies and low-fat milk

100% orange juice Popsicle

Half a sandwich and 1/2 cup 100% fruit juice

Black olives and feta cheese

All-fruit Popsicle

Air-popped popcorn

Toast with butter and jam

Toast with nut butter and banana

English muffin with butter and honey

Banana muffin and 6 oz. milk

Deli meat wrapped around a cheese stick

Snap peas and red peppers with spreadable cheese

Coconut yogurt and mini chocolate chips

Nuts and dried fruit

A cup of soup

Cheese and crackers

Peanut butter and pretzels

Mini bagel and cream cheese

Homemade trail mix (cereal, nuts, and dried fruit)

Red grapes and cheese kabobs

Pepperoni mini pizza (pita, sauce, cheese, and turkey pepperoni)

Tuna fish salad and crackers

Frozen yogurt Popsicle

Chicken salad and green grapes

breakfast, Dan was more satisfied after eating and less inclined to eat constantly after school.

STRIKING THE RIGHT FOOD BALANCE

It's good to know what kids need in terms of calories, but don't spend too much time crunching numbers. Most American children and teens are meeting or exceeding their calorie needs, but many of the calories they are consuming are poor sources of nutrition. As a result, many kids are getting too much sugar, salt, and fat in their daily diet, while missing out on important nutrients like calcium, vitamin D, fiber, and potassium.[7] Teenagers, in particular, are dining out, eating convenience foods, and snacking too much, plaguing their nutritional intake with nutrient-poor foods.[8] A key ingredient in successful meals is getting the food balance right, leaning toward wholesome, nutritious foods and away from highly processed, sugary, and/or fatty foods.

Sarah was embarrassed to admit that she really didn't know what a balanced and healthy meal looked like. "I was never really taught what I should include in a meal. I grew up with lots of frozen dinners," she says. Unfortunately, it's not uncommon for parents like Sarah to feel lost in the kitchen. Cooking skills, meal planning, and general nutrition education went away with home economics in the high school curriculum, leaving many of today's parents without the know-how to tackle this daily task. Sarah wanted to know what to include in her home-cooked meals.

I encouraged her to balance Nourishing Foods (the basics, including protein, dairy, fruit, vegetables, grains, and fats), Half-and-Half Foods (foods that offer important nutrients but also contain added fat or sugar, such as chocolate milk), and Fun Foods (foods that offer little nutritional value but lots of flavor, like candy or chips). To hit the right balance, I suggested she use the 90:10 Rule, where 90 percent of the foods offered were Nourishing and Half-and-Half

Foods and the remaining 10 percent came from Fun Foods—about one or two per day.[9]

When planning meals, Sarah should incorporate as many Nourishing and Half-and-Half Foods as possible to assure a wide variety of nutrients are presented. I reminded her that kids are typically accepting of fruit, which can be especially helpful with finicky eaters, and can add a good source of nutrition, especially if vegetables are hit or miss (they contain similar nutrients).

Sarah started including milk, a bowl of fruit, and a few slices of bread on her meal table, in addition to the entrée and sides she had planned. At first, her kids gravitated to the fruit and bread, but after a while, they included all sorts of food on their plates. She also asked her children for input on meals during the week to create more excitement and buy-in. She made sure to rotate different foods from the food groups to cover a wide range of nutrients and avoid boredom. Using a thematic approach to meal planning was also helpful: pasta night; meatless Monday; poultry dinner; kid's choice; and Mexican night were just some examples of the weekly themes. Sarah helped her kids plan for Fun Foods, taking care to include special events, dining out, and school treats. For example, when a birthday party was on the calendar, Fun Foods weren't part of the meal plan at home. Sarah was able to use this system to get balanced meals on the table and introduce new foods, while setting limits on sweets and unhealthy snack foods.

I also encouraged Sarah to include one or two familiar items in the meal, as this would help her children warm up to the meal, and perhaps feel more comfortable and secure. Sitting down to a table of unfamiliar foods can be a turnoff for any child, and a tough sell for a teen, who may become more particular with age.

Handling Mealtime: A Matter of Attitude and Action

Traditionally, mealtime has been a touch point for the family, an opportunity to communicate and strengthen family bonds. But today, family mealtime can be filled with pressure, angst, and chaos, with a little bit of guilt thrown in. Parents may pressure children to eat this or that, or threaten to take privileges away if eating isn't good enough. Chaos comes with disjointed meals, where family members are anywhere but at the table, and parents are retrieving alternative food items for the child who "won't eat." Feelings of guilt exist because mealtime isn't a source of pleasure or bonding, but one of argument, disappointment, and, let's face it, dread. The truth is, for many families mealtime has become more of a chore and less of a bonding experience for everyone.

Have you ever stopped to think about whether the vibe of mealtime is getting in the way? Forget the perfect meal. Forget the manners. What about how you interact with your child at mealtime? What about your beliefs about how your child should be eating?

Success at the table is as much a matter of attitude and action as it is about food. The attitudes and actions you bring to the table are what researchers call feeding styles and practices, and they may be setting you up for failure. From worsening picky eating to promoting excess weight gain, feeding styles and practices are an emerging area of childhood nutrition research that give insight into how the interaction at the table affects eating, for better or worse.

Feeding styles are the attitudes you carry from your own childhood experience with eating, and the general approach you use in the process of feeding your child.[10] Feeding styles are transgenerational, that is, they are passed down from generation to generation, as the "way things are done when feeding kids." *Feeding practices* are the daily strategies, or tactics, used to get children to eat, or not.[11] These practices are related to your feeding style but may also stem from outside pressure and fear. Let's examine some feeding styles.

AUTHORITARIAN: TRYING TO CONTROL A CHILD'S EATING

Tammy was a picky eater as a young girl and often faced foods she didn't like for dinner. Her father made her stay at the table to finish her meal. Sometimes she was at the table after bedtime, trying to choke down her milk. Tammy's experience with tight control at the table is what researchers call an *authoritarian feeding style,* characterized by high demands on the child ("eat all your food") and low sensitivity to hunger, fullness, and food preferences. Generally, few food choices are offered to the child. As a result, children who are raised like this may have a hard time regulating their appetites (they eat too much or too little), may eat vegetables and fruit less well, and may have a higher weight status.[12] They may also be building negative memories of their childhood food experience.

Tammy felt *pressure* to eat from her dad. He wanted her to eat everything, and not waste food, but often Tammy wasn't hungry enough to finish her meal, or she didn't enjoy eating some of the foods included in her meal. The problem with pressure to eat is that it may override a child's fullness signal. Research tells us that over time, children raised with pressure to eat may lose this sense, which is associated with the important cue to stop eating. In other words, they learn to overeat.

Parents also use pressure in the case of the picky or poor eater. Intending to get the child to eat more, or better, the parent nags or reminds the child to eat, what's known as *prompting.* Some children react to this pressure by eating less, what researchers define as early satiety (getting full early, before a significant amount of food is eaten).[13] Sometimes for the picky eater, the more pressure he feels, the less well he eats—the exact opposite reaction from the one parents are looking for! This "pressure to eat/retreat" cycle is repetitive and ineffective, and is often seen with picky eaters.

Alternatively, parents who worry that their child is eating too much may use *restriction* to control eating. Stopping a child before he is satisfied, reducing portions on her plate, or using only low-calorie food options are just some examples. Despite trying to help the child, parents who control their child's eating through restriction may see her lose control with eating at parties, hoarding food, or sneak-eating. The research in this area suggests that children who experience restriction may be more likely to eat when they are bored, or feeling emotional, or for other reasons unrelated to hunger.[14]

Last, to motivate kids to eat well or to eat something desired by the parent, rewards such as dessert are used. *Rewarding* has been shown to be effective in getting a child to eat or try something new, but may not be effective in getting a child to *like* the food in the long term.[15] In fact, rewarding promotes the reward, thus raising the value of dessert in a child's mind, while demoting the foods (vegetables, for example) the parent wants the child to eat and like. Rewarding may not work to mold positive behavior or attitudes about specific foods, and may even make them worse. It does, however, elevate the status of rewards like desserts and other treats.

While pressure, restriction, and rewarding are not *intended* to cause negative eating reactions, the truth is, for many kids, they do.

PERMISSIVE: BEING TOO LAX AT MEALTIME

As an adult, Tammy carried negative memories of eating and food (especially milk!) from her childhood. Some parents who had food experiences like Tammy's reject their childhood feeding style and adopt an opposite style. In Tammy's case, she promised never to make her children sit and finish their food. Instead, she was more lax with table rules and let them leave the table when they wanted to (sometimes several times during the course of a meal). She also allowed them to dictate the foods for dinner, which resulted in her preparing several meals and a chaotic mealtime.

Being too lax about food and mealtime is also known as the *permissive*, or indulgent, *feeding style*. While it is not demanding of the child with regard to eating, it is highly sensitive to a child's hunger, fullness, and food preferences.[16] This may make the parent overresponsive to the child, meeting food requests at every turn, or having a hard time saying no. Children may have more control over the meal content than is healthy. Children raised with the permissive feeding style may be out of touch with their appetite, eating more sweets and fatty foods, and either gaining weight or eating poorly due to picky eating.[17]

A common practice of the permissive feeding style is catering, where the parent is making separate meal items in addition to the family meal, or making exceptions for the child in other ways, such as in meal venue and timing. Parents believe they are doing a favor by making the child what he wants. Ironically, what they don't realize is when children are catered to, their limited food choices may become reinforced.

Sean, age seven, eats very few fruits and protein sources, no vegetables, and a lot of pasta and milk. Mom Maggie observes, "He just won't eat what the rest of us are eating. I've tried to bribe, reward, and discipline him, but it doesn't work. The only way we can have a relatively calm meal is if I make a separate meal for him." You can see that Sean has no incentive to branch out to new foods. Catering is a self-perpetuating problem: the more you cater to your child's food wants and desires, the more catering he will want and expect, and this will end up choking out food variety and balanced nutrition, and may be problematic as he gets older, interfering with social activities, and perhaps self-esteem.

Maggie needed an alternative approach to catering, a way to serve meals that freed Sean to make his own food choices from what was served and that offered *some* foods that Sean liked, as well as others. Maggie started to add different foods to the set menu, alternating between a bowl of fruit, raw veggies, cheese, peanut butter, and yogurt. This way Sean could have a cheese stick instead of a pork chop, or crunchy cucumber coins instead of a tossed salad. The new rule was "we eat what is on the table—no alternatives." This was tough on both Sean and Maggie at first, but everyone quickly adjusted, once the policy was in place and Maggie followed through.

AUTHORITATIVE: THE MIDDLE GROUND SECRET TO MEALTIME HARMONY

The secret to achieving harmony at the table lies in the delicate balance of boundaries, choice, and sensitivity, what researchers call the *authoritative feeding style*. This middle ground is an approach that is effective in helping your child eat well while keeping you in charge of food and feeding. It is characterized by high demands around eating (limits and boundaries) as well as sensitivity to your child's appetite and food preferences.[18] Parents who are authoritative with feeding have a predictable rhythm to meals and snacks, are sensitive to a child's appetite, and allow reasonable choices.

Mary is an excellent example of this feeding style. She serves meals at about the same time every day, and in the same location, usually at the kitchen table. "We try to eat most meals together, whether at home or out," she says. Mary understands that family meals are one of the strongest ways to build family cohesion, reduce adolescent risk-taking behaviors, and improve nutritional intake.[19]

Between meals and snacks, Mary "closes" the kitchen. "If they get hungry, they are allowed to have fruit, but they have to ask me first," she explains. Mary also involves her children in meal planning, asking for their menu suggestions, letting them have a kid's choice night each week, and picking new foods to try. When she introduces new foods, such as artichokes or quinoa, she makes sure to have an item or two on the table she knows the kids will eat, like fruit or bread, so they don't feel overwhelmed by unfamiliar food. She sticks to her meal structure (timing and location of meals), sometimes letting her child choose *not* to eat a meal and head off to bed. Mary knows it's more important to keep a rhythm with meals going, and let her child learn that if she decides to go on strike at dinner, or isn't hungry, that is fine. The meal system is in place, and another meal will be available in the morning. Mary knows no well-nourished child has perished overnight because of a missed meal, and the greater lesson—the self-regulation of appetite—is a key to healthy eating. She is sure not to react with emotion when her child isn't eating the way she expected or wanted.

If you have a teenager, you may find late-night snacking stirs up a concern. While it is more difficult to direct the teen away from the kitchen and food, you can suggest Nourishing and Half-and-Half Foods for a late snack. You will also want to check hunger levels. You might say, "Were you able to get enough to eat at dinner? Are you feeling hungry?" If hunger is the issue, make sure you are providing satisfying meals and snacks—your teen may be in a growth spurt and need more food.

Late-night eating may be related to pleasure or habit, rather than hunger. This is where you can step in if you see a negative habit forming, with reminders such as "I know that munching on chips while you do homework is soothing (or keeps you occupied); would you like to try something else, like carrots or celery sometimes, to help balance your eating?" or "I know it's pleasurable to cozy up on the couch with a pint of ice cream while you watch your favorite show. Are you making adjustments to your eating during the day to account for this Fun Food?" Remember, teens are beginning to be more independent and self-regulate their eating (and make mistakes along the way!), so you'll want to communicate about nutrition and guide your teen to stay on track, using the food balance discussed earlier.

Meal Service with Style

Mary planned one nutritious meal for the whole family with most food groups represented and served them "family-style." Rather than plating meals ahead of time, the family-style meal allows children to choose which foods they will eat and the amount that is right for them. This is accomplished by placing plates and bowls of food in the center of the table and letting family members pass the food around, selecting which foods, and how much, they will eat. A 2013 study in the *International Journal of Obesity* suggests that children who experience the authoritarian or permissive feeding styles may take more food with self-service.[20] I have seen this happen as a transitional phase, while the child figures out that he can be in charge of his own eating. Overall, my experience has been that children eat better (more variety and realistic amounts) when they are in charge of serving themselves.

Family-style meal service is authoritative in nature and aligns with Ellyn Satter's Division of Responsibility, where the parent decides the content of meals and snacks, when and where they will occur, and the child determines whether he will eat what is served, and the amounts that are right for him.[21] It gives some choice and control to the child, lets him eat to his appetite, and improves mealtime enjoyment. If you are skeptical about this approach, test it for two weeks and see what happens!

Why is the authoritative feeding style successful? First, it reflects a trust between the parent and child. The child trusts that the parent will have nutritious, satisfying, and timely meals in a pleasant environment and that his food preferences will be acknowledged. The parent trusts that the child knows when to eat, when to stop, and which foods taste good.

Second, the parent allows the child to make a choice, from a reasonable pair of options, usually within the same category. Examples of this are:

> *To a young child:* Would you like peas or broccoli?
> *To an older child:* Are you having soda for lunch or ice cream for dessert?
> *To a teen:* Are you eating dinner with us at 6:30 or having a dinner plate later when you get home?

Third, setting limits around mealtime (and food), like closing the kitchen between meals and snacks, setting a rule of asking first before eating outside of regular times, and limiting sweets to one or two per day help support the mealtime structure, curtail extra eating, and keep the parent in charge.

Because nothing is ever perfect, even authoritative parents have their obstacles. One challenge is getting the recommended three to five sit-together family meals each week.[22] It's estimated that only one in four teens eats a meal with his family each day.[23] We know family meals are beneficial to children and teens on many levels, including academic performance, better nutrition and weight status, lowered risk-taking behaviors, and improved family cohesion.[24]

Today, family meals can be next to impossible, though. In my own family of three teens, one middle-schooler, and a commuting husband, finding the opportunity to eat together in the midst of activities, sports, and late work schedules is difficult. I have to carefully look at everyone's schedules and plan strategically. Some nights we have only a half hour to be together, and only one or two nights during the school week. We almost always have Sunday-night dinner together. I look at breakfast, lunch, and snack as opportunities, as any meal or snack can qualify as a family meal. And, thankfully, it takes only one parent in attendance to show a benefit.[25] Once you have your family meals mapped out, make it clear to your family that these meals are sacred—in other words, a must-do for everyone, especially those teenagers!

Another challenge for parents of teens is the new driver. Once a teen gets a driver's license, some parents feel they start to lose all control of nutrition. If you're the parent of a teen who is driving, you'll want to set and review the boundaries for out-of-home eating: how frequently, where, what to order, and how much money to spend. These boundaries will help your teen keep nutrition a priority, as well as save some money.

You can implement healthy boundaries for elementary-age children, too. Look at the school lunch menu together and plan what will be ordered during the week, such as when dessert can be selected; set the rule for what to drink when dining out, such as water; and outline acceptable after-school snack items, such as yogurt or cereal and fruit. Be careful not to be too controlling with your limits. Review reasonable foods and amounts, and offer reasonable choices, based on the event. For example, you wouldn't want to declare a no-sweets rule when your child is heading to a Halloween party. That probably won't work, and may even be counterproductive, making your child want sweets even more. Be flexible with sweets, using the 90:10 Rule, and allow them on special occasions.

Mastering the Art of Mealtime Success

To sum up, the day-to-day feeding style and practices that are used by parents really do add an important dimension to how well your child eats at mealtime. If you find that your current methods aren't working—change them! It's never too late to start on the path to authoritative feeding. I've seen countless families switch over to this feeding style and drop unproductive feeding practices—and many have lived to tell the tale of pleasant family meals, decreased dinner drama, and fewer (if any) food battles.

Remember Tammy? She was raised with the authoritarian feeding style, but adopted a permissive feeding style with her own children. It turns out one daughter was very picky, and Tammy catered food to get her to eat while managing her husband, who was more demanding of his daughter's eating. She came to me because food and meals were stressing her out and she didn't know how to change them.

I worked to educate and transition both parents to an authoritative feeding style. We came up with a family-style meal service that included one or two items her daughter would eat, and allowed everyone to choose their own food from the items that were offered on the table. I also encouraged Tammy to hold the line with a no-alternative-food rule. Tammy could say, "I'm sorry you don't like what we have to eat tonight, but I am confident you will find something here to satisfy your appetite. If you'd like to make suggestions for tomorrow night, I'd be happy to consider them." With a better understanding of feeding, and time, the parents were able to take the helm at mealtime and enjoy each other's company without stress and whining.

Adopting an authoritative feeding style that honors your child's appetite and food preferences but keeps you in charge will be your ace in the hole. Don't be afraid to set the ground rules around food and mealtime, and hold them steady. Remember, children will always follow your lead, so be a good role model and leader, too.

Mealtime is challenging for many reasons, but it doesn't have to be. You don't have to be frustrated, overworked from cooking, or worried every time you sit down at the table about who's eating or whether the meal's healthy enough. You can have pleasant meals at which you communicate with your family, laugh, and enjoy one another's company. You can have nutritious meals that include a variety of old food standbys as well as new foods, while pleasing your family and promoting their health. And you can navigate the ups and downs of the ever-changing childhood experience with confidence and know-how.

1. B. Wansink, *Mindless Eating* (New York: Bantam Books, 2010).
2. V. Scafida, "The Family Meal Panacea: Exploring How Different Aspects of Family Meal Occurrence, Meal Habits and Meal Enjoyment Relate to Young Children's Diets," *Sociology and Illness*, April 2, 2013. Doi: 10.1111/1467-9566.12007 [epub].
3. R. Brown and J. Ogden, "Children's Eating Attitudes and Behaviours: A Study of the Modeling and Control Theories of Parental Influence," *Health Education and Research* 19 (2004), 261–71; Y. Wang, M. A. Beydoun, J. Li, Y. Lui, and L. A. Moreno, "Do Children and Their Parents Eat a Similar Diet? Resemblance in Child and Parental Dietary Intake; Systematic Review and Meta-analysis," *Journal of Epidemiology and Community Health* 65 (2011), 177–89.
4. H. Patrick and T. A. Nicklas, "A Review of Family and Social Determinants of Children's Eating Patterns and Diet Quality," *Journal of the American College of Nutrition* 24 (2005), 83–92; J. L. Harris, J. L. Pomeranz, T. Lobstein, K. D. Brownell, "A Crisis in the Marketplace: How Food Marketing Contributes to Childhood Obesity and What Can Be Done," *Annual Review of Public Health* 30 (2009), 211–25; M. Story and S. French, "Food Advertising and Marketing Directed at Children and Adolescents in the US," *International Journal of Behavioral Nutrition and Physical Activity* 1 (2004), 3. Doi: 10.1186/1479-5868-1-3.
5. P. K. Samour and K. King, *Pediatric Nutrition*, 4th ed. (Burlington, MA: Jones & Bartlett Learning, 2010).
6. B. Wansink, M. Shimizu, and A. Brumberg, "Association of Nutrient-Dense Snack Combinations with Calories and Vegetable Intake," *Pediatrics* 131 (2013), 22–29.
7. U.S. Department of Agriculture & U.S. Department of Health and Human Services, *Dietary Guidelines for Americans, 2010*, 7th ed. (Washington, DC: U.S. Government Printing Office, 2010).
8. R. S. Sebastian, J. D. Goldman, and C. W. Enns, *Snacking Patterns of US Adolescents: What We Eat in America, NHANES 2005–2006*, USDA Food Surveys

Research Group Dietary Data Brief No. 2 (September 2010). Retrieved from www.ars.usda.gov/SP2UserFiles/Place/12355000/pdf/DBrief/2_adolescents_snacking_0506.pdf.

9. J. L. Castle and M. T. Jacobsen, *Fearless Feeding: How to Raise Healthy Eaters from High Chair to High School* (San Francisco: Jossey-Bass, 2013).

10. C. Lachat, R. Verstraeten, D. Roberfroid, J. Van Camp, and P. Kolsteren, "Eating Out of Home and Its Association with Dietary Intake: A Systematic Review of the Evidence," *Obesity Reviews* 13 (2012), 329–46.

11. L. Webber, L. Cooke, C. Hill, and J. Wardle, "Association Between Children's Appetitive Traits and Maternal Feeding Practices," *Journal of the Academy of Nutrition and Dietetics* 110 (2010), 1718–22.

12. K. E. Rhee, J. C. Lumeng, D. P. Appugliese, N. Kaciroti, and R. H. Bradley, "Parenting Styles and Overweight Status in First Grade," *Pediatrics* 117 (2006), 2047–54; H. L. Burdette, R. C. Whitaker, W. C. Hall, and S. R. Daniels, "Maternal Infant-Feeding Style and Children's Adiposity at 5 Years of Age," *Archives of Pediatrics and Adolescent Medicine* 160 (2006), 513–20.

13. J. K. Orell-Valente, L. G. Hill, W. A. Brechwald, K. A. Dodge, G. S. Pettit, and J. E. Bates, " 'Just Three More Bites': An Observational Analysis of Parents' Socialization of Children's Eating at Mealtime," *Appetite* 48 (2007), 37–45.

14. L. L. Birch, J. O. Fisher, K. K. Davison, "Learning to Overeat: Maternal Use of Restrictive Feeding Practices Promotes Girls' Eating in the Absence of Hunger," *American Journal of Clinical Nutrition* 78 (2003), 215–20.

15. L. Cooke, L. C. Chambers, E. V. Anez, and J. Wardle, "Facilitating or undermining? The effect of reward on food acceptance; A narrative review," *Appetite* 57 (2011), 493–97.

16. A. T. Galloway, L. M. Fiorito, L. A. Francis, and L. L. Birch, " 'Finish Your Soup': Counterproductive Effects of Pressuring Children to Eat on Intake and Affect," *Appetite* 46 (2006), 318–23.

17. M. S. Faith, K. S. Scanlon, L. L. Birch, L. A. Francis, and B. Sherry, "Parent-Child Feeding Strategies and Their Relationships to Child Eating and Weight Status," *Obesity Research* 12 (2004), 1711–22.

18. H. Patrick, T. A. Nicklas, S. O. Hughes, and M. Morales, "The Benefits of Authoritative Feeding Style: Caregiver Feeding Styles and Children's Food Consumption Patterns," *Appetite* 44 (2005), 243–49.

19. B. H. Fiese and M. Schwartz, "Reclaiming the Family Table: Mealtimes and Child Health and Wellbeing," *Social Policy Report* 22(4) 2008, 3–17; A. J. Hammons and B. H. Fiese, "Is Frequency of Shared Family Meals

Related to the Nutritional Health of Children and Adolescents?" *Pediatrics* 127 (2011), 1565–74.

20. J. O. Fisher, L. L. Birch, J. Zhang, M. A. Grusak, and S. O. Hughes, "External Influences on Children's Self-Served Portions at Meals," *International Journal of Obesity* (January 8, 2013, epub ahead of print). Doi: 10.1038/ijo .2012.216.

21. E. Satter, "Division of Responsibility," April, 2013. Retrieved from www .ellynsatter.com.

22. A. J. Hammons and B. H. Fiese, "Is Frequency of Shared Family Meals Related to the Nutritional Health of Children and Adolescents?" *Pediatrics* 127 (2011), 1565–74.

23. A. L. Prior and C. Limbert, "Adolescents' Perceptions and Experiences of Family Meals," *Journal of Child Health Care* (March 1, ahead of print). PMID: 23455875.

24. A. J. Hammons and B. H. Fiese, "Is Frequency of Shared Family Meals Related to the Nutritional Health of Children and Adolescents?" *Pediatrics* 127 (2011), 1565–74.

managing academics in the home and school: finding the balance

BY DAN PETERS, PHD, COFOUNDER AND EXECUTIVE DIRECTOR OF THE
SUMMIT CENTER, LICENSED PSYCHOLOGIST, AND FATHER OF THREE

I get ready to walk into the house at the end of the day. My wife has alerted me that she is having the usual homework struggles with our then second-grader. These struggles consist of him sitting at the kitchen table, staring at pages of math homework, while his mood and behavior range among refusal, whining, complaining, and crying. I walk up the backdoor steps, take a deep breath, and open the door. There it is, the usual scene: my wife sitting next to our son while he is crying and saying, "I can't do it . . . it is so boring . . . it is too hard . . . my hand hurts from writing . . . we already did this in class . . . why do I have to do this?" She looks at me and says, "Your turn, I can't do this anymore."

I sit down next to him, trying to be patient and supportive. I ask what he is working on and where he is getting stuck. I get back tears, yelling, frustration, and a head down on the table. After thirty minutes of this and getting nowhere, I am totally frustrated and my patience is gone. A powerful thought flashes in my mind: We just spent seventy-five miserable minutes as a family *again* over second-grade homework! This is ridiculous! Instinctively, I take his homework off the table and say, "You know what, I really don't care if you do your homework. Just tell your teacher you didn't want to do it." To my utter surprise, he looks at me and says through tears, "Dad, *please* let me do my homework, I *have* to do it!" Stunned and confused, as I did not anticipate this immediate response, I put his homework back on the table and say, "Do whatever you want," and walk out of the room to change my clothes. He was done in fifteen minutes.

I have reflected on this experience often and use it as an example to show the complexities of parenting that homework brings "to the table." I was so caught up in the usual struggle, I was not able to step back and realize that my son inherently wanted to be successful, did not want to disappoint his teacher, and was likely to "step up" if given the independence and space to do so. I also realized how important it was that I did something different in what had become a usual dance. When I changed my behavior, or moves, so did he.

Homework is often associated with the word *battle*. It is often thought of as busywork, and yet completing homework is often also seen as an essential skill for college success ("If you don't learn to do your homework on your own, how do you expect to do well in college?"). So what's the goal of homework? Is it for your child to gain mastery of academic material? Is it for your child to learn to be independent and responsible? Is it for your child to learn persistence and resilience? Although there is considerable controversy about the merit of homework, the answer to all of these is yes. Is homework, on the other hand, worth daily conflict and misery for you and your family? This answer is a resounding NO!

Taking a Step Back

When looking at the issue of homework as well as your child's learning and academic performance, it's important to take a step back and understand what your ultimate goal is for your child, as well as the forces that are at play in our current parenting climate. As Madeline Levine aptly stated in her 2013 book, *Teach Your Children Well*, and reiterated in her chapter for this book, it is important to remember that we are trying to raise good adults. That means we need to keep in mind that we have a long-term goal that requires a longer perspective, rather than a focus just on what's right in front of us—a homework assignment, test, grade, or project.

A critical factor or force that seems to be having a significant impact on us parents today is fear. Whether a parent is aware of it or not, fear and worry are often driving a significant amount of parenting decisions and behavior. Take a moment and think about your worries for your child and his or her future. You might be thinking, "I am worried my child is not going to get into college. I worry my child is not going to get into a good college. I worry my child is not going to get into the college he/she wants. I am worried that other children are going to be more prepared. How is my child going to compete? How is my child going to make it on his or her own? How is my child going to be successful? Am I doing enough to prepare my child for the future?" Do any of these thoughts sound familiar? I certainly have many of them, and so do my clients.

Now take a deep breath. I have some very good news. I want to tell you about an organization called Challenge Success, a nonprofit organization started by the Stanford Graduate School of Education, which will allow you to breathe easier. Challenge Success's mission is to provide research-based information to parents and educators that will aid in growing kids who are "resilient, successful, meaningful contributors for the twenty-first century." As is stated on its home page, "Success, after all, is measured not at the end of the semester, but over the course of a lifetime."

Denise Pope, Challenge Success cofounder, cites studies that found, with a few exceptions, that success is *not* dependent on what college your child goes to, or whether or not she spends her first two years at a community or junior college.[1] As an example, "Students who attended more selective colleges do not earn more than other students who were accepted and rejected by comparable schools but attended less selective colleges."[2] Yes, you read that correctly. Their future is *not* dependent on getting into "the" school, or the "best" school, or "one of the best" schools. And guess what? Recent statistics show that there are 4,726 colleges, universities, and junior colleges in the United States.[3] That means that there is absolutely a place for your child. It also means that you have an opportunity to change your thinking to a less worry-based focus on the task at hand: to grow healthy kids who are motivated and engaged in learning and life. So how do we do that?

The Nurturing Parent

In the early 1980s, two researchers out of Boston College set out to find the ingredients of creative children.[4] Through hundreds of hours of interviews, they found something they weren't looking for. They found that the parents of the creative kids in their study had similar parenting values and behaviors. Further, while they were originally focused on creativity, they also found that the kids in their study were responsible, honest, and caring people.

John Dacey and Alex Packer termed this parenting style the "nurturing parent," explaining that these parents nurtured their children's growth and autonomy. Nurturing parents tend to do the following:

Trust their child's judgment (based on developmental age and maturity).

Respect their child's thoughts and feelings.

Support their child's interests and goals.

Keep their child safe.

Model self-control, sensitivity, and values they believe to be important.[5]

What is key about this approach is that it produces responsible, honest, and caring children and adolescents who are considered "successful" by school personnel. Isn't that what we are looking for? This approach is based on giving a child room to grow, make mistakes, become responsible, and experience and learn from the natural consequences of his behavior (i.e., not doing well on a test, forgetting to turn in homework). However, this approach also sets appropriate limits when necessary: "No, you can't go to a concert with your friends on a school night. I understand that most of your friends get to stay out until 11:00 p.m. on school nights, but we feel that is too late."

In Carol Dweck's seminal book *Mindset*, she shows us that the way we think determines the type of learner we are—a fixed-oriented mindset thinks we are only as smart as we were born to be; the growth-oriented mindset believes the brain is a muscle and the more we exercise it, the smarter we will become. The fixed-oriented child is often focused on grades and performance, whereas the growth-oriented child is more focused on learning.

As you can imagine, parents (and teachers) have a significant role in how our child thinks about his or her learning. Staying with the idea of focusing on the larger picture, what are the overarching messages we are giving to our child? Here are some typical things we may say with the best intentions, "Good job . . . I am so proud of you ... Another A, well done ... You got a B? How come you didn't get an A? ... I know you can do better." You may be thinking a few things. First, "What's wrong with saying that?" And second, "Oh no, what have I done!?" Okay, time to breathe again. Most of us parents have said the above, and we have not ruined our children for doing so. The issue is that the statements above mostly focus on the outcome rather than the process, so they inadvertently promote and reinforce a fixed mindset. When we congratulate without considering whether our child put in any effort, we are reinforcing the grade versus the process of getting the grade (which doesn't take much effort for many kids). When we focus on the grade (A, B, or C) without considering the effort, we may be missing an important opportunity to reinforce effort and persistence, rather than the grade.

When we focus on raising a child with a growth-oriented mindset, we might say things like, "How do you feel you did? ... Are you happy with the outcome? ... Would you do anything different next time? ... I am proud of the way you approached this ... I know you worked hard on this, I am sorry it didn't turn out how you expected ... What is your goal?" See the subtle, yet important, difference?

When we focus on raising children with a growth-oriented mindset, we are helping them to see it is their *effort* that matters, and we are interested in what *they* think about their performance. Are they happy with *their* outcome? Would *they* do anything differently? I am not saying we should not praise our children. Rather, we should be mindful about what we praise and why, as our words are powerful and are internalized by our children.

Development Matters

The question of how much guidance and support to provide for our children gets more complex as they age and we have to factor in chronological age, level of development or maturity, and the academic environment they are in. Children who are mature for their age, have good self-control and organizational abilities, and do not have any learning or processing issues require less guidance and support at all grade levels. However, children who are slow to mature, have learning or processing challenges, and are in school environments that are challenging for them, require more support.

Think about the scaffolding you see around tall buildings that are being restored and painted; it allows the workers to do their job well, as well as get to the "high places." Similarly, children and adolescents who are immature for their age, or have attention, processing, reading, and writing issues, as well as those who may be more anxious or have challenges managing their behavior, will require more "scaffolding" or accommodations and supports to do their job—learn and produce schoolwork. They will need these supports both at home from you, as well as at school from their teacher(s).

Finally, it is important to consider brain development. During adolescence, as in toddlerhood, the brain undergoes a process that consists of prolific cell growth resulting in millions more neurons than one needs. This is followed by a "pruning" period, in which only the neurons and neural networks that are needed are kept, while the others die off.[6] During this time, the adolescent tends to be more distracted, disorganized, and emotional. This is not news to those of you who have adolescents at home. However, it is important to remember that their frontal lobes—the part of the brain responsible for emotional and behavioral control, as well as attention and organization—are in development mode and therefore often require some scaffolding. Interestingly, this is at a time when adolescents have increased expectations for organization and independence at school and generally do not *appear* to want much help from adults.

Our experience with our oldest, now thirteen and a seventh-grader, illustrates the challenges of considering multiple developmental levels when providing support and scaffolding for school. Due to her learning and processing challenges, she has always needed in-school and out-of-school tutoring and support to complete her work and keep up with the rest of her class. She also struggled to remember to bring her work and lunch to school when she was younger. Thus, during kindergarten through most of fifth grade, my wife drove her to endless tutor appointments and drove to school to bring her work and lunch when she forgot it, as she didn't need another thing going against her.

As our daughter approached middle school, we began to stress about the importance of her taking ownership of her work, and working more independently. She still required a lot of supervision, more than we expected; however, she still needed it. We continued to provide support by sitting with her, slowly having her do more of the work on her own without asking us for help. At the beginning of this school year, we decided to help her transition from her reliance on us to an organizational coach and her teachers. The timing was good, as she was entering adolescence and ready to turn her focus to more independence in life and to handling things on her own. To our surprise, she began to work independently in her room, clean her desk and backpack, and take personal pride in her work.

I offer this story because it shows how we needed to gauge her age and grade expectations for school performance, along with her developmental readiness and maturity, in determining how much support and scaffolding to provide. We did not provide this support so she would get As, but rather because she needed it due to her learning challenges. We were focused, and continue to be, on helping her meet her school obligations while helping her to develop the necessary life skills of independence, responsibility, and self-confidence.

Homework, Projects, Teachers, and Technology

It seems that parents have become much more involved in their children's schooling than in past generations. There are multiple factors responsible for this, such as increased academic workload, increased focus and priority on being an involved parent, and more demands and pressure on students (and parents) to keep up and get ahead. As discussed at the outset of this chapter, the increased pressure that parents (and children) face is largely fear and worry-based, with the positive intention of preparing children to be successful in the world. However, it also is important to raise kids who are responsible, independent people who make good choices and contribute to society, and to give our children the opportunity and space to learn and grow. Let's consider these parenting goals in the context of the daily challenges of school.

HOMEWORK (AND SCHOOLWORK): WHOSE JOB IS IT ANYWAY?

This chapter began with a real-life and common example of the "homework battle." Children are being given homework at younger ages than in the past, and more of it. Let's set aside the ongoing debate on the value of homework for another day. For now, it seems that homework is here to stay and we need to deal with it. Some kids are motivated to do their homework, and do so with little to no oversight, while others find it excruciating and have little to no motivation to complete it. If you have a child in the first category, you are fortunate, at least for now. Many parents don't, however, and daily and/or nightly homework battles are the norm for them. Further, some kids who are motivated to do homework at one developmental stage such as elementary school may lose their motivation in another developmental stage like middle school. This does not mean that your child whom you battle with now will always dislike homework, or that your child who once was motivated will never be motivated again. Rather, it means something is getting in the way of his or her motivation and ability to do the work.

When a child is intrinsically motivated, she is motivated to complete her homework and finds satisfaction in doing so. Often though, children don't see value in homework, find it boring, are just plain tired after going to school and their activities, and want to do other activities of choice when they are home. Additionally, many kids have attention, processing, and learning issues that make homework particularly challenging for them. We must remember that most things, particularly homework, are not worth the deterioration of a parent-child relationship. It is important to keep this in mind when you find yourself gearing up for battle (again). Further, you must remember that you have already gone to school and had your own homework. The homework assigned to your child is supposed to be *your child's* homework, not yours. Let's look at a few real-family challenges:

Sabrina, age eight and a third-grader, would much rather play than write sentences and do her math worksheets. Her mother usually needs to ask her three or four times to get her homework out after school. However, once she finally comes to the table, she doesn't mind doing her work. Her mother needs to be in the kitchen with her, though, to help her when she gets stuck.

Adam, age ten and a fifth-grader, doesn't like doing homework at all. He thinks it is stupid and that it gets in the way of all the other things he wants to do, like play on the computer, play with his Legos, and draw. He avoids doing his homework as long as possible, then gets worried that he will not have time to finish it because he has waited too long. His parents have tried having him doing it right when he gets home, but he is tired and needs downtime. They have also tried letting him wait until after dinner, but then he gets worried and runs out of time.

Leticia is twelve and in the seventh grade. She finds homework very challenging and exhausting. Now in middle school, she gets homework from at least three classes a night. She often feels overwhelmed, doesn't know where to start, and feels like she will never finish. Further, she doesn't believe she can do it herself. If her mom or dad doesn't sit with her and guide her (for the usual two hours), it doesn't get done.

Parker is fifteen years old and a sophomore in high school. He does well on tests and seems to grasp the material, but he is disorganized, doesn't write down his assignments, often doesn't do his homework, and, when he does, often fails to turn it in. His parents vacillate between micromanaging him and being hands-off. The first approach often results in conflict, and the second often ends with poor grades.

I am guessing that the kids above, or at least some of their characteristics, will sound familiar to you. That is because they are all normal kids expressing normal, yet different, challenges with homework. Depending on the child's temperament (as well as the parent's), the examples above can result in full-blown meltdowns each night, or developmental hurdles to work through. Let's take a look at each child in terms of his or her own temperament and developmental stage.

Sabrina is only in the third grade so she is just learning to monitor herself and work independently, which is developmentally appropriate for her age. She seems to be fine doing her homework but needs support transitioning to begin it. Once she does begin, however, she seems to complete it with minimal oversight, as long her mother stays nearby.

Adam, as a fifth-grader, is at an age when children are expected to work more independently and take responsibility for their homework. Adam has not achieved this developmental task yet. He seems to both avoid homework and become anxious about his ability to complete it. His parents describe nightly battles. No matter which approach they try, they get the same result. They wonder if there is something else going on with his learning.

Leticia, as a seventh-grader, is expected to manage her workload. However, many preadolescents are not developmentally ready to do so. Leticia lacks confidence in her ability to prioritize, understand her assignments, and complete them without support. Her parents find that sometimes they mostly need just to sit by her to give her confidence. She has yet to internalize a sense of competence.

Parker, a sophomore, does not want help from his parents, nor have them involved in his business. This is developmentally appropriate, yet he has not developed the expected skills of keeping track of his assignments and managing his workload. As with Adam's parents, there doesn't seem to be a "win-win" solution. The stakes are higher with Parker, however, because his grades now matter for college. Should his parents micromanage him so he gets better grades? Will he learn the skills needed for college if they do so? Should they let him do it on his own and hope he learns from his mistakes?

All of these children have some type of homework challenge. There is no absolute right or wrong way to support their—or your child's—growth. The answer usually falls in the gray area. When thinking about how, and how much, to intervene, remember your overall goal. Is your intention for your child to learn to persevere, or to get a perfect score or grade? Is it to help him learn to organize his work prior to beginning so he is not so overwhelmed, or to complete it as quickly as possible so he can have free time? Let's see what a few of the parents in the above examples came up with to reduce the homework battle and increase work completion.

Adam's parents had asked for his input on when he preferred to do his homework, after school or after downtime; however neither seemed to work. They decided to include him in an incentive plan. Realizing that they could not make him like homework, they focused on having him do his homework without excessive complaining. Adam felt that he would be motivated to complete his homework if he could earn extra game time on the computer. He was given the choice to do his homework after school or later in the day, knowing that he would earn an extra fifteen minutes of time for completing his work without a meltdown. Rather than focusing on what he didn't like, Adam was motivated by what he loved, and showed stamina and persistence to meet his goal.

Leticia's dad realized that a major part of her meltdowns related to her feelings of being overwhelmed and her anxiety about not knowing where to start or whether she would ever finish. Rather than just sit and encourage her, he helped her make a plan to complete her work by breaking it into different groups: easy, hard, enjoyable, and miserable. Leticia was then able to choose which she wanted to do first and check off assignments as she completed them. He essentially taught her "how to eat an elephant—one bite at a time." Leticia felt a sense of accomplishment when she completed a task and gained confidence in her ability to manage and do her homework.

"So what should I do? What's the answer?" As it did for the parents above, the answer lies in the *process* of figuring out why your child is struggling, what support he needs, and trying strategies that "scaffold" his abilities while helping him to become more confident, independent, and successful. It often takes trial and error and will likely change over time. As discussed, there is no right or wrong way to manage these complexities, and we need to remember to keep our eye on the ball—raising a good adult. So what should you do if your children have any of the above-mentioned, or similar, homework

challenges? I find it helpful to ask the following questions when deciding how to intervene:

> What support does my child need to complete her homework?
>
> What are my child's challenges: transitioning? organization?
> sustained attention?
>
> How can I offer the support she needs while also helping her to
> learn skills and gain confidence?
>
> Is she having challenges that are beyond my ability to help? Do
> we need to seek outside guidance?
>
> How much effort am *I* putting into my *child's* homework? Am I
> working harder than she is?
>
> Are the emotional meltdowns and relationship challenges worth
> the price of homework completion?

All of the above apply to everyday homework as well as the both
fun and dreaded science project. Ever find yourself spending hours
on the details of the science board and changing your child's hypothesis so it sounds better or the results come out better? Do you ever
jokingly say to your spouse, "I hope you get a good grade." Again, we
need to look at our goal for our child when determining how much
we are "helping."

This was the first year that all three of my kids (third-, fifth-, and
seventh-graders) were required to do a science project. The younger
two were excited about their topics, planning their experiments, and
gathering the supplies. My wife took on the younger two and I was
the point person for our oldest (I definitely had the easier task). As
days went on, I saw the younger kids' interest wane and my wife go
through the "battle" for the science projects. As the final nights approached, my wife was gluing and cutting while the kids were drawing, reading, and playing on the computer. I thought, "What is wrong
with this picture?" I cautiously pointed this out to her, and she stated

she would not be working harder than them again. Remember, this is a process. We laughed when I told her how proud of her I was for her projects. Humor is essential when parenting—and living for that matter.

Now to my job of supervising our oldest daughter, who, you remember from above, used to require a ton of support. I sat with her and asked her questions while she made her hypothesis, list of materials, and procedure. I was in awe of the change she had made over the past few years, now running her ideas by me rather than expecting me to come up with them. She conducted her study and asked for some reasonable help figuring out how to use the graph functions on the computer. She did a little work most nights the week of the deadline, with some prompting from my wife and me. Of course, she left a little more than she planned for the last night, and found herself rushing. However, she was working on her own.

When she went to bed, my wife asked me to look at the final project. Our daughter had used too much glue on her pictures and graphs (because she was rushing) so all of the sheets were wrinkled. Our daughter realized this and actually said, "Oh well." We had to stop ourselves from lecturing her about taking pride in her work, as she did most of it by herself, which was a feat in and of itself. My wife asked if we should let her turn it in looking the way it did. Since I was in the middle of writing this chapter, it was easy for me to say with a smile, "Yep, it is her work." The glue dried much better than expected, and her project actually looked good in the morning. It was hers and she was proud.

Homework certainly doesn't have to be a smooth process, but if it is regularly stressful, it is time to check in with your child's teacher, which brings us to the next topic.

Motivation, Resilience, and Reducing Pressure

"How do I motivate my child to do well in school?" This is a common and good question that parents ask. I touched on the difference between intrinsic or internal motivation, versus extrinsic or external motivation, above. Ideally, we would like our children to be intrinsically motivated to do well in school. We want them to find meaning in their learning, take pride in their work, and exhibit a strong work ethic. Research from Challenge Success found that one of the most important contributors to student success is engagement in school and learning.[7] Simply stated, children who are interested in what they are learning are motivated to learn, and do well.

Setting your child up to experience success is a critical factor in increasing motivation. When a child completes a task with success, he is more motivated to do it again and gains the confidence to take on a more challenging task. Remembering that success reinforces effort and appropriate risk taking, and failure reinforces avoidance and refusal, we must set up conditions where our child can get a "win." This may include chunking homework into smaller time periods, reducing the amount of homework so a child can complete it on his own, or reading a book at his reading and interest level.

If your child seems to be disengaged in school, it is time to talk to his teacher. Find out if the work is too easy, too hard, or just not grabbing him. There is always a reason for a child's lack of motivation and engagement. Also, remember that we parents are our child's primary role models. Our children watch us and take notes on how to be in the world. So what are you modeling? Are you engaged in your work? Do you work hard? Do you cruise by and work the system? Are you adept at reducing busywork and doing only what matters? Of course you have earned the right to do whatever you want at this point. But keep in mind that our children watch us and one of the main things we can do to increase motivation and hard work is to model it for them on a daily basis.

Increasing Persistence and Resilience

Low frustration tolerance is a primary culprit in the lack of motivation, homework struggles, and meltdowns. Thus, helping a child to improve her frustration tolerance, or "lengthen the fuse," is an important skill to cultivate. In his book *The 8th Habit*, Stephen Covey describes how successful people have a "space" between a stimulus and a response. This means that something happens, the person thinks about how to deal with the situation, and then that person reacts. People (of all ages) who exhibit difficulty with emotional and behavioral regulation often have very little or no "space" between the stimulus (homework hurdle) and response (meltdown). A major goal then is to help your child get some "space" between what he is facing and how he is going to respond to it. When this occurs, the child has more time to think and problem-solve before getting upset and shutting down. The more space, the more opportunities for solutions. A helpful strategy is to talk your child through this process, helping her to slow down, breathe, and allow herself the time to think.

Our youngest child is notorious for having a very quick fuse, which is often caused by her not getting a concept as quickly as she thinks she should, or her artwork not coming out the way she wants it to. We have learned to see her meltdowns coming most of the time. When one starts to happen, we say things like "You can figure this out ... Take a deep breath ... Let's take a break ... Maybe you can change your original idea." We have found that these suggestions work some of the time, and much more each year. Maturation and frontal lobe development are definitely helping. However, there are still meltdowns. That's when *we* breathe deeply.

Teach your child she has a great thinking brain that can power through challenges to come up with solutions. Teaching children about "self-talk" and how their thoughts determine how they feel and act can be very useful. Help your child understand what his negative and defeating thoughts are ("I am never going to finish this ... This is impossible ... I am so bad at this."). Helping your child to uncover his negative thinking allows him the opportunity to have more control over his feelings and behavior by changing or editing this thinking. Some examples of more adaptive thinking might be: "This is hard for me; I don't have to be good at everything," "Good is fine enough this time," or "Learning takes time." When a child can change his thinking, it allows him to have more space between the stimulus and his response.

Troubleshooting

If your child is struggling in his learning, is not performing to his perceived ability, seems to have trouble paying attention, is challenged with controlling his behavior, is having regular emotional meltdowns related to school, and/or seems disengaged in school, it may mean that he has a learning or processing challenge such as attention deficit/hyperactivity disorder (ADHD), dyslexia, dysgraphia (trouble with writing), or auditory and/or sensory issues that need to be understood.

School can be stressful for all types of children but especially for those with particular challenges. If a bright child is not performing at the level of her thinking abilities, it may mean she has a learning or processing issue. It is important to note that schools are often looking for "grade-expected" performance, so if your bright child is performing at grade level and he is frustrated and/or the schoolwork seems below his ability, further investigation is needed.

If any of the descriptions above fit your child, talk to your child's teacher. If the issues persist despite classroom interventions, request (in writing) that your child receive a comprehensive assessment to determine his learning and processing challenges. If you are unable to obtain an evaluation through your school, seek a comprehensive evaluation from a professional who has expertise in children with learning and processing issues. Children unfortunately internalize how smart and successful they are based largely on their school performance. If they continually struggle, their confidence in themselves will be diminished, and will erode further over time.

Bringing It Home

You play a big role in how your child views school, homework, and his future. If you worry less about your child's future, your child will most likely worry less. You will no doubt need to fight the cultural climate of worry among your friends, parent peers, and community, yet this is a battle worth fighting.

Show your child your confidence and trust in her. Ask her questions about what she is learning and not learning. Find out what is easy and what is hard for her. Give her suggestions about what she can do to meet *her* expectations. Provide a structure and mindset that allow her to focus on *learning* over grades, and on *effort* over outcome. Finally, model working hard, enjoying the meaningful parts of your work and life, and persevering through the difficult and mundane parts—just like we want our children to be able to do.

Let's go back to my original story about the experience with my son at the homework table. I walked into that situation blindly, and like all well-meaning parents, my wife and I found ourselves doing the same unhelpful thing over and over—we sat through whining and complaining without considering the opportunity for growth and learning. We were focused on the task of homework, rather than the larger job of helping our child build life skills.

Ever since that experience, I ask myself many of the questions posed above when helping my own children and when guiding my clients through their homework and schoolwork adventures with their children. I remind myself and them about our goals of raising hardworking, responsible, and resilient adults. I remember that the process is about what is right in front of us, and that each potential moment and struggle is an opportunity to guide and grow our future adult. I remember that each math worksheet or science project must be dealt with, but it needs to be done in the context of these larger goals. I also remember, and remind my clients, there is a school, job, and place for each child. That means yours, too.

---

1. Innovative Learning Conference, Nueva School, Hillsborough, CA, October 21, 2011.

2. Stacy Berg Dale and Alan B. Krueger, "Estimating the Payoff to Attending a More Selective College: An Application of Selection on Observables and Unobservables," *Quarterly Journal of Economics* (2002), 1523.

3. National Center for Education Statistics, *Digest of Education Statistics,* 2013 Tables and Figures, Table 317.10, "Degree-granting postsecondary institutions, by control and level of institution."

4. John S. Dacey and Alex J. Packer, *The Nurturing Parent: How to Raise Creative, Loving, Responsible Children* (New York: Simon & Schuster, 1992).

5. Susan Daniels and Daniel B. Peters, *Raising Creative Kids* (Tucson: Great Potential Press, Inc., 2013), 117–122.

6. Patricia Wolfe, *Brain Matters: Translating Research into Classroom Practice* (2nd Edition), (Alexandria, VA: ASCD Association for Supervision and Curriculum Development, 2010), 82–93.

7. J. Conner & D. Pope, "Why Full Engagement Matters," *Journal of Youth and Adolescence* (April 2013), 1–39.

how to raise successful and happy young athletes

BY JIM TAYLOR, PHD, CLINICAL ASSOCIATE PROFESSOR IN THE
SPORT & PERFORMANCE PSYCHOLOGY GRADUATE PROGRAM AT
THE UNIVERSITY OF DENVER AND FATHER OF TWO DAUGHTERS

Sports participation has become a rite of passage for many children, not only in America, but throughout the world. Children from preschool through high school turn out in droves to learn and compete in sports for fun, physical health, and self-esteem. In fact, according to recent surveys, about 70 percent of children in the United States play organized sports. But research also tells us that another 70 percent will drop out of organized sports by the time they are thirteen years old, suggesting there's a dark side to all of this.

From years of counseling athletes and their families, I can tell you with certainty that you parents may play the most central role in determining what type of athletic experience your child will have. Your own sports involvement, the attitudes and beliefs you hold about sports, and the expectations you have about your children's sports life will have perhaps the defining influence on the quality of your children's experience and whether it has a beneficial or harmful impact on their lives.

We want our kids to be happy when they walk onto the field or court or what have you, and to have fun when they get out there. But this can conflict with achieving success as it is so narrowly defined by our culture, which is usually in terms of victories. And the definition of success as winning is most definitely at odds with what makes playing sports a healthy experience: fun, camaraderie, and learning new skills.

So, instead of striving to achieve success, let's focus on making our kids *successful achievers*. In the former case, children are successful, for example, when they're the leading hitter on their baseball team, the top scorer on their soccer team, or they win a lot of races, but they are not always happy. In contrast, for parents raising successful achievers, success without happiness is not success at all.

How to raise successful achievers

Children become successful achievers when their parents foster in them certain essential beliefs. Drs. Aubrey Fine and Michael Sachs, the authors of *The Total Sports Experience for Kids*, offer a valuable summary of those beliefs (I have added the first and seventh ones, and the parenthetical comments):

I am loved. (sense of value)

I am capable. (sense of competence)

It is important to try. (value of effort)

I am responsible for my day. (sense of ownership)

It is okay to make mistakes. (acceptance of failure)

I can handle things when they go wrong. (response to adversity)

I enjoy what I do. (value of passion and joy)

I can change. (mastery)

You can raise happy, successful kids through sports participation by fostering what I call the Three Pillars of Successful Achievers—self-esteem, ownership, and emotional mastery—and by learning how to set healthy expectations and goals for, and with, your children.

Successful Achievers' Pillar One: Self-esteem

Unconditional love is only one piece of the self-esteem equation. The second part, which receives much less attention, is that children must develop a sense of competence and mastery over their world. Most basically, they must learn that their actions matter, that their actions have consequences. If they do good things, good things happen. If they do bad things, bad things happen. And, importantly, if they do nothing, nothing happens.

The only way for children to develop such a sense of competence is for them to try things, succeed, and, yes, experience failure, which means that playing sports is a great way for children to develop this sense of competence. Unfortunately, many parents make two mistakes in this arena: overpraising their kids and protecting their kids from failure.

First, parents try to convince their children how capable they are by telling them how good they are in their sports. The problem with this approach is that sports have a way of showing children who have been convinced that they are exceptional by their parents that, well, they really aren't.

Take Mark, for instance. A father who loves baseball and has the best of intentions, Mark wants to help his eight-year-old son, Tommy, get the confidence he needs to be successful and have fun playing Little League baseball. To that end, Mark is constantly telling Tommy how great a ballplayer he is, how he is so naturally talented, and how he is sure to be one of the best players in the league.

Not surprisingly, Tommy enters the season with excitement and the expectation of being a top player. Unfortunately, within just a few weeks, it becomes readily apparent that he isn't. Tommy struggles both in the field and at the plate. He quickly becomes demoralized, loses interest in the game, and drops out before the season is over.

Second, out of a misguided belief that failure will hurt their children's self-esteem, many parents do their best to protect their children from failure in their sports participation. In doing so, parents don't allow their children to learn from, and gain competence from, their mistakes. As a result, we often create the very thing that we want to avoid, namely, children with low self-esteem.

Suzanne had been playing tennis since she was a child and still played on a competitive league team. She also followed the women's pro tour closely. Her daughter, Lisa, began playing when she was five years old and, at age ten, was playing tournaments, though she wasn't particularly good. Lisa's losses were really tough on Suzanne. She started to put Lisa in tournaments with little competition so she could win more, and when she did lose, Suzanne would blame the opponent, the conditions, or the weather. Lisa didn't think her mom had any faith in her and she began to lose confidence in herself. After a while, she just quit because it was no longer fun for her.

When parents and coaches allow kids to play for play's sake and give them the space to fail—and to keep trying—sports can be a safe and fun environment for children to gain competence and build deep and resilient self-esteem.

Successful Achievers' Pillar Two: Ownership

Out of fear that their children won't become as successful as they want them to be, parents sometimes turn their children into "achievement projects," managing and micromanaging them to ensure they do everything they need to become successful athletes.

As a result, children feel no sense of ownership of their own athletic efforts and goals and will have little incentive to work hard toward those goals (except perhaps fear that you won't love them). And they can come to dislike a beloved sport if they feel forced to participate in it.

I worked with a young athlete who rose to the top of the junior world rankings in her sport and turned pro with much acclaim. Her father had always played a central and, arguably, overinvolved role in her athletic life. He drove her unmercifully with unforgiving expressions of anger. She steadily climbed the professional ranks and was on her way to a successful career in her sport. After working with her for several years, we parted company and kept in touch periodically. About two years after turning pro, she called and told me that she had quit, saying, "How could I possibly be successful and happy doing something I hate so much."

PARENT AND CHILD RESPONSIBILITIES

For your children to have a great sports experience, which means having fun, working hard toward goals, and developing essential life skills, both you and your children must understand and fulfill your respective responsibilities and those responsibilities alone. If family members fulfill their own responsibilities and do not assume others', then children will develop into healthy, mature, and successful people, and everyone is happy. However, problems arise when parents take on the responsibilities of their children.

Your responsibilities revolve primarily around providing your children with all of the basic stuff they need to pursue their athletic goals. You can give them opportunities to develop by putting them in a quality junior program in their sport, giving them appropriate training, and taking them to relevant competitions. Practical responsibilities include ensuring that your children have the necessary equipment, good (in every sense of the word) coaching, and transportation. Provide psychological and emotional support by offering love, guidance, encouragement, and perspective on their efforts.

Your children's responsibilities relate to doing what is necessary to maximize the opportunities that you provide them. This includes giving their best effort, being responsible and disciplined, listening to coaches, being good sports, being prepared, and being respectful of others. Practical responsibilities include participating in all training programs, getting the most out of their athletic experiences, being good teammates, and expressing appreciation for the opportunities they have received.

When you take on the responsibilities of your children, you are communicating two messages to them. First, that you don't think they are competent enough to adequately fulfill their own responsibilities, which will hurt their confidence and motivation. Second, that the sport is your thing, not theirs. For many children, it also opens the door to avoiding their own responsibilities: "Heck, why should I do it if my parents will do it for me?"

When your children begin a new competitive season, you should sit down with them and outline each of your responsibilities. Make a list of what you as a parent will be doing to help your children succeed. Also, ask your children what you can do to help them and what you should avoid doing. Next, have your children make a list of what their responsibilities should be, suggesting important things they miss.

Be clear, too, that there will be consequences for not fulfilling responsibilities. The best consequences are those that remove something of importance to your children and give them the control to get it back by acting appropriately, for instance, that they can't compete the next weekend unless they complete their homework on time.

I worked with a young ski racer who lost his skis (worth more than $700) at a race. The father didn't replace them immediately, so his son had to race several times on an old pair of skis. He required that his son work at his business for three months (at a reasonable hourly rate) until the skis were paid off.

Your children need to gain a sense of ownership of their athletic lives. This ownership means that they play their sport because they love it, because they see its value, because it is fun. From this ownership comes an internally derived motivation to give their best effort. They think: This is mine, so I want to do my best. This ownership also provides them with an immense source of gratification and pride from their efforts that further motivates them to strive harder in pursuit of athletic, and other life, goals.

Sample List of Parent Responsibilities

Enroll and pay for her season.

Buy the necessary equipment.

Get her to and from practices and games.

Ask about her sport experiences.

Attend games (but very few practices).

Focus on effort rather than results.

Be supportive following victories and defeats.

Sample List of Child Responsibilities

Be prepared.

Work hard.

Be a good sport.

Be a good teammate.

Be respectful and listen to your coaches.

Take care of your equipment.

Be grateful for the opportunity you have been given.

Successful Achievers' Pillar Three: Emotional Mastery

Emotional mastery is perhaps the most neglected aspect of children's development and one in which sports participation can easily play a central role. Think about all the emotions children experience in their athletic lives, from fear, frustration, and disappointment to joy, pride, and inspiration.

Also, parents have been led to believe that allowing their children to experience negative emotions, such as sadness and embarrassment, will somehow hurt their children's self-esteem. So they placate, assuage, comfort, and distract their children from these emotions and attempt to create artificial positive emotions (by praising them and buying things for them). The problem is that emotions are two sides of the same coin. Children can't experience love, happiness, joy, and excitement, unless they are allowed to experience anger, worry, and sadness.

Parents who protect their children from their emotions are actually interfering with their children's emotional growth. These children never learn how to deal effectively with their emotions, because they have little experience with them; they enter adulthood ill equipped for its emotional demands. Only by being allowed to experience the full range of emotions are children able to figure out what emotions they are feeling, what the emotions mean to them, and how they can express them in healthy ways.

Every competition season in every sport that children participate in is a potential source of great pride as well as deep disappointment. As for all sports parents, I'm sure it pains you to see your children suffer the "agony of defeat." After an unsuccessful performance, they may be sad, downtrodden, and seem to have the weight of the world on their shoulders. Your heart aches for their pain, and you want to do everything you can to relieve them of that disappointment. But that would be a mistake! Learning to handle disappointment early is key to achieving dreams later in life.

Placating your children doesn't allow them to understand what caused the disappointment or figure out how to not feel disappointed in the future. Your children need to be able to just sit with their disappointment and ask, "Why do I feel so bad?" and "What can I do to get over feeling this way?" Pacifying your children may also communicate to them that you don't think they are capable of handling and overcoming the setback themselves. Your reaction will only interfere with your children's ability to surmount future setbacks and obstacles, and it will make disappointment more painful in the future.

You should view your children's disappointments as training for adulthood. After your child has had a bad game, don't rush up and try to comfort him. If you do that, you are meeting your own needs, not his. Only by experiencing emotions, good or bad, will he learn to understand and deal with them.

You can teach your children to see stumbling blocks as opportunities to improve and grow. Offering your children a different perspective on their disappointment—"I know it feels bad right now, but what can you learn from it?"—gives them tools they can use to avoid or minimize their disappointment in the future, and to turn the obstacles to their advantage by increasing resilience, motivation, and confidence.

The father of one of my young clients used to rationalize his son's defeats by saying things like "It's no big deal" and "You shouldn't get so upset." But these sorts of comments, though well intentioned and meant to make his son feel better, actually did more harm than good for several reasons. First, they made his son think that he was wrong for feeling as he did. It would have been better for the father to acknowledge his son's emotions: "You are really disappointed with how you played." Second, the comments didn't allow his son to fully experience his feelings and, in doing so, learn more about his emotional life. Finally, these attempts to assuage his son offered him no guidance on how to better manage his feelings.

Emotional mastery is not the absence of emotions, but rather the ability to recognize emotions, understand where they came from, and express them in healthy ways. Children who do not develop emotionally can still achieve success—we see many very successful businesspeople, professional athletes, and actors who are acclaimed—but the price they pay is often discontentment and unhappiness in their successes (as expressed in, for example, immaturity, narcissism, alcohol and drug abuse, and divorce). Emotional mastery enables children to not only become successful, but also to find satisfaction and joy in their efforts, in other words, to become successful achievers.

How to respond to your children's disappointments

Don't downplay or distort the situation to make your children feel better.

Allow your children to express their feelings about the setback and offer a perspective that may give them another way of looking at it.

Support your children, but don't give them a consolation prize.

Be realistic about your children's capabilities; give them feedback that considers their true abilities.

Help your children find ways to surmount the causes of their difficulties.

Finally, tell your children that they will survive these disappointments and will achieve their goals if they keep trying hard.

Comments you might share with your child
after a disappointing performance

"You're disappointed in how you played." (acknowledgment)

"It's natural to feel bad after you have a bad game." (normalizing)

"I remember when I played Little League [or whatever sport] and I would be pretty sad if I didn't get a hit in games." (empathy)

"Tell me what you did well in the game." (perspective)

"How about you do batting practice a few more times this week, so you can get your hitting back on track?" (positive, future focus)

Setting Healthy Expectations and Goals

Setting expectations for your young athlete is an essential responsibility of parenting. Expectations tell your children what's important to you and establish a standard toward which they can strive. Unfortunately, the culture of achievement that permeates youth sports (and most of children's lives) these days—it's all about results!—has convinced many parents to set the wrong kinds of expectations for their young competitors. There are two types of expectations that you should *not* set for your children: ability expectations and outcome expectations.

Ability expectations are those in which children are expected to achieve a certain result because of their natural ability: "We expect you to win the tennis match today because you're the most talented player at the tournament" or "We expect you to qualify for the state championships because you're the best swimmer in the pool."

The problem with ability expectations is that children have no control over their ability. Children are born with a certain amount of ability and all they can do is maximize whatever ability they are given. Another problem with ability expectations is that if children attribute their successes to their ability—"I won because I'm so talented"—they must also attribute their failures to their lack of ability—"I failed because I'm just not good enough." And, though children can improve in their sport, for example, gaining strength or new skills, they can't gain more ability.

Our culture of achievement emphasizes results over all else, and as a consequence, parents often set outcome expectations in which their children are expected to produce a certain result: "We expect you to win today" or "We know you will beat Sam." The problem is that, once again, children are asked to meet an expectation over which they may not have control. They might play as well as they possibly can, but other competitors just happen to be better that day. So they would have to consider themselves to have failed despite what may very well have been a great performance on their part.

Outcome expectations are often set by parents and placed in front of their children without their consultation or buy-in, and kids often feel dragged—sometimes kicking and screaming—toward those expectations. Children have no ownership of the expectations and little motivation, outside of an implied threat from their parents, to fulfill them. When I ask young athletes about expectations, they usually grimace and say things like "That's when my parents get really serious and I know they're gonna put pressure on me" or "They're telling me what to do and I better do it or I'll get into trouble." Outcome expectations are also black and white: your children either meet the expectation and succeed or they don't and they fail. So, instead of ability and/or outcome expectations, set outcome *goals* and *effort* expectations.

Outcome Goals

Goals are very different from expectations. I believe that children are wired to respond to goals. One of the great joys in life is to set a goal, work toward a goal, and achieve a goal. Children want to set goals for themselves, with guidance from parents and coaches, and they want to pursue those goals. Importantly, goals aren't black and white, but about the degree of attainment. Not every goal is achieved, but there will almost always be improvement toward a goal and that progress defines success. When I ask kids about goals, they respond much differently. Their faces perk up and they say things like "It means I decide to do something and I really work hard to do it" or "I feel like my parents are really behind me and I'm psyched to do it."

For example, let's say your young athlete has been finishing in the top twenty in recent competitions and he sets an outcome expectation of finishing in the top ten in the next event. But he finishes twelfth. According to his outcome expectation, he would have failed because he didn't meet that expectation. But if he had set an outcome goal of a top-ten finish, then his twelfth-place finish would be a success because, though not fully achieving his goal, he showed significant improvement toward it. It's not black and white, succeed or fail.

The ski-racing great Bode Miller is my poster child for the unimportance of results early in athletes' sports participation. Miller was a late bloomer as a ski racer; at age fifteen, he hadn't shown any real signs of greatness. What is remarkable about Miller is that he has never cared about results. All he has ever cared about is, as he put it in his autobiography, *Bode: Go Fast, Be Good, Have Fun*, to ski "as fast as the natural universe will allow." Contrary to the beliefs of many parents, this attitude of not caring about results actually led to Miller getting the remarkable results that he wanted. And, thanks to that attitude, which his parents encouraged, Bode has become one of the greatest ski racers in history.

Effort Expectations

If you want your children to experience enjoyment and also be successful in their sports participation, establish effort expectations that encourage them to do what it takes to achieve the outcomes they want. Collaborate with them to set standards of effort in terms of motivation, priority, time, and energy that are entirely within your children's control; they can choose to work hard or not.

Examples of effort expectations may include "Our family expects you to give your best effort in practice and competitions" or "Our family expects you to listen to your coaches and focus during every drill." Regardless of the abilities your children inherited from you, or whom they might be compared with, they have the capacity to use effort expectations and the tools associated with them to be the best they can be in their sport (or whatever area of life they choose to pursue).

If your children meet the effort expectations they establish, they will, in all likelihood, improve, perform well, achieve some level of success (how successful they become will depend on what abilities they were born with), and gain satisfaction through their efforts. If your children don't meet the effort expectations, they are not likely to achieve their goals and must face the consequences of their lack of sufficient effort, for example, disappointment. In either case, your young athletes will learn essential life lessons that will not only serve them well throughout their sports participation—whether it ends after high school or carries them onto the Olympic podium—but also in future goals they pursue throughout their lives.

A Healthy Perspective

Whether your children have a positive sports experience is largely in your hands. If you have the right perspective on why they participate in sports, your children will probably adopt that way of looking at sports. This healthy perspective comes from the values that you hold about their sports involvement. It is no small challenge to adopt and communicate positive values in a youth sports culture that emphasizes accelerating development, unrealistic expectations, and winning, and also encourages the less-than-admirable role models that children see in many professional athletes. I recommend that you think through and discuss what you value most about your children's sports experience—for example, fun, camaraderie, hard work, and being a good sport—and ensure that you are sending those value messages to them through what you talk to them about and your behavior at games.

---

toughLOVE TIPS

Ten Values for a Great Youth Sports Experience

IT'S ABOUT FUN. If your children (and you!) are having fun out there, they are going to feel less pressure, be more confident, relaxed, and focused, and will likely perform as well as they can.

IT'S ABOUT THE PROCESS. Talk to your children about how they are performing, not about results. If you focus on the process and downplay results, they will too. And, as I noted earlier, they are more likely to get the results they want. Ask them about how they felt during competitions, what they did well and didn't do well. Then describe what you saw out there, for example, effort, focus, teamwork, and fun.

IT'S ABOUT HARD WORK. As I noted above, your children's effort is the only thing they can control. Also, if they work hard, they have a better chance of achieving their goals.

IT'S ABOUT RESPONDING POSITIVELY TO ADVERSITY. Your children are going to experience plenty of ups and downs in their sports participation and in life in general. What separates those who succeed from those who don't isn't whether they have experienced adversity, but rather how they have responded to the inevitable difficulties that arose.

IT'S ABOUT SUPPORT. You want to be a positive and supportive presence in your children's athletic lives, providing a healthy and calming perspective when they experience doubt or anxiety. My key message to you: lift the pressure off of your children rather than placing more pressure on them.

IT'S ABOUT CONFIDENCE. One of the most robust findings in the research on the value of youth sports participation is that it builds confidence in children's capabilities and overall self-esteem. Whether your children's sports involvement builds or crushes their confidence and self-esteem depends on your perspective on it.

IT'S ABOUT SPORTS AS AN INVESTMENT IN YOUR CHILDREN'S FUTURE. I'm not talking about their future as superstar athletes, which is a statistical unlikelihood. I mean where you see their athletic lives in preparing them for success in school, career, and life.

IT'S ABOUT A LONG-TERM PERSPECTIVE WHILE ALSO FOCUSING ON THE PRESENT. Sports are a marathon, not a sprint, and your children have a long way to go before they reach their ultimate athletic goals. At the same time, you should communicate to them that even a

marathon involves taking one step at a time and that they may periodically trip along the way.

IT'S ABOUT STAYING GROUNDED. Your children may have some inspiring athletic successes and some demoralizing defeats. Though
they will likely experience emotional ups and downs, it is important
that you stay grounded, meaning calm and even-keeled, and be a safe
harbor they can return to when their emotional seas get turbulent.
As I like to say, you want your children to "keep their heads on the
ground and their feet in the air."

IT'S ABOUT FEELING THE JOY. You want your children's athletic lives
to begin and end with "I'm so excited." At a very visceral level, your
children's immediate sports experience should elicit feelings of
exhilaration gushing forth through huge smiles on their faces and
the joyful tone in their voices. Perhaps the most important lesson
you should learn yourself and communicate to your children is that,
whatever the results, the biggest reason to compete in sports is for
the pure joy of it.

If you can instill these values in your children, they will be as successful as they can be and they will be happy. Your children will look
back as adults on their youth sports participation with fondness, and
they will see the value it brought to their lives. Anything that your
children gain from their sports participation beyond these ten values,
whether that means a Little League playoff, a high school all-star
team, a college scholarship, an Olympic medal, or a professional career, will be just icing on the cake.

screen-savvy parenting: tv, movies, and media messages in the digital age

BY JAMES P. STEYER, JD, FOUNDER AND CHIEF EXECUTIVE
OFFICER OF COMMON SENSE MEDIA AND DAD OF FOUR

We'd just finished family dinner on a school night when our young-est son, eight-year-old Jesse, jumped up from the table with that winningly sweet smile of his.

"Hey, Dad, can I use the computer for homework?"

My wife, Liz, and I nodded at each other across the table.

"Sure, Jesse," I said, "but only for half an hour. You know we don't like you spending too much time in front a screen. So after homework, why don't we go outside and play catch for a little before bedtime?"

"Okay, Dad," he said, dashing off.

Ten minutes later, I strolled into the family room, where we keep the computer, to see how he was doing on his assignment. Jesse was so fixated on the screen that he didn't know I was peering over his shoulder—at a cartoon he was streaming on a TV website.

Since Jesse hadn't been truthful with us, he had to turn off the computer, and he lost his television privileges for the coming weekend. It hit me, at that moment, how hard it is to control what, when, and where our kids watch in a digital world that's networked, mobile, and multiplatform. TV and movies have migrated from flatscreens and multiplexes to desktops, laptops, tablets, and smartphones. With an online connection, our kids can see anything, anywhere, at any time, often without our knowledge or supervision.

As they're growing up, kids from eight to eighteen are also spending much more time with entertainment media than they are with their families or in school—more than seven hours a day on average (nearly eleven hours if you include multitasking).[1] How do we know what messages they're absorbing about life? And what do we know about the impact of all that media on our kids' development and social and emotional health?

Taking Control of TV

These days, many parents worry more about Facebook and YouTube than they do about the content of TV shows. But television is still, by far, the single biggest form of media that kids are exposed to up to the age of eight. And the images and messages they see on TV at every age matter profoundly to their social and emotional development. That's why it's important to remember three keys to controlling your kid's TV habit: quantity, quality, and location.

Quantity may be the most crucial factor. TV is hypnotic, as any parent knows who's watched their kid spend hours gaping at the tube on Saturday mornings. Too often, I've had to stand right in front of my kids and block their view of the TV screen to get their attention. But here's the bottom line: according to the American Academy of Pediatrics (AAP), school-age kids should spend no more than two hours a day, *total*, in front of any and all kinds of screens, including TVs, computers, smartphones, and video game consoles. How you and your child choose to divide that time is up to you. Every family's different, and you know your kid better than anyone. The key is to set firm limits on screen time and stick to them, even if you have to use a kitchen timer to enforce the rules.

There are important reasons why the AAP says families should limit screen time. Watching TV—or spending too much time in front of any screen—is a sedentary, isolating activity, and it can take a toll. Studies have shown that excessive media use can lead to school, attention, and sleep problems, as well as eating disorders and obesity. And the more time kids spend in front of screens, the less time they're spending running around, playing, reading, and interacting with family and friends. According to a 2010 study by the AAP Council on Communications and Media, the more hours preteens spend watching a screen, the more likely they are to feel sad, lonely, and negative, no matter how much physical activity they get.

The quality and content of shows also has a big impact. The good news is that there are many terrific, high-quality, age-appropriate programs that can engage, inform, and inspire kids. Unfortunately, there are also lots of violent, raunchy shows that push the limits as channels compete with the Internet, Facebook, and cell phones for kids' attention.

TV, we all know, can expose kids to lots of things they might not be ready for. It may seem harmless to let your preteen watch popular shows like *Glee* and *The Vampire Diaries*, but they're often full of sexual themes and content that can distort your kid's understanding and expectations. A 2010 study by the AAP found that 75 percent of prime-time programs contain sexual content. They also talk about sex as often as eight to ten times an hour, but they rarely mention the risks and responsibilities of sex. Your fifth- or sixth-grader is years away from being sexually active, but what he or she sees now, according to the AAP, can influence the timing and impact of that experience.

Exposure to media violence can also contribute to aggressive behavior, nightmares, fear, depression, and desensitization to acts of violence. Sixty percent of all TV shows include violent scenes, and kids see nearly two gun-related incidents of violence every hour that they watch TV.[2] For more than three decades, studies have also shown that media violence can help cause an almost paralyzing sense of fear in some youngsters by depicting a violent world where aggression is normal. This effect is particularly strong in younger kids, who can't tell the difference between fantasy and reality.

The important point is to choose wisely. Stay informed. You can read reviews of shows at commonsensemedia.org and online parent forum and discussion sites. It's also a great idea to watch shows yourself to make sure they're appropriate for your kid and have some educational value. Research suggests that routinely watching media that's purely entertaining or violent and spending more than two hours a day in front of a screen can lower a child's academic achievement and contribute to attention, behavior, learning, and health problems. So be very picky. Keep a library of high-quality, age-appropriate recorded shows. Remember, too, to keep young or sensitive children away from television news. Repeated coverage of shootings and other tragedies can make youngsters worry that they're in danger and that frightening events are happening over and over again. Stayed tuned in to your child's media life and know what shows your kid is watching, at every age. And it's always smart to watch shows together, whenever possible. If your child does see or hear something inappropriate, you can use that awkward experience as a teachable moment. Ask your child what he thinks about what he saw, say what you think, and have a frank discussion about choices, consequences, and your family's values.

It's obviously hard to watch shows together when your kid is using Netflix, Hulu, Amazon, or YouTube to watch shows on a smartphone, tablet, or laptop. That's why it's important to be proactive. Plan ahead. Check out program listings and reviews, then save the shows that are a good fit for your child's interests. Point him to the good stuff and let him choose from a range of high-quality programs you've preselected.

With older kids, you have to be a reality check. Lots of TV programs your teen is likely to see—at friends' houses, if not at home—show extreme types of behavior to attract audiences. Producers of shows like *Jersey Shore* and *Buckwild* stage risky, alcohol-fueled experiences for the camera but don't show the consequences. It's up to parents to explain what's real, what's typical, what's not, and what kinds of behaviors kids should never imitate.

After quantity and quality, the third key to controlling TV is location, location, location. That's also the hardest to enforce, since TV watching has become so mobile and multiplatform. Still, there are a number of important tips to keep in mind. First, it's best to keep the family TV set in a common area of your home, where you can keep an eye on what your child is watching. Most important, resist the urge to put a TV in your child's bedroom. It might seem like a good way to avoid family arguments over what to watch, but it's a risky move. Kids who have a TV in their bedroom, research shows, have lower tests scores at school and a higher tendency to be overweight. They also have a greater risk of sleep problems, since watching TV increases alertness.[3] Growing up with a TV in the bedroom has been linked to more junk food consumption, smoking, earlier sexual activity, and significantly lower scores on reading, math, and language arts exams.[4]

Unfortunately, too many kids do have TV sets in their own rooms, including nearly half of all eight- to ten-year-olds and most thirteen- to seventeen-year-olds.[5] If your child does have a TV in her bedroom, it's a good idea to take it out, the sooner the better. It's also wise to keep all screen devices—including smartphones, computers, tablets, and game consoles—out of your child's bedroom and in common areas.

Making the Right Movie Choices

My friend Rebecca still talks about the day she took her ten-year-old daughter, Megan, to see the movie *Valentine's Day*. She'd heard it was a cute film starring two of Megan's favorites, Anne Hathaway and Taylor Swift. But by the time they'd heard the last line of the movie—"Let's get naked!"—Rebecca had been squirming in her seat for more than an hour trying to figure out how to explain phone sex and threesomes to her fifth-grader.

Rebecca's the first one to admit that she should have paid attention to the ratings. *Valentine's Day* was rated PG-13, but Megan had been begging to see it, and Rebecca gave in. That's a challenge that a lot of parents have to face. Tweens, especially, can be eager to "age up" and watch PG-13 movies, with edgy content, that teenagers are allowed to see. And some movies rated for kids thirteen and up are marketed to younger kids through previews "approved for all audiences," as well as merchandising and ads on TV channels like Nickelodeon and the Cartoon Network.

Bottom line, it can be tough to figure out which movies are fine and which are not okay for your kid to see. Ratings are a start, but they're problematic. Even G-rated films marketed for small children can have frightening scenes—especially these days, when producers often use violence as a way to add action or conflict to a movie. PG ("Parental Guidance Suggested") films almost always have some violence, sexy scenes, profanity, or references to drinking and smoking that are inappropriate. A PG-13 rating, meanwhile, means "Parents Strongly Cautioned," and that's a warning you should take seriously.

The truth is, both PG and PG-13 movies have been getting cruder, more explicit, and more violent over the years. Some of them are much too violent and sexually graphic for most eleven- and twelve-year-olds—especially because watching a movie is an intense, emotional, and immersive experience. A fifth-grader, for instance, may have loved reading The Hunger Games book series. But the PG-13 movie shows kids fighting to the death in realistic scenes of bloody brutality and violence. The intensity of that movie experience can be way too much for many kids to handle. Some other

PG-13 films, on the other hand—like *Harry Potter and the Deathly Hallows*—might be fine for a tween to watch with a parent, because they can talk about questionable scenes afterward.

The best strategy, with kids under thirteen, is to find out as much as you can about movies before deciding. You can read reviews at commonsensemedia.org, talk to other parents, and see the films yourself if you're not sure they're the right choices for your child. Answering these questions can help you make up your mind:

- **If the film has violence, does it show the consequences of pain and suffering?** Kids this age should not see movies where violent behavior is rewarded or that have scenes of gratuitous, realistic brutality or horror.
- **Does the movie have adult sex scenes or show risky sexual behavior without consequences?** Simple kisses and boy/girl social dynamics are fine for kids to see at this age, but risky or advanced sexual activity is out of bounds.
- **Does it have scenes of drug and alcohol use or abuse?** Unless the movie shows clear consequences, it's inappropriate.
- **Does it glamorize smoking?** Be careful. According to the American Cancer Society, kids who see a lot of smoking in movies are about three times more likely to start smoking than other kids.

Nobody knows your kid better than you do. If you decide that it's okay for your eleven- or twelve-year-old to see a PG-13 film, try to watch it together. If the movie's streaming or on a DVD, you can always skip over any scenes you feel are inappropriate. Personally, I've always loved showing my four kids the food fight scene from *Animal House*—but none of them got to see the rest of the movie before they were teens. The fast-forward button has been a big help in my household. Still, your tween will inevitably see some scenes where characters push the limits. If you're watching together, you can talk about unhealthy choices and consequences. Bad examples are great opportunities to talk about safety issues, right and wrong, and responsibility.

The older your kid is, of course, the less control you have. Still, you can ask your teen what movie he or she plans to see—whether in a theater or on a tablet computer or laptop—then take a few minutes to look up reviews on your smartphone. If you're not comfortable with that movie choice, speak up. Have a talk with your teen about values. Explain that some movies are filled with sex and graphic violence just to make money; those scenes don't reflect reality. The media is a "superpeer" that can normalize behaviors, so it's crucial for parents to help kids sort through messages and behaviors they see onscreen.

Many teens, for example, love the scary rush of watching horror movies, but these blockbusters often depend on extreme violence and carnage to shock the audience. The more kids steep themselves in violent story lines and images, the more willing they may be to see violence as an acceptable way of resolving conflicts. And brutal onscreen violence linked to sex is a truly toxic combination that can encourage misogynistic, exploitive behavior. The best advice is to do what you can to minimize your teen's exposure to grisly violence and talk openly and often about what movies—and conduct—you think are out of bounds.

And whether your kid is seven or seventeen, there are hundreds of great movies that you can watch together. My family's favorites are exciting action classics like *The Bridge on the River Kwai* and *The Great Escape*. But no matter what your family's tastes are, watching movies with your kids can be an opportunity to bond, share life lessons, ask questions, and laugh. Those family movie nights can make great memories. When I was little, for instance, my dad worked long hours. I didn't get to see him much during the week, and sometimes not on weekends. But when he was home, we would watch Marx

Brothers or W. C. Fields movies together. I must have seen *A Night at the Opera* twenty times. Those were special times that brought the two of us closer. The point I want to make is that when parents are thoughtful and selective about media, it can help create positive shared experiences that enlighten, inspire, and strengthen family ties.

Managing Multimedia Messages

I still remember when, fourteen years ago, our eldest daughter, Lily, then five years old, came back from a playdate where she had watched her first Spice Girls video. She ran into the family room, shaking her little booty and lip-synching "If you wanna be my lover" from her favorite Spice Girls song. At that moment, I totally grasped, for the first time, the incredible power of media role models.

Today, the Spice Girls are (mostly) ancient history, but I recently saw a YouTube video that, at first, I found almost impossible to believe. In the clip, a tiny girl, who is maybe three or four years old, is dancing in a little pink ruffled tutu, swishing her hips provocatively, and lip-synching the fairly explicit lyrics of a Lady Gaga song. At three or four, she's already familiar with this stuff!

The media industry has a phrase for this phenomenon. It's called "age compression." Marketers use this term to describe how kids at increasingly younger ages are modeling the behavior of older children and adults. Many fashion items and toys that were once deemed appropriate for teens are increasingly evident in the lives of preteens, even preschoolers. This form of age compression is particularly disturbing to child development experts when it takes on sexual connotations. Increasingly, younger children are modeling adultlike sexual behavior without having anywhere near the intellectual or emotional capacity to understand what they are actually saying or doing. Obviously, many parents and psychologists worry about the impact in the short and long term.

It's a complicated media world, filled with TV, smartphones, tablets, and computer screens. The explosion of digital media technology means more and more options, perils, and possibilities. Content comes at kids from everywhere, and YouTube is a case in point. Kids love it—it's been their number-one Internet search term. On YouTube they can find episodes of their favorite TV programs, popular music videos, and silly or inspiring clips posted by other kids. But they can also come across postings with mature content and rude and crude viewer comments even on age-appropriate videos.

The point to remember is that YouTube is not meant for kids under thirteen. Younger kids shouldn't explore it on their own. They may be watching something perfectly innocent, but the list of suggested videos that pops up may include clips that are wildly inappropriate, and it's too easy for kids to click on the links and see things that you wouldn't want them to. That's why it's a good idea to make sure your kid goes on YouTube only through a child-friendly web browser that lets her see only prescreened, age-appropriate postings. Otherwise, watch YouTube with her. You should also make a point of checking the safety mode box at the bottom of each YouTube page to filter suggestions and search results. Inappropriate videos can still slip through the filter, so it's always important to keep a close eye on what your kid is watching.

There's no doubt, though, that kids over thirteen can learn great stuff on YouTube, from how to play lead guitar to what life is like in other countries and cultures. Still, it's important to be a gatekeeper. Be proactive. Ask your younger teen what he's interested in, find great YouTube videos for him, and save them to a "Favorites" or "Watch Later" list. Keep the safety mode on, and stay tuned in to what your kid is watching. You can't keep him in a bubble, but you can focus him on the good stuff that's out there.

The reality is, our kids are growing up surrounded by sexual messages, and there's no way to completely shield them in our 24-7 media world. The fact that media is always on is a huge problem. It's everywhere we go, thanks to mobile devices, cellular data plans, and wi-fi, making it really tough for parents to filter the media and messages kids consume. Our instinct is to protect our kids and control their environment, but digital media makes that almost impossible.

It wasn't always like this. In the past, as the late media observer Neil Postman, former chairman of New York University's Department of Culture and Communication, noted, childhood was a "sequence of revealed secrets." Kids were protected from information that they weren't ready to understand. That innocence was once considered priceless, an essential element of childhood and growing up. But today, when unfiltered messages bombard our kids from every angle—in movies, ads, and on TV and the Internet—gatekeeping is difficult or impossible, even for younger kids. My friend Kate remembers that, after the September 11 attacks, she saw kids in preschool building towers out of blocks and pretending to fly planes into them. That's the world we live in. Information outraces our ability to control it, and we can't sequence secrets anymore.

We can't change that, and we can't go back. But we can—and we must—help our kids navigate this new environment safely so they don't get lost or hurt. We obviously can't shield them completely from all the images and messages that confront them, so it's vital to give them the tools and values to think critically about those messages and make good, commonsense judgments.

The truth is, if we don't educate our kids, the media will. Research by the Kaiser Family Foundation and others has made it clear, for one thing, that kids learn much about sexual standards and behavior from the media. Many of these images are played for shock value, some contain graphic sex, and sexual humor is a mainstay of adolescent entertainment. The only solution is to equip our kids with the critical-thinking skills to deal with this exposure. It can be pretty tough to have a conversation about sexual issues with a six-year-old who believes in the tooth fairy long before you thought you'd have to address them. But it's important for parents, whether we like it or not, to talk with our kids about these issues and images, as well as our own values, so they can develop healthy perspectives as they grow up.

Media violence is a major concern, too. Parent and consumer groups have long criticized the TV and movie industry for pushing violent content. In fact, public concerns about media violence were a critical factor in the Motion Picture Association of America's (MPAA's) decision to create the first-ever self-rating system, as well as the federal government's adoption of the ineffective television V-chip technology in the late 1990s. Leaders in the traditional entertainment industry have acknowledged for years that movies like *Natural Born Killers* and *Saw* can negatively impact young people and that violence is a public health issue for kids. Indeed, most top entertainment executives I know agree that violence is a real concern for families and that media and entertainment companies have a basic responsibility to address it. That said, violence, like sex, is clearly profitable, and media is a bottom-line-focused business. As Leslie Moonves, the longtime CEO of CBS, admitted, "Network presidents don't keep their jobs based on the number of Emmy Awards. Let's face it; there is more sensation and violence because it works."

When award-winning journalist Ken Auletta researched his fascinating 1997 book, *The Highwaymen*, about people who run the media business, he asked a very simple but pointed question to key industry leaders: "What won't you do?" What Auletta discovered about such powerful media moguls of that era as Disney's Michael Eisner, News Corp's Rupert Murdoch, and GE/NBC's Jack Welch was that they somehow disassociated what they did at work from what they permitted in their own homes. They wouldn't let their kids watch certain shows or movies, yet their networks and studios would go and make the very same films and programs that they wouldn't let their kids watch. Auletta saw a bifurcated personality at work. These media executives didn't take responsibility for the effects that their programs and content might have on other people's children. Their focus on profit trumped all other concerns.

As a result, parents are, without question, the first line of defense. We need to know what's happening in our kids' media lives. We need to talk with them about what they're seeing and hearing, and we need to teach them to think critically about the images and messages they encounter. We have to limit their access and exposure, starting when they're very young, with rules about screen time and high-quality content. As they get older, we can give them choices, with limitations. And we have to stay involved in how they process messages and images as they gain independence.

When our son Kirk was sixteen years old, for instance, he loved edgy TV crime shows like *CSI*. I'm a former prosecutor, and I watched lots of episodes with him. It gave us a chance to have great discussions about the criminal justice system and serious social and emotional issues. Those were important teachable, relationship-building moments for both of us.

Kirk, by the way, also liked to remind me that I was his "worst nightmare" as a parent, because I took a hard line about the amount and content of entertainment media that he was exposed to. But the fact is, parental involvement has a very positive effect. Research shows that it can make a huge difference in the amount of media that kids consume. That's important, because studies have shown that kids who spend less time with media have much better grades in school and higher levels of personal contentment.

A big part of our job is protecting our kids, as much as possible, from the marketing pitches that bombard them, from every screen, to get them to crave junk food, toys, and endless products. Marketers, in fact, specifically and aggressively target children as young as five and six, because they're especially vulnerable to ads. Kids this age can't easily tell the difference between fantasy and reality, and that's exactly what makes them so susceptible—and desirable—to marketers.

Companies also spend around $400 million a year on television ads aimed at kids under twelve, pushing sugary, salty, high-fat, and unhealthy food. Children, on average, see fourteen of these ads a day, and that doesn't include hidden marketing schemes, like product placements on popular shows. Studies show that the more hours kids spend watching TV, the more likely they are to eat while they watch, eat what they see on the screen, and eat more. Childhood obesity rates are higher than ever, leading too many kids to face an unhealthy future, because these marketing ploys are effective.

What can you do? Choose commercial-free TV programs, or use a digital video recorder (DVR) that lets you skip the ads. It's also important to teach your kid the difference between a commercial and a TV show and how to identify the ads on TV and videos. You can even make it a fun "advergame"—ask your youngster to guess when the commercials start, so she'll learn to spot the marketing tricks before they trick her.

Kids also get powerful messages about their body image from TV and movies. As adults, we know that the perfect appearance of media stars is due to an army of specialists who manage their food intake, workouts, hair, makeup, and lighting. Too many kids, however, believe what they see onscreen. When they compare themselves to these false icons of beauty, they often feel they don't measure up. As a result, they can have lower self-esteem and spend an unhealthy amount of time worrying about and trying to alter their appearance. Boys as well as girls can fall into this trap. Based on what they see in the media, many boys think they're not cool if they don't have sculpted muscles and six-pack abs. Like girls, they're under more and more pressure these days to live up to an unrealistic, media-driven standard.

As parents, we can balance these body-image messages by emphasizing our kids' inner beauty—their talents, creativity, and kindness. We can focus on their health instead of their weight, keeping them active and eating right. We can be positive role models by not obsessing about our own looks and what the scale tells us. We can talk to our kids about people we find beautiful who have different body types. We can also let our kids know that it's normal to have insecurities—that we have them too—and that nobody's "perfect," even models and movie stars. To prove your point, show your child the great Dove "Evolution" video on YouTube, which films an ordinary-looking woman who turns into a glamorous model for an ad campaign thanks to makeup and hair teams (and Photoshop whizzes).

Our kids' assumptions about the world, and their place in it, are also shaped, in part, by media stereotypes. It's subtle, if you're not paying attention, but it's a fact that there are many more male than female heroes in movies and TV shows. Minority heroes are all too rare, and women typically play love interests and sex objects. Over time, those kinds of stereotypes can influence your kid's perception of herself and others.

As a result, it's important to be aware of and counteract media role models. Try counting, with your kid, the different stereotypes you see on the screen. Talk about how many female or minority characters you see and what their roles are. Does race or gender affect how the characters look or act? Point out examples from real life that run counter to media stereotypes to help your kid think critically about what he sees onscreen. It's always great for kids to watch movies like *Brave* and *Frozen* and TV shows like *SciGirls* and *Wizards vs. Aliens* that have unstereotypical characters. Commonsensemedia.org has lots of recommendations for movies and TV shows that break the mold.

Put Your Family on a Media Diet

Bottom line, you're the guide, gatekeeper, and decision maker when it comes to your child's media life. In our mobile, multiplatform digital media world, it's harder than ever to keep track of what your kid is seeing on a screen, but it's also more important than ever that you do. One of the best ways you can take charge is by starting a family media diet. Just like you control your child's access to junk food, it's essential to control his access to media. Too much screen time can lead to a host of problems, including attention, learning, behavior, sleep, and self-esteem issues. In small amounts, with controlled content, screen media can be educational and entertaining, but too much of it can be as unhealthy as a diet of candy, sugary soft drinks, and french fries. So set limits by starting a family media diet and get the whole family involved in planning it.

Some families find that a Media Turnoff Week (or two) is a good way to start. Others find that it works best to change family media habits gradually, a few hours a week at a time. It can be tough to change, but when parents agree on media rules and enforce them, kids' behavior patterns adjust. The reality is, kids most often respond well to limits. Once they know what the limits are, they learn to live with them.

No matter how old your child is, the main courses in her day should be physical and creative activity, homework, and real-life, face-to-face interaction with friends and family. Watching TV and movies should be a treat, but for far too many kids, it's the main event. Many spend more hours a day watching a screen than they do with their families or in school. It's as if they're eating more junk food than anything else. So just as you're in charge of what your child eats, you need to manage the kind and quantity of media he consumes.

To start a media diet, each member of the family should keep a media diary for a week, writing down each time they use media and for how long. Everyone will quickly become a lot more conscious of the media they're using and how much time they're spending with it. The next step is to come up with a healthy media diet together, with clear limits on the total number of hours that each family member should spend in front of a screen. For kids, the AAP recommends no more than two hours a day. I'd personally recommend setting a lower limit, but you might want to make exceptions for occasional splurges, like the Super Bowl or a long family movie you want to watch together. It's also crucial to have media-free family time—at mealtimes, for example, and before bed. And take care that the TV isn't on constantly in the background, so your child isn't surrounded by the conversation-killing drone of programs and commercials. Make sure your kid knows the consequences if he breaks the rules, like spending a weekend with no TV.

The earlier you set the rules, the easier it will be to enforce them. If you have a younger child, it's also good to teach her to ask permission before using media. It's an easy way to get your kid to think that media is a privilege, not a constant distraction that she's entitled to. Kids learn to ask permission before taking something out of the fridge, borrowing a toy from a friend, interrupting a grown-up, or going outside, and it's a great way to train your kid to see media use as a special, occasional treat and reward for good behavior. It can also give you a chance to suggest other activities, like reading, playing outside, or doing something special together. Until a child is ten or eleven, asking permission to use media won't seem strange at all.

Be sure to lay down media rules about content, too, and make sure all the kids in your family understand them. Big brothers and sisters, for instance, are rarely willing to watch a "baby" show for kindergarteners just because their little brother or sister is in the room. That's why they need to understand there will be consequences if they watch an age-inappropriate show in front of your five- or six-year-old. Remind them that they have different privileges because they're older, as well as their own media rules about screen time and content. Make sure other adults in your home know the rules, too, so that everyone's on the same page.

As kids get older, they make more decisions on their own. They don't live in a bubble, and when they're away from home, it's much more difficult to control the media that they're consuming. When your tween is hanging out at her friends' houses, she's spending at least part of that time in front of a screen. But there are two things you can do to increase the chances that she'll stick to your family's media rules when she's away from home. Think of it this way: if your child had a food allergy, you'd make sure she understood the rules about what she can eat and the consequences if she didn't follow them. You'd also make sure to communicate those rules to the parent of any friend she was spending time with.

The same strategy applies when it comes to media. First, make sure your child understands the family media rules. Reinforce them clearly and often and explain what the consequences will be if your child breaks them. Second, speak up about those rules, in advance, to the parents of any friends with whom your child is spending time. Explain the rules to other family members, babysitters, and the parents of friends your child spends time with. Between their supervision and your child's understanding of rules and consequences, there's a good chance that you'll minimize her exposure to media that's out of bounds.

Still, kids learn how to make good choices through experience and occasional mistakes. Life isn't a walled garden. As a parent, you can reward the good decisions and enforce the consequences of bad ones. You can always mitigate the effects of inappropriate media exposure by discussing the issues with your child and sharing your values and point of view. He'll remember those words when you aren't with him, and they'll help him make better, healthier decisions for himself.

It's so important to pay close attention to your kid's media life. And because kids learn more from what you do than what you say, it's vital to be a role model. It's hard to encourage your seven- or eight-year-old not to eat junk food if you're always reaching for candy bars and bags of chips. It's the same with media—you have to lead by example. If you want your child to lead a balanced life that's not tethered to digital screens, make sure you unplug and turn off the TV during family time. What you do sends a powerful message. If you keep the TV on during meals and when no one's watching, if you're glued to a screen when your child's trying to talk to you or show you what she made at school, you're teaching her that media is more important than she is. If you're staring at a screen instead of making eye contact—or emotional contact—with your child, you're modeling behavior that he'll mimic as he grows up. So show him that you control your media life, it doesn't control you, and it's never a distraction that keeps you from real human experience and connection.

Our kids may be living in a world of revealed secrets, but we can counteract this loss of innocence by teaching them good judgment and the critical thinking skills they need to filter media messages. The world of digital, 24-7, mobile media is changing rapidly, but parenting hasn't changed. It's our responsibility to help our kids make good choices and grow up healthy, informed, and responsible in a complex world.

1. V. Rideout, U. Foehr, and D. Roberts, "Generation M2: Media in the Lives of 8- to 18-Year-Olds," A Kaiser Family Foundation Study (2010), 2.
2. S. Smith, E. Moyer-Guse, and E. Donnerstein, "Media Violence and Sex," the National Television Violence Study, the SAGE Handbook of Media Studies (2004), 542–546.
3. Heather L. Kirkorian, Ellen A. Wartella, and Daniel R. Anderson, "Media and Young Children's Learning," *Future of Children* 18, no. 1 (Spring 2008), 39–61.
4. E. A. Vandewater, V. Rideout, E. A. Wartella, X. Huang, J. H. Lee, and M. Shim, "Digital Childhood: Electronic Media Use Among Infants, Toddlers, and Preschoolers," *Pediatrics* (2007) 119:1006–1015.
5. Frederick J. Zimmerman, PhD; Dimitri A. Christakis, MD, MPH, PhD; and Andrew N. Meltzoff, PhD, "Associations Between Media Viewing and Language Development in Children Under Age 2 Years," *Journal of Pediatrics* (August 7, 2007).
6. Aviva Lucas Gutnick et al., "Always Connected: The New Digital Media Habits of Young Children," The Joan Ganz Cooney Center Publications (March 10, 2011).

going with the technology flow and raising good digital citizens

BY SANDRA BRYSON, MFT, MARRIAGE AND FAMILY THERAPIST, FOUNDER OF PARENT MINDFULLY, AND PARENT OF TWO GIRLS

Recently, Ana came into my office to proudly tell me about the limits she was setting with her twelve-year-old son, Theo, on his access to technology. Clear that she didn't want him to have a smartphone with a data plan, she decided to buy him an iPod Touch instead. She told me that she felt good that, despite the fact that all his friends had smartphones, she had stood firm on setting this limit. Ana gave Theo her ID and password so he could download games and didn't think much more about it.

One day, Ana walked in to find Theo talking to someone using his iPod Touch. In confusion, she grabbed it and demanded to know what he was doing. He explained to her that, with a password and ID, he had downloaded Skype. Despite the best intentions to limit his communications, she had unwittingly given her son the tools to call anyone, anywhere, at any time.

Parenting today can be downright confusing. In addition to the normal stresses and strains of raising children, parents now have to deal with the myriad issues surrounding technology. Not only do we have all of the perils of the Internet, we have social networking, smartphones, and video games to contend with. It seems that every day we hear about cyberbullying, Internet addiction, and online porn. The question looming is loud and clear: How do we protect our children from harm while teaching them how to protect themselves?

Technology has become part of the fabric of our lives. Computers, the Internet, and other digital technologies have changed the ways families live, learn, manage their lives, connect with the community, and gather information. When used wisely, digital tools can have incredible benefits: they empower children with amazing outlets for their creativity and provide skills that will give kids more opportunities as they enter the workplace. Instead of fighting against it, we need to focus on creating a new generation of good digital citizens who are moderate, respectful, and have the ability to function well in real life *and* online. Because, whether you like it or not, there is no stopping this train.

The facts seem daunting: The average young American now spends practically every waking minute—except for the time in school—using a smartphone, computer, television, or other electronic device, according to a study from the Kaiser Family Foundation.[1] Those ages eight to eighteen spend more than seven and a half hours a day connected to someone or something through such devices. And since so many of these kids are multitasking—say, surfing the Internet while texting and/or chatting online—they pack nearly eleven hours of media content into those seven and a half hours. More than two thirds of the time kids are doing homework on the computer they are simultaneously using it for something else. All of this screen time isn't just harmless fun: heavy media use is associated with several negatives, including behavior problems and lower grades.

All is not doom and gloom, however. I believe that technology does have a silver lining. As a therapist who specializes in helping families set limits on technology, I see the opportunities technology gives parents to pay closer attention, set limits, open the lines of communication, and help us truly understand our children's worlds. When it comes to technology, we need to be intentional, aware, and fully present. In this way, we can actually become better and more involved parents in the long run—while also protecting our kids.

Rule #1: Understand Technology

These days, it's not enough to know where your kids are. You also need to know what they are doing. Ana had the best intentions when she bought her son that iPod Touch. However, she simply didn't understand the risks involved.

Ana was lucky: her son only made a few calls to friends. But failing to understand technology can have far more serious consequences. Consider the heartbreaking case of four Iowa teenagers who met in an online game chat room through their Xboxes,[2] only to plan an escape and run away from home together. Chances are that their parents had no idea that kids can get online using Xbox (did you?). When I heard one of these children's mothers pleading on the news for her child's safe return, it broke my heart—and reaffirmed my conviction that parents must learn more about how their child's technologies work.

Although technology is scary for some parents, it doesn't have to be. In fact, learning about technology can be empowering. When you educate yourself, you will better understand when your children reach an appropriate age to have certain privileges like a cell phone or how much screen time they should have. You will have the confidence to clarify your own values, take a strong stand on the issues you feel are important, and convey clear values to your children.

When you understand the technology, you'll be fortified with the information you need to educate your kids. This hit close to home during a conversation with my nine-year-old grandson, who matter-of-factly told me that if a kid is under thirteen he can have a Facebook account with his parent's permission. I explained to him the facts: you must be over thirteen. This prompted quite an argument, with him trying to convince me that it's perfectly okay for an eleven-year-old to have an account because parents can give their permission. I even went so far as to explain the law to him—and he still insisted. By understanding this technology, I was able to stand my ground and help him realize that the "word on the street" was unreliable.

After Ana finally understood the capabilities of an iPod Touch, she did the logical thing: changed her password. She also took the time to explain to Theo why she felt he was too young to have a smartphone and negotiated getting him a bare-bones phone in the future if he demonstrated that he would behave responsibly with technology.

When we hand over devices to our children, we need to help them understand a few key things:

- These devices are a privilege, and you have to continue to earn that privilege by proper behavior with your device.
- There will be times when the devices will be turned off or stored, such as 7:00 p.m. to 7:00 a.m. on school nights or during family mealtimes.
- We will have ongoing conversations (i.e., family meetings) about the proper use of our devices, and together come up with reasonable guidelines for kids and parents alike. (This could include rules such as never give out passwords or personal information or never say anything in an e-mail or text you wouldn't say to someone's face.)

- When I first give it to you, we will learn about it together with a shared password. As you get older, you can gain some autonomy with your device by earning my trust.
- You need to demonstrate to me that you can function as well away from your electronic devices as you do in front of them—and I have to do the same. This includes doing activities together or separately with our devices turned off.

I urge parents to do research on every piece of technology they buy for their children, making sure they understand how it works and what it can do. Because most kids know technology better than their parents, this creates a wonderful opportunity to spend time with your children. Have them explain how they use it! Encourage them to do creative projects, and do some with them, such as learning Photoshop together or creating a how-to video of making their favorite cupcakes and posting it on YouTube. And why not play a video game with your children once in a while? This will help you understand their world. Afterward, you can ask them what they liked and didn't like, and set the stage for comfortable two-way communication in the future.

When you are educated, you can teach your children certain things about technology they might not know. Just as you wouldn't let your child drive a car without taking driver's ed and passing the driver's test, you shouldn't just expect them to know how to use every piece of equipment responsibly.

Take Immediate Action Item #1
Put parental controls on your computer.

We all want to trust our children. However, letting them self-regulate technological decisions is too big a burden to put on a child.

As Kimberly Brooks writes in the *Huffington Post*: "Technology is addictive and allowing children to attempt to regulate themselves is akin to helping them regulate their use of cocaine or alcohol."[3] If kids come across something inappropriate accidentally, this will cause them conflict. Find out the most appropriate controls for your child's age and implement them. When you do, you will have gone a long way in protecting your child. As kids get older and they show us they know what it means to be a good digital citizen, they can gain more and more privileges. Our goal is to shape their technology experiences so that by the time they leave home, we have the confidence that they can handle their online experiences responsibly and safely.

Rule #2: Set Limits

A counseling client, Susie, confided in me that her twelve-year-old daughter Maura was upset because all of her friends were on Facebook. Although according to the Children's Online Privacy Protection Act (COPPA), she needs to be thirteen to get an account, Maura blamed her mother for not letting her lie about her age to participate. After much begging on Maura's part, Susie caved and helped her daughter set up a Facebook account by lying and changing her birth date online. Susie didn't want to be the "bad guy." But, unable to set an appropriate limit, not only was she opening her daughter up to a whole world of online behavior with the associated risks, she was modeling that it's okay to lie just to get in the game.

Many parents don't like to set limits with their kids. It can be difficult and uncomfortable. But here's the truth: it's perfectly okay for them—and for us—to have that discomfort. It will go away. They will still love us, we will still love them, and they will be *far more* prepared for living in the Great Big World than they would be if we protected them from the emotional ups and downs of life.

Setting limits isn't just a good idea for parents, it's a crucial step toward creating independent thinkers with healthy mental and physical outlooks. When a child is up all night texting his friends, for instance, setting a limit becomes a health issue that needs to be immediately addressed. Kids internalize the limits we set for them—and can then set limits for themselves when we are not around. In the same way that repeatedly wearing a seat belt in the car creates an almost automatic behavior for kids, consistently setting clear limits helps them eventually have an easily accessible understanding about what is okay and what is not.

We need to help our kids understand the concept of moderation, and that includes screen time. We don't let our kids eat a whole batch of chocolate chip cookies. We talk to them about moderation, and how too many cookies can affect them. It's important they learn how to step away, whether from the cookies or the computer. With life moving at a breakneck pace, it's certainly easy to let our kids entertain themselves in front of a screen. It takes a bit more parental involvement and effort for them to be entertained in other ways. But it's worth it. And it often means turning off our own screens!

We can't just lecture our kids about our values and hope that the information sticks. We have to show them that we can survive without checking our phones or e-mail. If we give them a device to distract them whenever they demand one, we are not giving them a chance to experience frustration. Instead, we are actually depriving them of an opportunity to learn how to self-soothe or, god forbid, be bored for a few minutes.

Out of boredom comes creativity. If one of our values is to raise creative and productive members of society, then we need to model for our kids that time away from technology is important and consciously provide opportunities for them to experience that time so they can learn how rich it can be. This reminds me of a relative from the East Coast who recently went through a four-day power outage. He said the first day was torture for his wife, his two kids, and himself. But by the second day, they had all surrendered and were enjoying playing games, reading books, and sitting by their fireplace telling stories. As a result of this experience, the family decided to make Sunday a technology-free day each week. Why not institute a day when the whole family unplugs? We can play games, do puzzles, or cook together. In this way, we interact in positive ways with our kids—and avoid modeling the very behaviors we don't want our kids to engage in.

I had a client recently who said her child was glued to the computer playing Minecraft and was unable to self-regulate. I advised she say to him something like this: "I know you would really love to spend the next two hours playing Minecraft on the computer. I realize this is really important to you. However, we had an agreement that you would stop now, and while I realize that you don't want to stop playing, it's what we agreed on so I am going to turn the computer off. It's fine if you are upset. I understand, and we are still going to turn it off right now." This kind of communication might disappoint our kids, but it also validates their feelings and gives them the space to protest. For most kids it only takes a few days for them to be able to move on.

Take Immediate Action Item #2
Set limits on screen time, cell phones, and social networking.

When you set limits, your children won't like it. They might have a fit or slam doors. This is okay, and it will pass. Figure out what limits work for you. You can set weekly hours, take the phone away at certain times, or get a pay-as-you go phone. Beyond keeping your kids safe and helping them deal with disappointment, setting clear limits gives them a structure so they know what to expect. When kids know what to expect, they feel safe, loved, and protected.

When determining the right age to give your child a cell phone, several factors need to be considered. First of all, does your child need the phone in order to communicate with you for safety reasons? Is the child responsible enough to use the phone properly?

The answers to these questions can depend on your child's age. If it's an elementary school child, getting the simplest phone possible and programming in one or two numbers will do the trick. For middle-schoolers, choose a phone that's not a smartphone, be sure to set limits on calling and texting, and establish clear rules about use, which might include not texting during class and turning over the phone to you at night. If these rules are not followed, there need to be real consequences. High school–age kids might legitimately need to have smartphones for school these days because they have to access the Internet for schoolwork, which adds a layer of complications. Have high-schoolers demonstrate that they can behave responsibly and have consequences if they don't adhere to the rules. Parents can check the phones and phone plans to see when and where kids are communicating and then establish guidelines and appropriate limits.

Guiding your child through social networking takes some paying attention. When it comes to younger kids, many sites for five- to eight-year-olds have robust safety features, and parents can explore these sites along with their children. Middle school presents other challenges. While you can't technically have a Facebook account until you are thirteen, plenty of kids get around this by lying about their birth dates. Find out if your child has an account and make a decision about what will be allowed in your family. Talk about specific guidelines, such as not posting anything that's harmful or mean, understanding privacy settings, and remembering that what goes out on the Internet is permanent. Have conversations about cyberbullying and sexting to open the lines of communication. By high school, kids should already be well schooled in online etiquette. But ongoing conversations can always reinforce this knowledge. Talk to your kids about the fact that colleges and employers look at applicants' Facebook pages, and that posting questionable activities can have grave consequences for their future. By understanding social media and by paying attention to what your kids are doing online, you can ensure that you are raising a generation of good digital citizens.

Whether it's screen time, phone time, or social networking, establish rituals, such as rules for earning screen time or when all devices must be put away. Take away offending media devices until homework and chores are done, or have a media-free rule during the school week. Whatever you do, avoid negotiations once the rules are set. Setting limits with your children's input, thoughtfully and with intention, can lead to more clarity, peace, and understanding down the road.

Rule #3: Reduce Multitasking

Helene called me in a panic over the fact that her daughter seemed to be doing her homework, texting, and listening to music all at the same time. She was very concerned that this would affect her daughter's performance in school. She had heard that all teenagers multitask, but she wasn't so sure it was such a good idea. She asked my advice about how to work with her daughter on this issue, and expressed her concern that her daughter would hit the roof if she were told she couldn't study with music on and answer texts at will.

Multitasking can be detrimental. At least one recent study[4] has shown that while kids are good at going back and forth among different activities, they do get distracted and they do have trouble remembering what they are studying. In particular and most important, the next day they have trouble remembering what they studied. As a result, their grades might start dropping and it might just be taking them longer than necessary to complete tasks. Constant distractions can keep a child from learning new tasks or concepts. And when we attempt to learn something while multitasking, our ability to remember it later, or use it in other contexts, is diminished. The truth is that there really are negative consequences to multitasking for kids, including trouble remembering, underperformance at school, and relationship difficulties.

Once Helene understood the downside of multitasking, it was easy for her to clearly explain the rules: no TV, Facebook, YouTube, IM, or texting while doing homework. (It's best to establish these boundaries when kids are young.) When her daughter did have to be in chat rooms to discuss homework, I encouraged Helene to monitor her carefully so she knew when her daughter switched gears. All parents should heed this general advice: pay attention to your children's Internet use, and what is happening in school. If their grades are slipping, set stronger limits about what goes on at home during homework times. If you are paying attention, you will know when multitasking becomes a problem.

Another solution? Encourage your children to read more. The more kids (or anyone, for that matter) read, the more they strengthen the brain's ability to focus, improving their reflective and analytical skills.

Take Immediate Action Item #3

Keep the computer in a family space and the Internet out of bedrooms.

This simple solution helps on many levels: it ensures that you know what your children are doing and how much multitasking is going on, it maximizes the chances of communication, and it creates an environment where computers are a family affair. Also: don't let your child have Internet access in her room. And if you don't want your kids using technology often, engage them! Create fun projects, outings, and experiences so they will be happy to unplug.

Rule #4: Keep the Lines of Communication Open and Don't Overreact

Debbie, a longtime client, came in to tell me that her twelve-year-old daughter was Googling online and came across the word *intercourse*. When she looked it up, graphic sexual images came on the screen. When Debbie glanced into the living room and saw these images, she started screaming at her daughter: "Get off the Internet! What are you doing?"

Seeing a disturbing image on a computer is one thing. But seeing a disturbing image on a computer—and having a parent freak out and make a huge deal about it—totally compounds the issue and can leave a lasting negative impression on a child.

When you see Internet use gone awry, which happens in even the most aware families, don't go ballistic. Understand that kids will come across these adult images, and if you handle it the right way they aren't going to be scarred for life. By keeping the lines of communication open and assuring them that they are not in trouble, there is a much better chance they will come to you again in the future and talk about what they've seen.

If you find that your kids have discovered something inappropriate online, don't take their smartphone and smash it into bitty pieces. After Debbie's daughter's incident, I encouraged Debbie to keep the lines of communication open by talking candidly. Debbie started the process by giving her daughter her full attention, away from any distractions. Instead of chastising her daughter, she apologized for overreacting. Without being judgmental, she asked her daughter about her reaction to what she had seen, and how she felt about it. While it's important during these kinds of conversations to listen and not lecture, Debbie also took the opportunity to explain the differences between normal healthy sexual expression and deviant activity that shows up the Internet. Finally, Debbie asked her daughter to come to her when she had questions in the future. A few months later, Debbie happily reported to me that her daughter was confiding in her more often since she had opened these lines of communication.

Open communication applies to any situation. For example, if you find your child sexting (sending explicit photos or messages on mobile devices and computers), take the chance to talk about it immediately. Tell him about the legal consequences of his actions, since a teen can be charged with distributing child pornography. Talk about the emotional consequences of sexting, such as how a friend could betray him and send a sext to others, or how a photo could become archived online (even with Snapchat and similar apps that supposedly "disappear" photos after a short amount of time). Discuss peer pressure, and give him advice on how to react to it in a healthy way. Tell your child that no matter how intense the social pressure is to send a sext, the potential downside is much worse: the sext he is sending could end up humiliating him in the short run or potentially haunting him forever. In addition, if an image is sent across state lines—even inadvertently—it's a felony!

What to Teach Your Kids About Sexting

- It's illegal.
- It can be emotionally damaging.
- Tell a parent or trusted adult if you receive a sext.
- Don't forward the sext; delete it immediately.
- Be a good friend and let the person who sent it know that it's the wrong thing to do.
- Find resources for dealing with sexting at parentmindfully.com.

Communicating also means teaching your kids how to think critically about their online communications. Educate them about the fact that people aren't always who they say they are, and how people can sometimes be mean and disloyal. Teach them online etiquette, and how to think about their own values when going online: kindness, compassion, and honesty. And don't forget to remind them about the importance of staying in the present, not just staring at a screen, so they don't miss out on their own lives.

Teaching critical thinking and online etiquette begins the moment we first hand our kids a screen. When a child is fussing in a car seat while we are driving, if we hand back our iPhone to keep him quiet, we are sending a big message: that it's not okay to be upset, frustrated, or bored. A great time for conversations about online etiquette is during one of your technology-free dinners. Talk about what it's like to be intentional about putting your phones away. Have each person around the table give an "appreciation" and a "resentment" about technology. "What I appreciate, Mom, about you having a cell phone is that I can always get ahold of you. What I resent about you having a cell phone, Mom, is that it's hard to get your attention when you are talking to someone when you pick me up at school." Or, "I appreciate my laptop. And I resent that I have to turn it over to my parents when they say so."

In the same way that we teach our young children that violence on television is not real, we can teach them to question what they see on a computer screen. By partnering with them and paying attention to what they are doing, we can ensure that they explain to us what they are thinking about. More listening than talking is always best. Be curious and elicit conversation, such as "Tell me about your world." When kids are school age, they will most likely already be hearing about empathy and compassion as part of antibullying campaigns. We can generalize these ideas to online communications, and talk to them about how important it is, for instance, to never say anything in an e-mail or text that you wouldn't say to someone's face.

Communication is a lot of work. You need to be vigilant. But use these discussions as opportunities to connect with your kid. Even when your teen seems uncomfortable, or as if he's not listening, it's likely that something is getting through. It's our job as parents to push through the discomfort—our child's and our own—and keep the conversation going.

Take Immediate Action Item #4
Create a written contract with your kids for online safety.

A written contract can include pledges not to give out personal information, send photos, or see in person anyone they met online. Kids can also promise to talk to a parent if something is uncomfortable or doesn't feel right. Items in a safety contract become talking points to kick off open discussions between you and your kids. Download contracts from the Internet (find good ones at common sensemedia.org) or make your own.

Rule #5: Pay Attention

A mom called me to say that she had noticed some changes in her son's behavior. He seemed depressed, suddenly stopped using the computer, and had lost interest in playing video games. She had observed that he seemed anxious when he was receiving text messages, and she noticed that he seemed more withdrawn from his family and friends than usual. He was having trouble sleeping.

Without even having to see this family, I suspected that the boy was most likely a victim of cyberbullying.

Cyberbullying is a huge and growing problem; 20 percent of

teens have been victims of cyberbullying and the same percentage admits to having cyberbullied at least once in their lives.[5] Cyberbullying is not something to minimize or ignore. It should be dealt with immediately. And it's important for kids to feel they can trust you, that you have their backs and that, no matter what, you will support them.

Good thing this mom was paying attention. After seeing the warning signs, she came to see me. I helped her with a strategy for dealing with her son in a nonconfrontational way. I explained that her goal was open communication and letting her child know that she was supportive and would protect him. I then saw the mom and boy together, and reinforced how the boy could deal with bullying, both online and offline.

The boy felt empowered and supported by his mom and me. He felt comfortable enough to talk to some of his close friends about how they could together deal with the bullies in their school. He was also brave enough to tell the yard supervisor the next time someone said something inappropriate to him in the school yard.

Rules for Dealing with a Cyberbully

- Ignore the harsh or threatening messages and don't respond or retaliate.
- Block the sender.
- Save the evidence.
- Tell a parent or trusted adult.
- Have a parent help you report the incident to the website or the authorities.
- Now that you know what it feels like to be bullied, don't bully others.
- If you are aware of someone being bullied, support them against the bully.

Take Immediate Action Item #5
Teach empathy.

Technology opens the doors for teachable moments in your child's world. Let's say that your kid is being cyberbullied. This creates an opportunity for talking about empathy. To get the conversation started, ask your kids over dinner: What is it like to be bullied? What are the lasting dangers of being someone who bullies another kid on the Internet, through a text or a tweet? What do you do if you are a victim of cyberbullying? Have your children take turns role-playing on each side, imagining what it would be like to be someone who was being cyberbullied and then someone who was a cyberbully. It can be really fun to get playful and dramatic, so the discussion is enjoyable yet gets the important points across.

Rule #6: Clarify Your Values

Recently, a mom came to me because she and her husband were in conflict over whether to limit their daughter's total screen time. She told me that her husband often gave his iPad to their toddler to keep her entertained. She was furious with her husband because she wanted him to be interacting with his daughter, not setting her up with an iPad.

It's imperative that parents figure out how they want to integrate technology into their own family values. For example, when difficult feelings arise and you tell your kids to watch a movie to calm down, this is teaching them a powerful lesson about how to deal with upsetting emotions. Ask yourself, "What is important to me?" "What are the lessons that I want to teach my children?" "What are my values?" "How do I maintain my integrity?" If these questions seem overwhelming, try writing down the answers. When you start with clarifying your values as parents, the rest becomes a little easier.

I congratulated this mother for her good instincts, which were right on target: The American Academy of Pediatrics[6] advises that, for children older than two, screen time should be less than two hours a day of educational, nonviolent programs. Ideally, this time should be supervised by parents or other responsible adults.

When I met with these parents, we strategized ways to better align Mom's and Dad's different parenting styles and values so they could parent more consistently and effectively together regarding screen time and media use in their home. I emphasized that this was a perfect time to begin learning how to communicate openly with each other, and we discussed how to begin these conversations with their children. One good way is to have family meetings at which you establish healthy, open communication about a variety of issues families face. Start with nonthreatening topics like chores and bedtimes, but don't be shy about eventually broaching important subjects, such as bullying and other social issues the children might be dealing with. It's okay to ask them directly, "Have you ever been bullied or seen someone being bullied?" You might be surprised at how this opens up the lines of communication.

Take Immediate Action Item #6
Model moderation.

Kids pay attention to everything. When we are plugged into technology and distracted they know it. How can we expect them to use moderation when we aren't modeling this behavior? So be a good role model—be mindful of your own screen time and limit it during important family times.

Be willing to put your handheld devices aside, set them on silent, and make family connection time more important than immediate responses to incoming messages. Modeling good behavior automatically leads to another ideal behavior—staying present. If you aren't always plugged in, you have many more opportunities to stay attuned to your kids' needs.

Your kids are watching. Here are some comments from fifth-graders at a local elementary school who were asked about when the adults in their lives use screen time.

"While having dinner at home, my parents sit down and act like I'm not even there and are talking on the phone—especially at Sunday-night dinner."

"During a school performance."

"At the movie theater, the person in front of me on their iPhone was texting and they start laughing, even though it is silent in the movie."

"In a restaurant—they should be talking outside."

"When I'm fighting with my brother who is trying to kill me, and the babysitter is on the phone."

"Talking to Mom and she starts texting."

"Driving in the car with my parents and they say, 'This is a real important call' and you just sit there and they don't talk to you and it really isn't important."

"My mom is on the phone in the car, and I think she is talking to me so I answer her."

"At a quiet Italian restaurant and everyone's texting and not talking with friends."

"When I'm playing a soccer game and parents are texting and don't see you score a goal or hit a home run and it is your big moment."

"I come home from school and ask where Dad is, and Mom says he is outside on the phone."

"On a camping trip and parents keep complaining that there is no service."

Rule #7: Watch for Addiction

A terribly distraught mom was referred to me by her son's pediatrician because both he and the mother suspected that her fifteen-year-old boy was addicted to online gaming. Although he spent an inordinate amount of his time shut in his room gaming, the extent of his dependency hadn't come to light before this because his grades were good and he was participating in the family. Recently, however, his grades began to slip and he was less available at home. And when his parents suggested he stop playing his games, or wanted him to join in a family outing, he completely lost his cool and got violent. This frightened the parents, so they just gave in and let him do what he wanted.

Typical signs that a child is addicted to a form of technology include:

Spending most hours not in school on the computer or playing video games

Grades slipping, or falling behind in school assignments

Choosing to play on the computer rather than spend time in the "real world"

Getting irritable when not in front of the computer

Getting up in the middle of the night to check online activity

If you see any of these signs, get help. Internet addiction should be treated in much the same way as any other addiction, with a formal program (find resources at parentmindfully.com) and/or by talking to a psychotherapist who specializes in it. Addictions involve secrets, but solutions involve open family communication and working toward common goals.

Take Immediate Action Item #7
Learn mindfulness.

Mindfulness is what it sounds like: staying present and aware. Paying attention to the present moment challenges busy parents. However, those who deliberately try to stay present for each interaction with their children often discover that it totally transforms the parenting experience. Learn how to become more present with yourself and your children, which in turn helps you become a less reactive and more loving parent.

I coach my clients in a technique called mindfulness meditation. It's easy to do. (For instructions, go to parentmindfully.com /resources.) When we practice mindfulness meditation, for even as little as ten minutes a day, we learn to tune in to our moment-to-moment experiences in a calm and reflective way. By learning to be in the present with ourselves, we gain the skills to be present with others as well. This is enormously helpful in parenting. With mindful listening, we truly hear what our children are saying to us and can calmly take it in without overreacting. In addition, by tuning in to ourselves as we listen, we can respond calmly and authentically.

The Bottom Line

Those are my seven golden rules for good digital citizenship and accompanying action items, very specific ways that you can help your children evolve into good digital citizens. When you have the core philosophy down—pay attention, get more involved, and keep communicating—it's much easier to apply solutions to any given situation.

In this daunting technological age, parents have major concerns: What is the right age for different kinds of technology? How much screen time should my kids have? How do I set limits? How do I understand the technology? How do I keep my kids safe from cyberbullies and predators? How do I relate with my child in this online age?

My rule of thumb is simple: no matter how much emphasis is on technology, your children should be able to function as well without it as with it. In other words, they should be able to entertain themselves, come up with creative ideas, and just enjoy quiet time. One family I worked with came up with a creative solution for their technology-oriented son. Each year, he goes on a wilderness camping trip for two months, immersing himself in nature and not going anywhere near a screen. In this way, everyone wins: his family knows that he can get along without technology, and he gets the chance to nurture a lifelong love of the outdoors, while learning things that technology can't teach.

Perhaps the most important thing parents can do is to pay attention. It's hard work. It's challenging and often overwhelming. But when we actively commit ourselves to doing this, we become much better parents. Working with your children on setting limits, modeling behavior, understanding technology, and staying present gives you the opportunity to fine-tune your parenting, and ultimately have better relationships with your kids. And this is something that goes far beyond technology; it's a gift that will serve your family for a lifetime.

------

1. Kaiser Family Foundation, 2010. "Daily Media Use Among Children and Teens Up Dramatically from Five Years Ago."
2. D. Lohr, "Xbox Romance Runaways," *The Huffington Post*, 2012.
3. K. Brooks, "If I Were Queen, Kids and Screens," *The Huffington Post*, 2012.
4. A. Gorlick, "Media Multitaskers Pay Mental Price, Stanford Study Shows," Stanford Report, 2009.
5. J. Patchin, Cyberbullying Research Center, 2010 Research Study of 4,441 Youths ages 10–18, 2013.
6. American Academy of Pediatrics, "Media and Children," 2014.

sex ed for the modern parent

BY LOGAN LEVKOFF, PHD, A NATIONALLY RECOGNIZED SEXUALITY EDUCATOR
WHO DESIGNS PROGRAMS FOR MANY INDEPENDENT SCHOOLS AND
COMMUNITY ORGANIZATIONS, AND IS MOM TO A SON AND DAUGHTER

Imagine that your twelve-year-old daughter comes home and says that she and her friends saw something, as she calls it, "inappropriate," on the computer. She implies that it was sexual. What do you do? What do you tell her? What if it was your twelve-year-old son telling you instead? Would the information you give him be different?

This is only one particularly challenging conversation about sex that you will have during your child's early years and adolescence. There will be many others, on topics including sexual readiness, negotiation skills, and your own personal experiences. Whether we like it or not, pornography is a part of our culture and is more accessible than ever before. And remember, this "inappropriate" sexual image seems fairly ambiguous—it may not even be pornography. It might be an advertisement for a strip club that initiates this dialogue. It doesn't really matter what it is, but underscoring any talk you have is the knowledge that our culture's unhealthy preoccupation with sexuality manages to seep into our children's lives and there's nothing we can do about it.

That being said, you should know right off the bat that I am not a defeatist nor an alarmist. I am an opportunist. Wait, that sounds bad. What I meant to say is that as parents, we have a tremendous opportunity to shape how our children see the world and themselves in relation to their sexuality and sex in general. But I'm not about to tackle this particular situation just yet. Before I tell you how I would and how I have dealt with this issue in my own home, it's time for a wake-up call. Your kids are sexual beings. That does not (I repeat, that does not) mean that they know, care about, or are interested in doing anything sexual. But it does mean that they have an innate sexuality, one that we need to support and nurture from a very early age.

Sex Ed from the Start

I know that you may find this hard to believe: sex ed begins at birth. Or at least it should, if we are doing our jobs right. We have this strange notion that the big sex talk only counts if we are communicating about sexual intercourse. But that's not the case. So pat yourself on the back, you've probably been having more sex-related conversations than you thought. That's the good news. The bad news is, we are not doing enough of it.

As a sex educator, I am in roughly fifteen classrooms each week, with children and teens ranging in age from eight to eighteen. In each of those rooms, with every class I teach, I encourage my students to go home and talk to you. Yes, you. I beg them to share what they have learned, to ask any follow-up questions, and just to let you know that they want to talk. I would love to tell you that my "homework" is accomplished regularly, but I am very certain that is not the case.

My job as an educator is small; as parents, *our* job is huge. I won't beat around the bush here. We need to step it up. Stop worrying about whether or not you're doing it wrong. Doing it—talking to your children about sex and sexuality—is part of what you signed up for when you became a parent. Can it be embarrassing? Sure, but guess what? Your kids need you. And if you are embarrassed, you inadvertently teach your kids to be embarrassed, too. Not to mention, they will not come to *you* for information and guidance if they think that you'll just shoo them away.

Before we talk about the details, you need to have an honest conversation with yourself and any parenting partner about what it is you want for your child. Do you want her to feel good about her body? Do you want him to avoid any potentially negative outcomes from sex? Do you want her to have pleasurable experiences? Do you want him to be a virgin until he (maybe) gets married?

Are these trigger questions? Sort of, but that's the point. If you cannot identify what your values are as they relate to sex, it is going to be impossible to engage your children in a conversation about it. And you should really try to be on the same page as whoever is parenting with you. You do not want to send mixed messages.

And don't assume that you and your partner share the same views. For some reason, when the subject is sex, it often feels like all bets are off. I remember a particularly uncomfortable parenting workshop I conducted during which a couple started a fight over what they wanted for their daughter. Needless to say, I'm pretty sure the conversation continued at home. And it should. Because you need to check in with your partner before you check in with your child.

My Philosophy

There is no better sex education than one that is sex-positive, fact-based, anatomically correct, critical of language, and both challenges the sexual double standard and teaches young people to take ownership of their sexuality. This is not my philosophy for teens; it is my philosophy for everybody. I believe that honesty is always the best policy when it comes to talking about sex, no matter how young or old your children are. This is not just what I practice in the confines of my classrooms, it is what I practice in my own home with my seven-year-old son and three-year-old daughter.

Really. There is nothing that I would share with you here that I would not or have not shared in my own home. So let's break down what all of this means.

Being sex-positive. Sex should be enjoyable. Pleasure is good. Let's not lie about it and pretend that it is all bad, because I can assure you that there are plenty of sources that will happily contradict the negative message that you may want to convey. And sex can be emotionally and physically fulfilling. It should be, otherwise why on earth would we want to do it?

Let me alleviate any anxiety. Research has backed this up; talking to kids about safe sex and pleasure does not encourage them to initiate sex at earlier ages. But I can understand your hesitation. How do I explain that something feels good? How do I tell them that sex is something positive but something that they should wait to have? Like this: "Sex is something that can be—and should be—a wonderful part of your life when you are older and more mature [if that's what you want to say, of course]. It should be pleasurable to your body and make you feel good emotionally, too. Sex should be an intimate experience that people share when they care for each other deeply and can handle the responsibilities that come with it. And having sex (of any kind) when you are not being fulfilled emotionally and physically doesn't feel good, nor does it make you happier."

Let me explain this further: In my first book, *Third Base Ain't What It Used to Be,* I shared how my father taught my sister and me about sex. He always told us that sex should be this wonderful part of our lives and that he would be comfortable with whatever decision we made as long as it was something we wanted to do (with our total consent), we were protected physically and emotionally, and it wasn't at the behest of an overeager partner. You may think that his "permission" of sorts and the emphasis on the positives would make sex seem so enticing that I rushed right into it. You would be wrong. I didn't have sexual intercourse until I was eighteen years old and in a monogamous, loving relationship with someone whom I had known most of my life. When you know how good it should be, you don't want to waste it.

Being factual. In the United States we spend over one billion dollars on abstinence-until-marriage education. That type of programming fosters many problematic ideologies, including heterosexism, shame, and, believe it or not, medical inaccuracies. Yes, many young people in this country have been told lies in an effort to curb early sexual experimentation. Does it work? No. Shame and lies do not stem sexual experimentation; they just limit a young person's ability to make an informed and safe decision about sex. The perfect example of this is the purity pledge movement, programs that encourage teens to make public virginity pledges. Unfortunately, these are not effective. More than half of the young people who participated in a federal study became sexually active before marriage regardless of whether or not they had taken a pledge. However, teens who took virginity pledges scored ten points lower than those who had not taken pledges when it came to taking precautions to prevent sexually transmitted infections and pregnancy.

Beyond that, haven't we all heard of Google? Look, I am not saying that all sex education on the web is good or accurate. What I am suggesting is that it is not hard to find out that you have been lied to by a parent or a teacher. The minute our children realize that we have been untruthful is the minute we lose them. They will no longer seek out our counsel and they will tune out our words, even if they look like they have been listening intently. I have been in classrooms where a child figures out that she is the only person who was told that babies come from kissing. Not only is she embarrassed; she is angry. We owe it to our children to do better than that. And this applies to all ages. I hope that by now you've gathered that I'm not the type of person who believes in creating some elaborate ruse about how God and the stork and the magic of love join together to make a baby. Those ideas are nice, but not realistic. And if you give a five-year-old a simple definition of how a sperm and egg meet, he will file it away as just another answer to a question that his mother answered for him. How do I know this? That's my child we're talking about.

Using anatomically correct language. I am a stickler for language, especially as it relates to our bodies. I have a completely involuntary physical response to the word *vajajay*, or anything like it. In addition to being juvenile and silly, I find it distressing that we need a more palatable term for female genitals because apparently the original one isn't good enough.

And on the subject of female genitals, let's call them what they really are. The vulva. The vagina is inside a girl's body and the only part of it that you can see from the outside is the vaginal opening. At least a boy's body is more familiar to them. What boy doesn't know that his penis is called a penis? My wordsmithing may sound silly to you, but consider the implications of not knowing about your body. How can you talk to doctors about your development? How can you identify when something isn't right for your body? Are you going to say, "I have a problem down there"? Words have negative power when used incorrectly or when the correct words are avoided altogether. I bristle if my students cringe when they hear words like *vagina* and *penis*. (They don't do this at the word *vulva*, because most of them haven't learned what it means yet.) I never want people to feel like their bodies are something shameful or dirty. It's the same reason that I detest the phrase *private parts*. When you tell young people something is private, they assume it means that they can't talk about it. What if they have a question about their genitals? What if something hurts or is (god forbid) touched inappropriately? We need a universal language for anatomy—no matter what gender we are.

Being critical of language. Part of what I love about adolescence is that the words teens use to describe, well, anything, are ambiguous at best. And quite frankly, that is the brilliance of them. Consider the following terms:

Sex: What is sex? I ask my students this on a regular basis only to hear that no one shares the same definition. Most people say that sex refers to intercourse, or as I like to call it in my classes, penis in vagina (PIV) sex. But what about the other sexual behaviors—what about oral or anal sex? Do those "count" as sex? I like to think that they do, otherwise we are all fairly heterosexist. If only straight people can have sex, what does that mean for anyone who doesn't identify as heterosexual? We should teach our children that sex can be oral, anal, or vaginal. They are all intimate, personal, sexual behaviors with both positive and potentially negative outcomes. So even though my students laugh when I teach them to use the term *PIV sex*, there is a method to my madness; I don't want their definition of sex to be limited to one act. Ask your children to define sex. See if their definition matches yours. Get them to understand that sex is a range of behaviors. Of course, if you disagree with me, that's fine, too. Just keep in mind that when we talk to teens, we often tell them, "Don't have sex." We do not offer them our thoughts on other types of sex or help them with how to identify when the decision to have sex with a partner is a good one. If we want to master this whole parent–sex educator role, we need to teach our young people how to evaluate readiness, not just give them a blanket "Don't do it."

Readiness: "What do you think *readiness* means? What would make someone (in your opinion) ready to have sex?" Based on your teen's answer, you are in a great position to craft your own responses and fill in the gaps. Now if you were to ask me, I would say that key components to readiness are: self-confidence, positive body image, comfort in communication about sex/relationship issues, knowledge about outcomes and protection, commitment to seeing an OB-GYN, commitment to getting tested for sexually transmitted infections (STIs), ability to consent, and comfort buying condoms at a drugstore. But feel free to add to this list.

Hooking up: In the spirit of full disclosure, this happens to be my favorite ambiguous term. Depending upon whom you ask, where he lives, how old she is, this term has a multitude of definitions. It may mean: making out (with or without tongue), oral sex, vaginal sex, everything but sex, or the fact that you just met someone to hang out with, i.e., "we hooked up." What I love about this term is that someone may have told you everything or nothing at all. What is problematic though is that we apply our own personal definitions to this term when we hear it, leading us (and more importantly, our children) to make incorrect assumptions about the people in their lives. Think of how many girls have been called a "slut" based upon the gossip surrounding whom she "hooked up" with.

Abstinence: This has always been a loaded term, used to identify one's personal values about teen sexuality. Is abstinence the best choice for most young people? Yes, however it is not the only option nor is it responsible for us to offer only this type of education and information to our children. One of my issues with abstinence is that we need to be as critical of it as we are of other terms. What is abstinence? That depends upon whom you ask. If someone is abstinent, he doesn't engage in sex. But that depends upon one's definition of sex. See where I'm going here? Abstinence only works in preventing sexually transmitted infections and unintended pregnancies if abstinence is defined as not engaging in oral, anal, or vaginal sex. That may be your definition as parents, but many children and teens would not share that view.

Most of my students do not view oral sex as "sex." They think that it is perfectly acceptable to call yourself abstinent but experiment with oral sex behaviors. And is that really surprising? We often put so much pressure on our children to be abstinent that it isn't a surprise when they explore other behaviors as a means of expressing their sexuality while still trying to adhere to our "rules." We all know how savvy teens are.

Virginity: By now you should have picked up on the fact that I am highly critical of words, especially those that pertain to sex. I want our young people to be critical, too. I want them to learn to explore words instead of making assumptions or taking something at face value, just because. *Webster's* defines a "virgin" as "a person who has not had sexual intercourse" or "an absolutely chaste young woman." Interesting to note is that the burden of maintaining or preserving chastity falls to the woman, as if it is acceptable for boys and men to be sexually active. Moreover, without further exploration of this concept, this would suggest that anyone who isn't heterosexual (or has never had heterosexual sex) is a virgin indefinitely. I know plenty of people who would adamantly disagree with this notion. Beyond the definition, consider how virginity (or the lack thereof) is commonly referenced among young people: "She lost her virginity," or "He popped her cherry." In addition to the latter sounding absolutely disgusting, violent, and nonconsensual, having sexual intercourse in the best of relationships shouldn't be a "loss." It should be a shared experience, not a gaping hole that you can never fill again. I would much rather we ask our children to think about what this virginity means and whom it applies to, and encourage them to think in broader terms than intercourse. Virginity isn't about one particular act but a series of acts that are as much an emotional rite of passage as a physical one.

Challenging the sexual double standard. I believe that the most important part of what I do is teach young people to deconstruct the sexual double standard. This is the idea that when it comes to sex, boys and girls, men and women, are not equal. It is the system that supports (and elevates the social status of) boys who talk about, are interested in, or have sex of any kind but denigrates a girl who does the same exact thing. It is the concept that a boy is a "player," but a girl is a "slut."

Slut: The most grotesque, demeaning, and damaging word to call a female. Now I'm sure that you are wondering about the word *cunt*. Demeaning, yes. But *slut* connotes the idea that female sexuality is bad. *Cunt* doesn't do that. A word that has no male counterpart. You can brainstorm all you like, but there is no term that demeans male sexuality in such an ugly way as the word *slut* does for girls and women. Maybe you think that I am making a big deal of this. I can assure you, I'm not.

As parents, you need to understand that perpetuation of the double standard has actual physical consequences for girls and boys. It affects their present and their future. It affects the choices they make, whether they speak up and demand protection or pleasure, and impacts their ability to communicate with one another.

I know many girls who have been so belittled that they cannot speak up for their needs. They're sexually active but they don't carry condoms because they don't want to be perceived as a slut. There are real-life implications here: Not using protection. Not having healthy, balanced, and respectful relationships and partners. Not feeling comfortable speaking out and saying yes, or no. Demeaning a girl's sexuality affects everything.

Interestingly enough, our kids are not the only ones to implicitly buy into the sexual double standard. It is often perpetuated in our own homes and all done under the guise of having the best of intentions. Were you ever told that "boys were only after one thing"? Were you told or did you tell a daughter that she needs to "protect herself from those sex-crazed boys"? Have you implied to a son that playing the field is a natural and cool part of boyhood?

Supporting the old "boys will be boys" ideology is not helpful to anyone. This creates a huge wedge between genders. We are told from an early age that we cannot trust one another because boys' desire for sex always gets in the way. Girls also feel guilty about any innate (and very natural) sexual desires or feelings because most of us never bothered to tell our daughters that those feelings were okay. Internalized guilt about sexuality only ensures poor decision making, low self-esteem, and compromised sexual health.

And don't for a minute think that there are not negative outcomes for boys in this archaic system. A boy who is uninterested in sex or is uninterested in sex without emotional attachment is considered "less of a man." Sometimes he is called "gay" or a "pussy." Masculinity is not linked to sexual desire. It takes much more to be a man than wanting to have sex at all costs.

This also means that boys aren't given the freedom to be physically affectionate with their male friends (as girls often are with their girlfriends). But I have worked with many teen boys who have expressed frustration because they can't show affection with their friends (i.e., throwing an arm around his shoulders or giving him a hug) without someone questioning their sexual orientation or "manliness." What a shame it is that male friendships must be "toned down" for the sake of appearances.

Last, the sexual double standard as we present it to our children makes the assumption that they are all heterosexual. They are not. Teaching them the perils of trusting someone of another gender doesn't help them navigate the world; it makes them feel worse about it.

So to whittle it down for you: the double standard gives our children guilt and teaches them to feel shame. I would think that is counterintuitive to our job as parents. Of course, while I say that, I recently spoke on a parent panel at an all-girls school. After offering my perspective on the sexual double standard, a mother of a fifteen-year-old girl raised her hand and said, "Well, what if I *want* my daughter to feel guilty about sex? And what if her friend *is* a slut?"

I was floored by this mother's very public admission. She had no idea how damaging it could be for her daughter. Teens (of either gender) who feel guilty about their bodies, desires, and sex will be less likely to speak up for themselves—less likely to demand protection, equality, pleasure. They will be more likely to find themselves in unhealthy, even abusive relationships. Guilt has never worked as a means of stemming sexual curiosity, though it has done wonders for the psychological and psychiatric professions. People spend years in therapy trying to undo sexual guilt and shame. It affects personal choices as well as relationships.

And if you hear your child saying that someone looks or dresses *slutty*, challenge that, too. Clothes may be inappropriate for a particular environment but they don't dictate what someone does with their body. And that's what we do when we say someone looks slutty. We even say this if a girl is more voluptuous than we are. Make no mistake, we walk into dangerous territory when we teach our kids to associate what someone does sexually with their appearance. It is exactly the same as someone saying that a girl who was raped "asked for it" because she was dressed a certain way. If that statement makes you uncomfortable (as it does me), then we'd better stop our children (and ourselves) from using it.

Teaching about ownership of voice. There is nothing more important than having the ability to speak up. Having a voice (in any situation, not just sexual ones) is essential. Having a voice ensures you have the ability to consent, to speak up for your needs, to protect your feelings, and to be part of an equal, balanced, respectful relationship (even a platonic, nonromantic one). Of all the things we should be teaching our children, this is the one that has the biggest impact on their emotional and physical health.

Why is this helpful? The United States has an awful record when it comes to sexual health. We supply young people with fear-based, hypocritical, inaccurate information and expect that they will remain abstinent until adulthood. This has led to the highest rates of STIs (an estimated one out of four teens) and teenage pregnancy of any industrialized nation (yes, our teen birth rates are officially at an all-time low (31.3 births per 1,000 women), but we still have more work to do. The time to act is now. Putting our heads in the sand or adapting Nancy Reagan's old "Just Say No!" policy to sex behaviors isn't doing our young people any good. We want our children to avoid drug use indefinitely. We wouldn't (we shouldn't) say the same thing about sex.

This is also a job for parents. And I'm saying that as someone who teaches young people about sex. I cannot do your job for you. I cannot share personal stories and values and tell my students how I want them to experience the world. I can give them facts. I can teach them how to critically evaluate language, media, relationships, and the world around them. But I cannot be the storyteller. Our stories are what connect us to our children. They make us look human, not like authoritarian automatons who have never been young before. Sure, their world looks different from the one we grew up in, but that doesn't mean our perspectives are unimportant. They give context to our stories; they explain why we are concerned when they take photos with their cell phones (any of which can be misused or misrepresented) or search for sex education on the Internet. Your children should also know that we are sexual beings, too. We may be grown-ups, but we're human.

Your children need you. The proof is out there: A 2008 study found that teens who perceived having had a "good talk" about sex, contraception, and STIs with their parents in the last year were two times more likely to use condoms at last intercourse than those teens who don't talk to their parents as often.

Young people's engagements in sexual risky behaviors are fewer when parents are comfortable and responsive when they talk to their children about sex and sexuality. What you say and how you say it matters!

Challenges

I understand that there are challenges to the recommendations I am making. You may not have been given any information (or got just plain bad information) about sex from your parents. You may not be up to date on all of the issues that your teens are dealing with today. You may need resources. SIECUS (the Sexuality Information and Education Council of the United States) and Advocates for Youth are two great places to start.

No one said that this would be easy. In fact, everywhere we turn there is information that contradicts or just plain undoes the good messaging that we have tried to impart to our children. So we need to be vigilant. We need to talk with our kids about what they see and what they say. And we cannot expect that someone is going to do a better job than us. We have our child's best interests at heart. We may not have all of the facts, but our motivation is unmatched.

The elephant in the room (and the one that began this entire conversation) is pornography; it has not only changed the landscape with respect to how young people see and understand sex, but it has impacted our ability to have a meaningful dialogue about sex because it greatly skews our children's expectations. Now you may not think that your child has viewed anything pornographic, and that may be the case. However, they (and their peers) do have access to it. It is estimated that nine is the average age at which someone sees something pornographic for the first time. But don't freak out; just be aware of this. It may clue you in to the questions your children ask or the topics that their friends may be talking about.

Pornography may exist to turn people on (or off for that matter), but it is not representative of the average sexual relationship. It does not present sex as something consensual or negotiated, it does not (okay, rarely) show the use of condoms, it presents unrealistic expectations of people's bodies (pubic grooming, size of breasts and genitals, etc.), and if you expect that sex is going to look like (or be like) what you see on the screen, you'll be very disappointed in real life.

Our children need to be pornographically literate. They need to be critical of it in the same way that they should critique advertisements, television shows, and music lyrics. It may be entertainment, but it is definitely not education.

So, Back to the Beginning

If your child has opened the door to a conversation about sex and pornography by telling you about an "incident" at a friend's house, consider yourself lucky. (Yes, I know that your heart is sinking because you don't want pornography to be your child's first image of sex, but you really are lucky.) Your child came to you to tell you. If she didn't want to talk about it, she would have kept it a secret. She's quietly asking for your feedback.

This is an opportunity (remember, I'm an opportunist, sort of) to start a bigger conversation—not just one about pornography, but one about relationships and sex in general. So try posing the following questions, and before you jump to any conclusions, listen to your child. Really listen. And don't panic.

Ask her what she saw (or at least what she thought she saw).
Was this the first time you saw something like this?
How did you come to see it? Were your friends looking for
   it? Did it pop up on the screen? (You'll get some significant
   information from this question.)
How did it make you feel?

Ask her if she has ever heard of pornography. What do you
think that word means? (Then you can define it for her.
"Pornography is pictures or videos of people engaging in
sexual behaviors.")

Acknowledge that people have a variety of feelings and responses to pornography and all of them are understandable. It is
very normal to be curious about naked bodies and sex, but it is very
important to know that what you see in pornography isn't what sex is
like in real life. From there, you should be able to talk about the differences between real-life relationships and on-screen ones (including those in mainstream TV and movies, too).

If you want a script for how to talk about pornography and sex
(in general), try this: "Honey [or choose your own term of endear-
ment], pornography may show people having certain types of sex
[see that—certain types, not just one!], but that is not what sex looks
like in real relationships. Sex should be loving, consensual, and private. Couples have to talk about what they want to do, not just do it.
But I want you to know that sex can be a wonderful part of grown-
up relationships and I am so happy that you came to talk to me.
Please know that I am always here for you if you have any questions."

The truth is, I could have given you any number of potentially
complicated situations to explore: Where do babies come from?
Why do people have oral sex? When did you have sex for the first
time? Would you let me get a prescription for birth control pills?

No matter what the subject, the format of the answer is the same:

1. Listen.
2. Get a sense of why your child is asking and what he already
   knows.
3. Using this information, craft your sex-positive, honest, fact-
   based (and so on and so on) response.

Don't be afraid of your children. Don't be afraid that you are doing it wrong. Nobody said that teaching about intimate matters was easy (especially when you may not have had your own childhood model of it), but there's no better person to do this than you. Be an opportunist—use the opportunities you have to create a generation of sexually healthy, empowered, and confident young people. Because whether you are ready to think about it or not, your children will be sexually active at some point in their lives. We need to make sure that they do it smartly, safely, and respectfully.

SOURCES

Hannah Brückner and Peter Bearman, "After the Promise: The STD Consequences of Adolescent Virginity Pledges," *Journal of Adolescent Health* 36 (4) April 2008, 271–78. Doi:10.1016/.2005.01.005. PMID 15780782.

V. Guilamo-Ramos and A. Bouris, *Parent Adolescent Communication about Sex in Latino Families: A Guide for Practitioners*, The National Campaign to Prevent Teen and Unplanned Pregnancy, 2008.

J. E. Rosenbaum, "Patient Teenagers? A Comparison of the Sexual Behavior of Virginity Pledgers and Matched Nonpledgers," *Pediatrics* 123 (1) 2009, e110–120. Doi:10.1542/peds.2008-0407. PMC 2768056.

John Santelli, MD, MPH, Mary A. Ott, MD, Maureen Lyon, PhD, Jennifer Rogers, MPH, Daniel Summers, MD, and Rebecca Schleifer, JD, MPH, "Abstinence and Abstinence-only Education: A Review of U.S. Policies and Programs," *Journal of Adolescent Health* 38 (2006), 72–81.

M. Weinman, E. Small, R. S. Buzi, and P. Smith, "Risk Factors, Parental Communication, Self and Peers' Beliefs as Predictors of Condom Use Among Female Adolescents Attending Family Planning Clinics," *Child Adolescent Social Work Journal* 25 (2008), 157–70.

getting it right for kids
when parents part

BY CHRISTINA McGHEE, MSW, DIVORCE COACH, AUTHOR OF
PARENTING APART, AND MOM/BONUS MOM (AKA STEPMOM) TO FOUR

Rachel felt heartbroken. She had tried for several years to make her marriage work but at the end of the day neither she nor her husband, Ethan, was happy. Unfortunately, the one thing they were in absolute agreement about was the need to split up. Like most of the parents I encounter, Rachel was seeking my help because she desperately wanted to get it right for their two young children.

When I coach parents, one of the first questions I ask is, "If you could take one thing away from our conversation today, what would that be?" It doesn't take Rachel long to get to the point. "I want you to tell me what I can do to make sure our divorce isn't going to destroy the kids. I need to know the *perfect* way to handle this."

I can tell from the quiver in her voice that Rachel is really struggling. She's not just feeling guilty; she's worried sick about how this decision is going to change her kids' lives. "My kids are happy, healthy, and the light of my life. I can't let this screw them up."

Getting It Right: What Does It Really Take?

Hands down, one of the toughest parts of being a parent is watching your kids hurt. No matter how old your children are, it guts us to see them struggling, upset, or in pain. To make matters worse, when we become the ones responsible for their heartache, it's hard not to feel as though we're the ones that have screwed up.

Like Rachel, you may be worrying:

"Are they going to be okay?"

"Will this affect the rest of their lives?"

"How can I protect them?"

"What can I do to keep this from hurting them?"

While there's no way to make divorce a pain-free experience, it's important to realize that the choices you make from this point forward definitely will make a lasting impression on your children's lives. My question to you is . . . what kind of an impression do you want your divorce to make?

Will your children simply get through it or get through it simply? By no means am I suggesting that you can make divorce a simple process for your kids. Divorce is hard. How you handle the hard stuff is what will make or break things for your kids. Still, I firmly believe that it's possible to successfully parent children through family change and raise happy, secure, and confident kids. When parents split up, families don't end—they change.

Whether you're parenting on your own, never married, newly separated, in the throes of divorce, or struggling years down the road from your divorce, this chapter is designed to help you get clear about where you stand and how to get it right for your kids when parenting apart. Keep in mind that everything offered might not apply to where you are right now. Over the years, I've coached, spoken to, and educated thousands of parents. Although there are some expected transitions every separating couple faces, experience has taught me that no two divorces are alike. What works for one family may not work for yours.

I don't believe in cookie-cutter solutions. Rather, these stories of real-life moms and dads are designed to help you identify key issues and what it's going to take to get your kids to the other side. And, while many of the concepts I discuss are related to separation and divorce, this information isn't just for divorced parents. It is intended for any parent who shares children and parenting responsibilities with another adult living in a separate household.

Molly, Playing Supermom

Determined to counter the effects of a contentious divorce on her two boys, Molly early on adopted the philosophy of just pushing through. When she wasn't busy being Supermom and compensating for the discord between households, she filled her spare moments with catching up on work, doing household chores, and wading through a mountain of paperwork related to her pending litigation.

On an average day, Molly would run at full speed until she was completely exhausted, only to wake up at the crack of dawn and start all over again. During all of this Molly made sure to keep a tight lid on her feelings. After all, she didn't want to make things worse for her kids. While Molly was doing a lot of things right, as one day rolled into the next her resolve began to wear thin.

Emotional meltdowns became a regular occurrence after the kids came back from Dad's house. Following their "reentry," they would consistently challenge rules, fight with each other, and say hurtful things to Molly when they were angry. Although Molly understood, eventually it would get to be too much and she would end up snapping or shouting. After the explosion was over, she would immediately feel guilty and mentally beat herself up for not handling things better. Arguments with her ex and problems with the kids occupied her thoughts for hours on end, leaving her distracted at work. Every day felt tainted with divorce drama. No matter how much she gave, it never seemed like enough. She just couldn't imagine how life was ever going to feel normal again.

Sound familiar?

Without a doubt, there are many different factors that will play a part in how your kids are able to pick up the pieces, move forward, and adjust to a new normal. Unfortunately, when it comes to weighing those factors, most parents tend to overlook the one thing that packs the most punch: taking care of themselves.

Contrary to what you might think, managing divorce well isn't about sacrificing yourself at all costs to keep life humming along flawlessly for your kids. Yes, there will be times when you may need to let your immediate needs take a backseat to stabilizing life for your kids. However, don't make the mistake of cutting corners when it comes to taking care of you.

Digging deep, day in and day out with no time to recover, comes with a hefty price. As Molly discovered, not only does it wear you out physically and mentally, but over time your parenting will inevitably start to falter. You may find yourself regularly feeling numb, mentally checking out, more reactive to simple situations, frequently distracted, unable to focus, less tolerant of your kids' bad behaviors, resentful of your ex, or just plain overwhelmed. Bottom line: no matter how much you love your kids, if you completely tap yourself out you'll have a much harder time being the parent your children need you to be during this tough time.

I know, I know, right now the last thing you want to hear is someone drone on about putting the oxygen mask on yourself first. You may even be thinking, "Yeah right, whatever," or "Easy for you to say" but that's not what real life is like, at least not mine. As someone who has been a stepmom for almost twenty years and has lived in the trenches of divorce drama, believe me, I get it. I can remember times when I felt stretched so thin and was so emotionally raw that having a complete thought or taking a hot shower before midnight seemed like a total luxury. To be perfectly honest, I still have my moments; we all do.

Here's the deal: regardless of what life has thrown your way, your kids are taking their cues from you. While you may talk a good talk, *what you do will always carry more weight.* In order for your kids to know that life is going to be okay, they need to know that you're okay. So how do you get from here to there?

Taking good care of you isn't just about scheduling in a little me-time. Paying attention to how you're feeling, adjusting, and dealing with the split is critical. And here's why. No matter how educated, experienced, emotionally stable, or skilled you may be as a parent, divorce is devastating.

Like Molly, you may be doing your very best to keep your head down, hold it all together, and just get through it. Let's be honest, finding time to reflect on how you feel isn't usually a top priority. However, when strong feelings get stirred up, ignoring, avoiding, or discounting those feelings has some significant consequences. Not only will you probably be less patient and more likely to snap at your kids, but you also run the risk of your personal issues about divorce spilling over into your children's lives.

Case in point: A mom in one of my parenting classes told me that she had forbidden her children to give Dad their cell phone numbers. In her opinion, if he wanted to talk to them, he could just call the house phone. After all, she was the one paying the bill, not him. When I asked her who else the kids couldn't give their numbers to she was quick to reply, "No one, just their dad." I responded by asking, "What kind of message do you think that's sending to your kids; that everyone else can call their cells except Dad?" Mom's face suddenly tightened. Clearly this mom had not stopped to consider how her feelings about finances and child support were overriding her ability to see how the situation might feel for her kids.

Ever hear the phrase "It's hard to see the picture when you're in the frame"? When stress and emotional upset are in play, how we view the world and situations around us shifts. Our perceptions get skewed and our perspective often narrows. Much like this mom, when emotions are running high, we are all vulnerable to getting a bad case of tunnel vision. It's easy to do. Instead of seeing solutions you may hone in only on problems.

When issues come up with the other parent you might slip into the habit of reacting based on your feelings and not think about the consequences for your kids. The only way around that is to find a way to gain a different vantage point. And here lies the real problem. Getting that much-needed perspective usually involves connecting with someone who's outside of your frame. For many of us, there are major stigmas attached to asking for help or admitting we don't have all the answers. Whether it's working through your feelings about the end of your marriage, managing discipline differences with your ex, or trying to figure out how to best help your kids, seeing the whole picture when you're living it day in and day out is no easy task. Taking a step back and finding a way to look at your situation with a fresh set of eyes can make a huge difference for you and your kids.

For some it may involve confiding in a trusted friend, reading a book, or attending a parenting class. Others may really benefit from becoming involved in a support group, working with a life coach, or engaging in counseling. Do what works for you. But do find some way to step outside the frame of your life.

Taking Care of You: The Basics

While loving your kids and doing what you can to smooth out the rough road of divorce is healthy, making them the focus of your every waking moment is not. To avoid burnout, do your best to regularly make time for things that you want to do. If the idea of having time for you seems overwhelming or ridiculously impossible, start small.

BLOCK IT OUT

Every day make a point to block out at least twenty minutes in your schedule to take a break from being Mom or Dad. Be sure to write it on your calendar, just like any other important appointment. Consider having coffee with a friend, taking a run in the park, watching a show that makes you laugh, or just stepping away from your desk at lunch to sit outside and read a good book. Whatever you do, be sure it is something that reenergizes and renews you.

SHARE AND PAIR

If taking that first step seems daunting, ask for help. Enlist the support of a trusted friend, family member, community group, or professional coach. Sharing your goals with another person not only allows you to gain insight on what's holding you back, but it also makes you accountable. To keep your motivation from waning, consider either pairing a needed self-care activity with something you routinely do or hooking it to a more enjoyable activity.

USE KID-FREE TIME WISELY

Not having your kids with you when you are divorced can be a huge adjustment, especially in the beginning. It can feel strange, upsetting, or incredibly uncomfortable. Avoid giving in to the angst or discomfort by cutting yourself some slack and using kid-free time to recharge. Instead of waiting for the weekend or overnight emptiness to hit, plan ahead. A couple of days before the kids are scheduled to be with the other parent, spend ten or fifteen minutes making a list of things you'd normally consider self-indulgent or haven't had time to do. Not sure where to start? Ask yourself.

When's the last time I got so caught up in enjoying myself that I forgot about the time? What would it take to do that again?

What's an activity or hobby I used to enjoy that I might want to pick up again?

Is there something I've been putting off doing because I didn't have time?

Is there someone I enjoying spending time with who leaves me feeling energized?

Cecelia and Marvin, Accepting That Change Means Change

Marvin and Cecelia definitely had their share of ups and downs. What started off as a passionate romance quickly became overshadowed by daily clashes that ranged from incessant bickering to all-out brawls. Unfortunately, ten years and three kids later, things had gone from bad to worse.

Not surprisingly, their children were struggling terribly. Meltdowns and temper tantrums had become daily occurrences. The two oldest went from doing well in school to barely getting by. Their youngest daughter became increasingly anxious and clingy. After a particularly gruesome fight, Marvin and Cecelia came to the agreement that things had to change, and they jointly filed for divorce.

Despite their differences both Marvin and Cecelia agreed they needed to put their parenting relationship before any personal feelings they had about each other or the divorce. Both readily acknowledged that even though they didn't make a good couple, there was no reason they shouldn't parent their three daughters together. To their credit, they established a flexible parenting schedule and worked at maintaining a high level of togetherness for the kids. When one of the girls had an event, Marvin and Cecelia could usually be found sitting side by side. But it didn't stop there. Along with daily phone conversations, they also frequently scheduled joint family outings, trips to the zoo, and dinner out, as well as hosting birthday parties together. On average, the kids probably saw their parents together after the divorce just as much as they had when they were married. An ideal situation, right? Actually, no.

Turns out that anytime Cecelia and Marvin were together, an argument was not far behind. Even though they were divorced, poor communication, ongoing resentments, past expectations, and unresolved hurts were still very much a part of their relationship. Family events became tainted with tit-for-tat arguments. Expectations from the marriage spilled over into their coparenting relationship. If Cecelia's car was acting up or she had a DIY repair, she'd phone Marvin and ask him to fix it. Sometimes he didn't mind. Other times he'd say yes only to throw it back in Cecelia's face the next time they argued. Likewise, when Marvin got in a bind at work, he'd expect Cecelia to change her plans and care for the kids. Sometimes she was fine with the arrangement. Other times she would rant in front of the kids about how Marvin was shirking his responsibility as a father. End result: While they had divorced to end the fighting, they continued to act like a married couple in all the worst ways. As you can imagine, nothing got better for the kids.

It's been said that "when you always do what you've always done, you'll always get what you always got." While the circumstances of your divorce may be very different from Marvin and Cecelia's, the dynamics of "always doing what you've always done," play out in lots of different ways when you split up.

You and your ex have a history together. That history covers a lot of territory. As a married couple you began life together with shared hopes and dreams. Throughout your relationship you developed ways of talking to each other, interacting, making decisions, parenting your kids, handling differences, and managing life. Some areas of your relationship worked and others didn't. It's important to evaluate where you need to make shifts away from the history you had as a couple and how you will redefine your relationship as parents. Let's talk about what it takes to move forward.

Remember in your marriage vows when you said something like, "'til death do us part"? Sorry to be the bearer of bad news, but when you have kids, that part of your vows has some serious staying power. Although you're now living separate lives, your connection as parents remains a lifetime gig. Striking a balance between honoring your need for independence while supporting your children's ongoing need for connection is essential. A central component to achieving that balance involves shifting your focus from what you don't have in common to what you do—your kids.

Redefining your relationship takes more than just living apart. To illustrate, let's take another look at Marvin and Cecelia. To help them along, I encouraged them to view themselves as business partners with a lifetime investment in raising successful, happy kids. To sidestep arguments, when they talked with each other they both worked at keeping conversations focused on issues involving the kids. Although it wasn't always easy, they also did their best to steer clear of past issues and old arguments.

Along with their new focus, Marvin and Cecelia found that timing and location played a big part in how they managed their new partnership. Most of their past parenting chats typically took place while they were exchanging the kids. While it seemed like an ideal time to discuss schedules or upcoming events, emotions were usually running high for both parents and kids. Inevitably an offhanded comment struck a nerve, tempers flared, and the kids would end up having a ringside seat to another nasty spat.

Moving forward, Marvin and Cecelia decided to stop having conversations about their kids during pickups and drop-offs. Instead they would either hand each other a quick note about "need to know" items (i.e., an English test on Tuesday) or arrange a time during the week when the kids were out of earshot to have a structured discussion. To avoid getting off topic, before picking up the phone, they both made a habit of jotting down what they needed to talk about (agenda items). When bigger issues cropped up, rather than hashing things out around Cecelia's kitchen table, Marvin and Cecelia would arrange to meet at a local coffee shop. Having public chats in a neutral place not only eased tensions but also helped them stay better behaved.

Over time, Marvin and Cecelia also made adjustments to their relationship in other areas. Instead of calling Marvin every time her car needed an oil change, Cecelia found a reliable mechanic. Likewise, Marvin made an effort to minimize schedule changes when things came up at work. Now Marvin made sure to ask if Cecelia wanted the option of having the kids, rather than assuming she would drop her plans. If there was a scheduling conflict, Marvin would contact a dependable sitter. Although they still occasionally hit a bump in the road, shifting their expectations and setting new boundaries helped keep their resentments at bay. Eventually the children's behaviors started to level out, making transitions between households less stressful and joint occasions more enjoyable.

Although Marvin and Cecelia eventually got to a better place, by no means was it smooth sailing. In the beginning there were lots of times when they both totally dropped the ball and reverted to their old ways. The key was that they stayed committed and pushed through. Remember, breaking free of past issues, developing new skills, and adjusting expectations don't happen overnight. These things take intention and effort along with a healthy dose of commitment and patience, and lots of deep breaths.

To develop a successful coparenting relationship

Stay focused on what matters most—your kids.

Communicate with each other in a respectful manner.

Gain emotional distance from old hurts and past issues.

Learn to compromise.

Redefine your roles and gain new skills.

Find common ground.

Minimize opportunities for conflict.

Okay, okay, I know what you're thinking: "If I could get along with my ex, I'd still be married." For some parents the idea of having a workable relationship with their former spouse seems about as easy as nailing jelly to the wall. When I talk about developing a business-like relationship, I almost always get a little pushback from parents. It goes something like this: "Okay, Christina, that all sounds great when you have a reasonable or willing ex. What about an ex who has a 'my way or the highway' attitude? What do you do then?" Good question.

Phil and Mary, Stepping Back from the Drama

Phil felt completely defeated. Even though he had been divorced for more than two years, things with his bullying ex, Mary, never seemed to let up. Despite his best efforts to get along, Mary was constantly doing things to undermine his relationship with their seven-year-old son, Andrew. If Phil called the house to talk to Andrew, Mary would find some reason to cut the conversation short. Yet, whenever Andrew was with Phil, Mary gave Andrew a cell phone so he could call her as much as he wanted. If Andrew was having a good time and didn't call Mom, Mary would make a point to phone him right before bedtime to make sure he wasn't homesick or missing her too much. Any guesses as to how easy this made bedtime at Phil's house?

Mary also never hesitated to draw Andrew into financial issues. When Andrew asked to do something like go out to eat or buy a new toy, Mary would always tell him she wished she could say yes but Daddy never gave Mommy enough money.

Typically, communication between the households was just as one-sided. Mary rarely included or informed Phil about important parenting decisions. More often than not, bits of news would filter to Phil through random things Andrew said. If Phil tried to talk to Mary about it, she would either hang up or fly into a rage. Not surprisingly, most of these exchanges were followed by a barrage of angry e-mails. First, Mary would send a nasty note that dredged up lots of past issues. Phil would then labor over a lengthy well-worded response that countered her accusations and defended his position. No matter how logical or rational his points, nothing ever changed. Most of the time, Phil would give up and let Mary have her way just to keep things from getting worse for Andrew. When Mary threatened to take Phil back to court for the umpteenth time, he knew things had to change.

In taking a look at his ongoing relationship with Andrew's mom, Phil quickly launched into a long list of "if only's." If only Mary would quit fighting . . . if only Mary would be reasonable . . . if only Mary could move on and stop being angry. You get the idea. Like lots of conflict-averse parents, Phil had gotten caught in the trap of seeing himself as helpless against Mary's bullying behavior. And who could blame him?

What Phil didn't understand was that as long as he focused on what Mary did or didn't do, all of his actions were simply reactions. In reality, Phil would never be able to change or control Mary. If Mary wanted to be nasty, there wasn't one thing Phil could do about it. The only area he did have control over was his attitude and how he *reacted* to Mary. Understanding that allowed Phil to turn over a new leaf.

Instead of immediately responding to Mary's outbursts and defending his position, Phil began approaching his interactions with calm confidence. When Mary sent a cutting e-mail that dredged up past issues, Phil resisted the temptation to reply right away. Rather than be at Mary's beck and call, he gave himself time to cool off and think things through. If a response was necessary, Phil worked on keeping it short and focused on Andrew.

When Phil needed to talk with Mary directly, he would think through the conversation and how he would handle things if Mary lost her cool. Not only did this help him stay on task, it also allowed him to stay calm, which took some of the wind out of Mary's sails when she got riled up. While it wasn't always easy to emotionally detach from every interaction they had, over time Phil got better at stepping back from the drama. Phil's new focus also helped him do a better job of addressing Andrew's needs when conflicts cropped up. Although Phil's situation was far from ideal, as he continued to stay consistent, Mary's antics became less frequent.

Without a doubt, dealing with a contentious ex feels unfair and one-sided. Resisting the temptation to give what you get is harder than hard. Yet consider this: if you and your ex were in a boat on the ocean and one of the kids fell overboard, what would you do? Jump in and save him, or sit in the boat fighting with your ex over who was the best swimmer?

Jumping in requires taking the higher ground instead of fighting the good fight. To be clear, jumping in doesn't mean rolling over. In order to deal with a difficult ex, you need to have good boundaries. When issues come up, sort out what's worth standing your ground for and what's not. Ask yourself, What difference will this make one month from now? How about six months from now?

> ## When coparenting with a difficult ex
> Manage your reactions.
> Stay consistent with your communication.
> Avoid giving back what you get.
> Shield children from conflict.
> Limit the energy you give to divorce drama.

If you have an ex who is nice one day and nasty the next, remain consistent in your communication. That means no matter how your ex behaves, you continue to use positive coparenting strategies. Staying consistent also helps you limit the amount of energy you give to the conflict.

It's also important to realize where you start may not be where you end. Believe it or not, once the dust settles, things do get better for most couples. Whether you think your ex will come around eventually or not, do your best to engage in good coparenting etiquette. Regardless of how the other parent acts, whenever possible share information, include them in important decisions, and support their role in your children's lives. While you may not feel like you owe it to your ex, you do owe it to your kids.

---

toughLOVE TIPS
Eleven Key Points for Postdivorce Parenting

---

1. DON'T EXPECT YOUR EX TO BE WHERE YOU ARE. Initially Eddy was very optimistic about his coparenting relationship with his soon-to-be ex, Kristen. In contrast to most of the parents I encounter, Eddy initially talked about Kristen in glowing terms. Although devastated when she learned Eddy was having an affair, Kristen went above and beyond to keep things amiable for their ten-year-old son, Cameron.

During their lengthy separation, Eddy and Kristen worked cooperatively as parents and approached legal matters in the same way. Instead of hashing things out in court they jointly decided to work with a local mediator. In talking with Eddy, it was clear he was ready to move on with his life and develop a relationship between his new girlfriend and Cameron. Since he and Kristen were getting along so well, he felt certain she was ready to forge ahead too. Much to Eddy's surprise, however, when it came time to start meeting with a mediator, Kristen slammed on the brakes and everything came to a screeching halt. In contrast to Eddy's all-systems-go attitude, Kristen painted a much different picture.

Even though Kristen had initially taken the high road, she had been silently struggling with the reality that her marriage was ending. Contrary to Eddy's perspective, she felt it was really unfair that Eddy was charging ahead with his new, improved life. She resented having to pretend everything was okay when clearly it wasn't. How dare Eddy even think about Cameron spending time with him and his girlfriend? Cameron wasn't ready for that. Kristen felt angry, betrayed, and alone. In her mind, things were moving way too fast.

No matter which side of the fence you're on, how you and your ex each are coming to terms with the divorce plays a big part in how you move forward. While you all may be going through the process of divorce at the same time, you, your ex, and your children will likely have different perceptions and feelings about it. Along with keeping tabs on how you are handling the process, be sure you take stock of how your ex is managing. When adult feelings are left unattended, it can definitely muddy the waters and skew perspectives on lots of different levels.

For example, Eddy could easily make the mistake of thinking that Kristen is dragging her feet out of jealousy or to punish him. In turn, Kristen may see Eddy as irresponsible and thinking only of himself. Those individual perceptions also have the potential to impact each parent's position about Cameron. Eddy may need to realize that just because he's ready to move on doesn't necessarily mean Cameron is ready to jump on board. On the flip side, just because Kristen is having trouble accepting the divorce doesn't mean Cameron is too. Make sure you're keeping your feelings and issues separate from your kids' needs.

2. STEP AWAY FROM THE BLAME GAME. When you've lost that loving feeling it's hard not to point the finger and focus on all the ways your ex has done you wrong. Although you may feel quite justified in your perceptions of your ex's shortcomings, hanging on to old hurts will only undermine your ability to parent your kids successfully. When talking to your kids about divorce, resist the temptation to place blame squarely on the other parent's shoulders. Taking a look at your part in things not working out is essential. Placing blame also tends to make things even more confusing for children. They may be more likely to take sides, feel emotionally responsible for a parent, get caught in the middle, or be drawn into adult issues.

It's important for kids to understand that two good people don't always make a good couple. In order to redefine your relationship as parents, it's essential that you believe that too. While your ex may have been a lousy spouse, it doesn't mean he or she can't be an awesome parent. Whatever it takes, honor your children's right to have a healthy and loving relationship with both of their parents.

3. DON'T REACT—RESPOND. While you're absolutely certain your ex put a little 'tude into the e-mail or text she just sent, do your best to take a step back from knee-jerk reactions. Let's say Heather shoots a quick text to Rick saying, "Hey, could you please be on time when you drop the kids off this Sunday."

Suppose Rick's MO is that he is always late. His lack of timeliness was a constant source of strain in their marriage. Rick's first impulse is to take Heather's comment as a dig. To top it off, right before her text came through, Rick's boss jumped on his case about a report he should have had done an hour ago. As Rick reads Heather's text, he feels his blood begin to boil. While he's tempted to hit Reply and let Heather know what she can do with her text, he decides to get up from his desk, grab a cup of coffee, and take a few minutes to regroup. Rather than send a nasty jab, Rick replies, "Sure, no problem." Heather quickly returns with, "Thanks! Surprising the boys with tickets to a baseball game and want to make sure I have enough time to get them seated before it starts."

I realize that every e-mail or text exchange you have with your ex may not result in a happy ending. In the Rick/Heather scenario, Heather's comment could have had snarky intent written all over it, making Rick's initial irritation completely justifiable. That's not really the point. Regardless of Heather's intent, Rick took control of the situation by making a conscious effort to respond instead of react.

When your ex is looking to stir the pot by sending a nasty e-mail, letter, or text, unless it's an emergency, remember you don't have to respond immediately. Instead, give yourself time to think things through. It can also help to ask yourself, Is this something I need to respond to? How will my response hurt or help the situation? Will it make things better or worse for my kids?

4. SUPPORT A TWO-HOME CONCEPT. Although your marriage relationship has ended, your roles as Mom and Dad last a lifetime. Children need to be reassured that the love you have for them will endure. However, telling children is not enough. You also need to back up your words by supporting the idea that both parents will be an ongoing and permanent presence in their lives. The best to way to do that is by using a two-home concept.

Regardless of how time or parenting responsibilities are shared, children need to feel a sense of connection and belonging with each parent. Avoid using terms like *visiting* or *visitation* when referring to time with a parent. Sometimes parents think making a distinction between households offers kids a sense of security. Actually, it often has the opposite effect. When one household gets cast as their "real" home and the other as a place kids "visit," it suggests that parents no longer have equal value in children's lives.

Implementing a two-home concept means no matter how time is spent between Mom and Dad, children feel a part of a family in each household. So instead of using words like *visitation* or *visiting*, you talk about time with Mom and time with Dad. Rather than the children having one home, you support children having a home with Mom and a home with Dad.

Creating a home isn't about how many hours kids clock in under your roof; it's about connection. Your family hasn't dissolved, it has changed. Kids need to be reassured that their family will go on. Remember, while your relationship has changed, your children's needs have not. Support your kids in maintaining a strong sense of family by talking about each household as a home.

To help your children feel connected to both homes:

Make sure kids have a special space in each home where they can keep their things.

Provide two sets of everyday items such as clothes, personal items, toys, etc., in each home.

Maintain a sense of family. Balance fun with everyday activities like eating dinner together, doing homework, and helping out around the house.

Create stability for kids by establishing predictable routines and structure in your home.

Speak positively about the other parent's household and allow children to feel proud of both homes.

5. FORGET FAIR. When developing a parenting schedule and figuring out how to share responsibilities, my advice is to forget fair. Crafting your children's future isn't about who is the better parent or making things equal, it's about what's best for your kids. In planning for the future, consider what life was like for your children before you separated. Then ask yourself, what about your child's life needs to stay the same and what needs to change? For example, maybe every Thursday Mom takes Trent to swim meets. Suppose Dad is the one who does homework with Becca every afternoon. Whenever possible, work together to maintain that level of sameness for your kids.

If you don't have a cooperative ex, focus on what you can do to minimize disruptions to your children's lives. Sometimes that may mean compromising or giving ground when you don't feel like your ex deserves it. Again, although it may not feel fair, short-term sacrifice can yield long-term gain for your kids.

6. MAKE LIFE IN YOUR HOME PREDICTABLE. Do your best to help your children manage everyday transitions and changes by making sure they know what to expect when they are with you. Be clear about your rules and expectations while providing them with love and consistent limits. You can also pave the way for smoother transitions for younger children by making color-coded calendars to note where they will be when (i.e., blue days mean kids are with Dad, yellow days they are with Mom). Children also may feel particularly anxious about where they will be for holidays, birthdays, and other special events. Make an effort to think out plans and arrangements ahead of time so you can include those on calendars as well.

For teens and tweens, instead of hanging a calendar in your home, think about creating an online or shared calendar that they can access on the go. Keep in mind that when your kids get older, arrangements may need to be more flexible.

7. FIND MIDDLE GROUND. You and your children's other parent may have decidedly different approaches to parenting. Instead of getting into a push-pull over whose approach is the best, put energy into identifying where you agree.

To get started, think about what values you share as parents. Do you both want the kids to be successful in school? How will you engage your children in activities that promote self-confidence? Is it important for them to be respectful, to have a strong sense of family?

Once you have identified areas of common ground, then begin to work out how each of you can support those goals.

8. AGREE TO DISAGREE. When you were married, chances are you and your ex didn't see eye to eye on every single parenting issue. Although you may not have been happy with your ex's "it's okay to have doughnuts for breakfast" policy, you probably tolerated it. Now that you're parenting apart, things you used to put up with often become a breeding ground for some serious clashes.

Cooperative parenting doesn't mean you have to do everything exactly alike. Rather, good coparents learn early on to find common ground on big-ticket items (i.e., education, safety, respect, etc.) and agree to disagree on less critical day-to-day parenting issues (bedtime, chores, general household rules).

While it's great when parents can mirror a similar structure and identify shared values, don't overlook the fact that your kids are adaptable. They can deal with differences if they know what to expect. Just think about it. How do your children manage in school? Does every teacher have the same rules or teach the same way? Probably not. However, the school does have guidelines, expectations, and rules that every teacher supports. In the same way, do your best to get on the same page about important parenting issues while leaving room for kids to benefit from your individual differences.

9. KEEP CHILDREN INFORMED. With divorce comes lots of change. In order for kids to manage those changes successfully, they need to be prepared. An important part of setting the stage involves keeping them informed. While talking to your kids about divorce seems like an obvious thing to do, lots of parents fall into the trap of saying very little or nothing at all. Sometimes it's because they're worried about saying the wrong thing or maybe they don't know what to say. Others may fret over the best time to break the news, while another group may put it off because they don't want to rock the boat or make things worse.

The problem with saying very little or nothing at all is that it puts kids in a position of having to figure things out on their own. When this happens, kids may misinterpret situations or put their own spin on things. Case in point: I worked with a mom who had been separated and divorced for almost two years. At the outset she and her husband jointly told the kids that they had decided to separate. Initially it was tough, but after several months, everyone seemed to settle into the idea that life had changed. The kids seemed happy, were doing well in school, and transitions between homes felt seamless. According to Mom, the kids never even talked about the separation. From her perspective they had adjusted remarkably well. During this time, she and her husband decided not to reconcile and moved forward with the divorce. The only problem was they never bothered to tell the kids. In their minds, the kids were fine. Nobody was talking about it; why stir things up?

Several months later, Mom got a major reality check when visiting her son's school. In his classroom, she noticed a project he had done about what made him the same as or different from other children in his class. At the top of her son's project he had written, "My parents aren't divorced." This mom felt both stunned and incredibly guilty. It never occurred to her that her son might still think of his parents as married.

As this mom learned the hard way, it's important to keep kids in the loop. Even when your children seem fine, there still may be questions, concerns, or inaccurate perceptions brewing under the surface. Do your best to keep the lines of communication open.

10. STAY IN CHARGE OF COMMUNICATION. While chatting with your ex may not be at the top of your favorite-things-to-do list, avoid putting children in charge of communicating details to the other parent. Even though it seems fairly harmless (i.e., "Tell Dad you need to be home early on Sunday" or "Remind Mom that you need to take your medicine after supper"), kids shouldn't be responsible for managing your relationship. Although communication can be challenging after a split, make a commitment to share information with the other parent—even if it's not reciprocated.

Unsure where to draw the line on sharing? Ask yourself, if you were still married to your ex, how would you handle the situation?

11. SPEAK POSITIVELY OF THE OTHER PARENT. Although you may have lost that loving feeling for each other, don't forget that a significant part of your children's self-esteem stems from Mom and Dad. When you judge, criticize, or make cutting remarks about the other parent, it's no different than directly criticizing your child.

Even when you keep bad-mouthing in check, remember that kids pick up on subtle overtones too. For example, when Jessica makes a comment about how pretty Mom is and Dad ignores that comment, you can bet Jessica notices. If José makes a big mess in the kitchen and Mom's response is "You're just like your dad; he never cleaned up after himself either," it sticks. Over time, those negative comparisons and comments can take a toll on your children's self-worth.

If warm fuzzies for your ex aren't pouring in, consider shifting your perspective. A dad once told me he didn't ever have trouble saying something positive about his ex. When he was talking to his kids, he just reminded himself he wasn't speaking about his ex, he was talking about his children's mother.

Having trouble finding something good to say? Try seeing what your kids see and make supportive comments based on how your children view the other parent. For example, if Noah comes home talking about how awesome it was that Dad hit a home run at baseball practice, you could say something like "You're really proud of Dad. Sounds like having him for your coach is pretty cool."

Throughout this chapter, we've covered a lot of ground and yet in many ways we've only scratched the surface. While the concepts that have been offered provide a solid framework for parenting after you part, it is by no means the end of the story. Whether you are recently separated, newly divorced, or years down the road, one thing is for certain: life will continue to change for you and your kids. And as life changes, how you parent will need to change along with it.

In order to stay ahead of the curve, stay connected to resources and supports that will help you go the distance. Keep in mind, there may be times when you feel stuck, get caught off guard by your kid's reactions to a new change, or have an unexpected clash with your ex. In those moments you may be faced with making a split-second decision or struggling to rein in a gut reaction. You may make mistakes, regret something you said, or wish you had handled things differently. No parent gets it right every time. What's important is that you learn from those experiences and stay committed to making things better for your kids.

Remember, parenting children through divorce is a marathon, not a sprint. Getting it right takes dedication, patience, persistence, and the ability to look beyond the immediate moment. While I realize all this is easier said than done, take a moment to ask yourself: Years from now when my children look back on this time, what will I have done to make them proud of how I handled the divorce?

it takes a vital village to raise great kids—and great parents

BY JANET TAYLOR, MD, COMMUNITY PSYCHIATRIST, WHOSE COLUMN, "ASK DR. JANET," APPEARS MONTHLY IN *FAMILY CIRCLE,* AND MOTHER OF FOUR

It may take a village to raise a child, but it takes a community to keep the parents sane.

—SOBONFU SOMÉ

I remember feeling so isolated when my children were young because I didn't live near my family. In fact, one of my emergency contacts on my daughter's school forms was my mother—who lived in another country! After we moved from Wisconsin to Vancouver, Canada, it occurred to me that I had to take an active role in settling in. In other words, I couldn't wait for my new neighbors to find me. I reached out to friends in faraway places asking for any connections or suggestions that would help me tap into my new home. At community centers, on my walks, or in exercise class, I would approach strangers who had seemingly happy, well-adjusted kids and ask about preschools, summer camps, and other good programs for kids. Venturing out of my comfort zone was painful at times and felt risky, but I had no choice.

The good news is that it is in so many ways easier than ever to find and connect with a supportive community. I wish I'd had all the Internet tools available now when I was so far from home. I know I would have Skyped my mom constantly and tapped into all manner of social media to find both real and virtual communities of moms and dads going through the same things I was.

Few of us would disagree that being a parent is one of life's biggest blessings, and at the same time an even bigger challenge. No matter our circumstances, studies show we want the same things for our kids. Whether married, single, cohabitating, same-sex, fostering, even incarcerated, parents tend to have the same long-term goals for their kids. We want to raise thriving, happy, motivated, kind children. Yet this single purpose requires multiple skills—and more resources than many realize.

The idea that it takes both a village and a community to raise children highlights a fact we rarely talk about. Not only do parents need help with parenting, but also parents sometimes need to be parented themselves. How many times, during feverish nights or teen tantrums, have we just wished our own moms or dads could be there?

We cannot underestimate the value of family and friends in helping raise our children. Family and friends serve as confidants for parents, but also as role models for children. Aunts, uncles, and grandparents give parents much-needed breaks, and they provide advice and support, and help teach kids about family history and traditions. They model cultural and moral values. That is, if you're lucky.

People with supportive family and friends may be surprised at how many parents don't have such a ready source of emotional support or good advice, and need support from other sources. Access to an online community with experts and the virtual support of like-minded parents can help fill that gap, as, of course, can a real-world community of friends and neighbors. We all need a vital village of family, friends, and community, both real and virtual, to support us throughout the challenges—and share with us in the many joys—we encounter as parents.

What Is a Family Today?

Family life has transformed since TV's *Ozzie and Harriet* view of the 1950s ideal family. Families have grown smaller, less stable, and more diverse. Today, 66 percent of all married women with children—and an even higher proportion of single mothers—are part of the workforce, compared to just 16 percent in 1950. Half of all marriages end in divorce—three times the rate in 1950. Three in ten children are born to unmarried parents. In 2012, the US Census found that 66 percent of households were family (at least two members are related by birth) households, down from 81 percent in 1970. The share of households that were married couples with children under eighteen decreased from 40 percent to 20 percent. During the same time period from 1970 to 2012, the proportion of one-person households increased from 17 percent to 27 percent.

The family has been reconstituted: dual earners, single parents, blended families, same-sex parents, and empty nesters. The changing face of the working family has created a so-called crisis in caregiving. Many parents have found it increasingly difficult to balance the demands of work and family life. Not to mention that working parents not only care for children, but for aging parents as well. Family-values crusaders blame all sorts of society's ills, from crime to drug abuse to academic failure, on career moms, unwed parents, absentee dads, and gay parents.

But the truth is that, in many respects, the family is stronger than it was in that '50s "ideal." Ninety percent of Americans still choose to marry and raise families. Parents who get divorced are remarrying and continuing to raise families. Parents are making greater emotional and economic investments in their children than in the past thanks to increasing financial resources from two working parents and fewer numbers of children in each family. Fathers are more active in child rearing, and the rise of work-at-home options and the virtual office have made it easier for moms and dads to work from home. In addition, increasing life expectancies mean couples are more likely to grow old together and families are more likely to experience the benefits of living grandparents.

Kevin, a father of four who works two jobs, is an example of how modern parenting and families may well result in the need for the support of the experts and colleagues in a vital village. "I'm thrilled my kids' extended family includes eight living grandparents. On the one hand, we have a lot of love and support around us, but on the other hand my kids are seeing living examples of failed marriages and disrupted families. I worry about that." Not to mention the fact that Kevin's family will most likely have to adapt to the added responsibility of caregiving for at least a few members of their extended family in the near future.

What Is a Community Today?

Throughout history, communities were woven into the fabric of our children's personal character and learning experience. In Nigeria's Ibo culture, for example, children were called *nwa ora*, meaning "children of the community."

In colonial America, families accepted how local authorities and neighbors intervened in family life. For example, selectmen of New England oversaw ten or twelve families at a time, ensuring that fathers carried out their responsibilities as head of a household. If parents were deemed "unfit," the selectmen could remove children from a family.

On slave plantations until 1860, networks of extended kin became functioning parents because slave spouses often resided on separate plantations. It was not unusual for grandparents, aunts, uncles, and cousins to coparent or even informally adopt those orphaned children.

Fast-forward to post–World War II when the 1940s and '50s spawned single-family track homes in the booming suburbs. Neighborhoods became the community. "I remember if I was caught doing something I wasn't supposed to be doing, Mrs. Mannara, who lived at the end of our street, got the bad news back to my mom before I even got home," says Don, a 1950s inner-city kid who recalls how normal it was for kids to walk to school through the neighborhoods, picking up friends along the way and stopping on the way back home for playtime and snacks.

Indeed, the communities so crucial to supporting and influencing families throughout history are changing. Today's school kids are picked up, dropped off, monitored, or escorted by adults every step of the way. Susan, a 1960s suburban kid, recalls her childhood: "I spent a lot of time riding my bike and bouncing from house to house. My parents knew I was 'around somewhere' with my cousins or my friends." Susan remembers that playtime was organic, compared with today's more scheduled approach to playdates. "These days, playdates keep both kids and parents connected. Sure, it's more structured than in the 'old days,' but it is my opportunity to share experiences with other parents and it gives my kids a better chance to interact with other adults outside our family," says Susan. Still, Susan admits that most often she finds herself in a hurry—picking up, dropping off, and squeezing in as many errands as she can in between. She ends up getting most of her peer socialization when checking into her online communities after the kids have gone to sleep.

Meanwhile, economic swings have witnessed businesses contracting and closing, scattering job-seeking workers everywhere.

The global workforce, a concept that has taken hold in less than a generation, relocates families efficiently and expeditiously. "My husband and I didn't even have to think twice about saying yes to a job opportunity with a Fortune 500 company in Singapore," says Ruth, a Kenyan-born, American-schooled mother of two. She couldn't imagine forgoing the opportunity to expose her children to one of the world's most important emerging cultures. So her family of four, having once before said good-bye to family, schools, and friends in Kenya to come to the United States, uprooted themselves a second time for a move to Asia.

Where Is Community Today?

Some of our traditional centers of community life, such as schools and churches, are shrinking, consolidating, and in many cases struggling for relevance among remaining members. "For our family, I strongly believe our church community is central to raising morally balanced children," says Karin, now a stay-at-home mom who interrupted her career to raise a family of four and who is involved with the Catholic Church in everything from policy making to youth group education. "I have to say, the Church is undergoing such dramatic changes that working through issues and processes is a difficult and frustrating job. I sometimes feel very isolated in my beliefs and views."

We live in a time when parents and kids are looking for peaceful environments in which to thrive, worship, grow, and learn. Geoffrey Canada, the founder and CEO of the Harlem Children's Zone, encourages more than 8,000 children a year to excel academically while navigating the unforgiving streets in New York City. Geoffrey knows that "a child's education can't be separated from where they live." Literally drawing a line around community, he realizes that if our kids are safer, better educated, and motivated to achieve, the community will thrive, and will raise good citizens who in turn will give back to the community.

Allison, a working mother of two in Washington, DC, knows how incredibly fortunate she is in terms of her kids' school. They go to a public primary school that is a model of excellence because it is a *true* neighborhood school. Everyone in the neighborhood has a vested interest in the students at this elementary school and in their performance.

Holly Searl, principal, explains why the school has such a strong community focus. "We're small: 150 students with only one class in each grade level. Most of the kids walk, bike, or scooter to school with an adult and we have open playground early each morning where parents, both moms and dads, get to know each other well. You can't be anonymous at our school—and I tell parents that when they apply. Everyone is involved in everything from PTA to school fund-raisers. Even community members who don't have kids at our school get involved, for example, with our fund-raising auction. We reach out to the community through my blog, through the community newspaper, and I even have two members of the community on my advisory board. It's kind of like Mayberry; everyone is going to be in everyone's business," she says.

Allison calls the school her lifesaver. "At any one time I have at least eight backup parents I can call on if I need someone to watch my sons at the last minute. The school has fostered this strong parenting network that gives all of us incredible peace of mind." According to Holly, "The entire neighborhood benefits from our strong school model, not only in maintaining home values, but also in making the community like a small village where everyone watches out for everyone."

We all know we need to create more schools like the one Allison's kids attend, but it's been an uphill battle in recent decades as schools compete for limited resources—both financial and human—

with other institutions in the community, including other schools. One result of that has been smaller schools consolidating with larger ones, encompassing many more neighborhoods.

Where else can we find community?

What Does It Mean to Be a Village?

A village is usually a rural or small community of people. Villages were often named for an environmental feature: Left Hand Bay, Alaska, or Weed Patch, California; or for an aspect of functionality: Boring, Maryland, and Truth or Consequences, New Mexico. Urban areas can have a "village mentality" because many people live together in close proximity sharing a defined space, as in Greenwich Village, New York, or The Villages, Florida. The focal point or core of the village comes from its history and its character. What began in the twentieth century as a bohemian artist community, Greenwich Village today is upscale and fashionable, but still "The Village" in a true sense of the word. The heart and soul of a village are its residents and the spirit of what they represent.

The concept of a village hasn't really changed through history, although the context surely has. Today's village is better understood in this modern, transient world we've been discussing, one that knows no global or informational boundaries. What we cling to is no longer the village of the past, but our constantly evolving community of the moment. And even as it closes off some of our more traditional avenues to finding community, it also opens up many new ones. As parents we must learn to adapt to the new context, borrow from it, use it to our best advantage, and rely on it for help.

What We Need Is a New Community, a Vital Village

In her book *The Gifts of Community*, Anne Marie Durham reminds us that community is a gift that enriches our personal and collective universe. On a grand scale it is a gift *exchange*—from the Latin *comm*, meaning "together," and *unis*, meaning "gift." Community is a coming together that produces positive outcomes, some tangible and some less so, in which families, neighborhoods, cities, governments, institutions, countries, and cultures can thrive. Community in support of parenting is a powerful and purpose-filled road that we all can benefit from traveling. How can parents reconnect, reinvent, and feel reinvigorated by community in our lives?

Imagine a community anchored by shared values and beliefs, a common mission, and the ability to both protect and sustain itself through positive encouragement and the achievements of its residents. Imagine that each home and family joins the vital village. What would it look like? How would it function to maintain the promise of raising its children and keeping parents sane? And what does it take to put one together, even if you are geographically far away from friends and family?

Villages thrive when people are encouraged to join, play, have fun, and participate in being part of a growing, mindful culture. Villages make you feel welcome because you find common ground, people with shared values and similar goals—in this case, parents who want to raise happy, kind, successful, well-adjusted children; parents who are seeking information and best practices from credible sources to guide their family's growth and development.

Building Your Vital Village

We think about the word *vital* as meaning "effective" or "necessary," as in *vital organs*, the essence of sustaining life. That could be a great definition for the vital village—the essence of sustaining or nourishing life. We need to recognize, identify, and gather all the support systems to create our own vital village, so that they are in place when we need to tap into them, or simply to lean on them. Here are just some of the places to begin the search.

FAMILY AND FRIENDS

Healthy parent-child relationships are, of course, central to this village. Raising kids in a household with minimal conflict and maximum communication is the foundation for success in parenting. Talk about what's working and what isn't working. As a parent, you don't have to be perfect, but you do need to be present and active in your pursuit of parenting skills—and, as mentioned before, you can't underestimate how much it helps to have the support of family and friends.

Susan, an urban mother of two boys, was vacationing in Maine. "My fifteen-year-old seemed withdrawn and distant for a time and I hoped a family vacation might help bring him out of his funk. I was shocked and totally devastated by what my husband and I found. My son was a 'cutter,' which we now know is a form of self-injury caused by extreme anger, frustration, and pain. We were clueless and guilt-ridden. How could we have missed the signs? Were we that bad at parenting? How were we going to help our son? As I look back, without the help from family and friends, I doubt we could have coped with this low point in our lives. On the other hand, the loving support we received from those around us turned this potential tragedy into a triumph of sorts. I don't think our family ever had more raw and real conversations as we had during this incident. We learned how to open our hearts to each other and talk about feelings."

NEIGHBORHOODS

Being involved in your neighborhood and getting your kids involved in projects that give back to your community are the best ways to teach children to be kind and empathic. Get involved and become a dynamic part of the village. Take notice of the positive things that are working well, and evaluate what needs mending. Boundaries and discipline are important and are most effective when enforced in ways that show care and concern or when used as teaching moments. How well the village functions is a by-product of its citizens' involvement; whether you live in a small rural town or a huge metropolis, find the neighborhood within.

In 1999, the small town of Massillon, Ohio, was in danger of imploding from increasing crime, high unemployment, and a lack of job opportunities. Rather than giving up or giving in, the town rallied. Citizens banded together by organizing neighborhood associations. Small grants allowed them to install streetlights, rehabilitate a neighborhood park, pave driveways, and put up neighborhood address signs. Pride and involvement replaced crime and hopelessness. Like the Cinderella team no one thought would get to the playoffs, they didn't give up. Get involved. Seize opportunity and take the initiative for change in your own neighborhoods.

Katrina Adams was a rising junior tennis talent whose parents had the will but not the financial resources to support her dream of becoming a professional. Her parents actively participated in their South Side Chicago community and had the connections and networks to ask for help along the way to support their daughter's dream. The community responded generously, giving Katrina the opportunity to take her talents to the next level. She eventually won a tennis scholarship to Northwestern University. "Even the gang-bangers in my neighborhood appreciated my growing skills as an athlete and showed their respect by protecting me," says Katrina. Her success on the wings of her own community took her to the ranks of the professionals. After her professional career, she became a champion of connecting youth, academic enrichment, and tennis in Harlem. She continues her community work and is also a vice president of the United States Tennis Association.

SCHOOLS

Schools and other institutions we belong to help prepare our children to be citizens of a community. Parent involvement in schools can improve children's self-esteem, behavior, and motivation. Not to mention how much parental involvement improves the health of our schools. Children can observe positive and constructive interactions between you, schoolteachers, staff, and team coaches to begin to understand how an organization functions. Relationships with your children's teachers and coaches also can help reinforce the values and lessons you teach your kids at home.

Kevin, a father of four, is actively involved in what his kids learn at school. "I recently wrote to my son's principal about how surprised and disappointed I was that the school's Chorale Cabaret performed a Billy Joel song about drinking and alcoholism," Kevin told me. "While I didn't believe the school condoned the ideas or behaviors, I thought that by teaching the lyrics, it romanticized the behavior. I thought the school should use better judgment about what was being taught. The principal's response assured me that the decision to use that song was discussed in advance with both the students and their parents."

Kevin appreciated the principal's honest, open communication and how it helped him generate discussion with his kids about the topics in the song. Involvement with schools and all the extracurriculars hopefully fosters a better understanding of how and what your children learn and what you might want to be talking about at home.

CAREGIVERS

More and more, busy moms and dads rely on caregivers to pick up, drop off, and/or tutor their children. It is critical that caregivers be vetted carefully. Check references, driving records, and most important, check in with your child. Ask daily questions like "How is it going with _____?" "Are there any issues that you'd like me to know about?" Ask your caregiver the same questions.

Parents who have dual caregiving duties for their kids as well as their own parents often find themselves stressed and overwhelmed. Check in with your health care provider to discuss support options. Websites with many helpful resources for elderly parents are www .eldercare.gov and www.strengthforcaring.com.

VIRTUAL NEIGHBORHOODS

Technology can be a source of group support, information tools, and parental guidance—without geographic limitations. Used selectively and with keen regard for the source, information from the web and the ability to form social connections with people we know and don't know are truly unique resources of the village. As long as we don't substitute electronic contact for the emotional and physical connections families need, technology has the capability to enhance our connectedness and our effectiveness in a rapidly changing landscape. The web provides an opportunity for parents to gain support, share experiences, and obtain information from the comfort of their own home. Social support online can combat feelings of isolation and increase connectedness. It often helps, too, to support an already strong network of friends, family, and neighbors.

Elizabeth was closely involved with her teenage son and his friends, often sharing experiences with the parents and connecting with neighbors in a close-knit villagelike community. Neighborhood parents often discussed all kinds of issues about their families, including drug and alcohol use. "We were content and complacent thinking that our kids were doing fine. My heart sank when I went into my son's room and discovered bags of empty beer cans and liquor bottles. When I discovered what my son was doing, my first reaction was panic. How was I going to deal with this?

"First I cried, then I screamed in anger, and then I realized I needed to seek advice from more neutral voices—my online community of peers—the friends and experts I'd come to trust in the virtual world. I'm the type of person who needs to poll a lot of people and then take all the input to form a plan. That's exactly what I was able to do. Their input helped me frame a cool-headed and empathetic discussion with my son about what was going on with him and why. I got advice on several local support programs for teens, but ultimately the discussions helped me decide to send my son to an Outward Bound type of experience, taking him completely out of his environment for a brief time.

"In the short term my strategy worked wonders for my son's attitude, and longer term, my support network helped me develop a much more open, honest communication with my son. Interestingly, my cry for help with my peers also opened up the communication among the group, as several of them actually feel more comfortable now sharing similar issues they're facing with their teens."

Having your vital village at the ready will certainly help if you end up in a situation like Elizabeth's. It also helps to just stay informed about what might be going on with your kids. Don't be caught off guard. Read books about issues your kids will face and visit sites like toughLOVE.com and Mom.me. Go to parenting workshops and start conversations with other parents. Staying connected to your vital village happens when you engage. What are your best parenting skills? Commit to sharing those passions with others in the village.

Whether in your family, at work, or in your neighborhood or

community, connecting with others helps define who you are as a parent. You accept rather than judge. You open yourself to ideas. You learn from others. You feel deeper connections and a greater inner peace than would be possible on your own. Creating a home and a community that is loving, healthy, warm, and safe for our children is a fundamental charge for parents. Within the vital village we are better together, exchanging our innate gifts to create meaning and purpose for our families, our world, and ourselves.

SOURCES

Laura T. Kessler, "Community Parenting," *Journal of Law & Policy*, vols. 24–47 (2007).

Samantha B. Berkule-Silberman, et al., "Sources of Parenting Information in Low SES Mothers," *Clinical Pediatrics* 49 (6), June 2010, 560–568.

Lisa S. Badanes, "Understanding Cortisol Reactivity across the Day at Child Care; The Potential Buffering Role of Secure Attachments to Caregivers," *Early Child Care Research Quarterly* 27(1), 2012, 156–165.

Robert D. Laird, "The Social Ecology of School-Age Child Care," *Journal of Applied Developmental Psychology* 19(3), 1998, 341–368.

Mark E. Feinberg, et al., "Effective Co-Parenting, Parenting and Child Self-Regulation Effects of Family Foundations 1 year after Birth," *Pres Sci* 10(3), September 2009, 276–285.

Deb Ramacher, "Parent Peer Supports: Impact on Children with Mental Illness," research paper.

Susan B. Hillis, et al., "The Protective Effect of Family Strengths in Childhood against Adolescent Pregnancy and Its Longterm Psychological Consequences," *The Permante Journal* 14 (3), Fall 2010.

Matthew R. Sanders, et al., "Theoretical, Scientific and Clinical Foundations of the Triple P. Positive Parenting Programs: A Population Approach to the Promotion of Parenting Compliance," *Parenting Research and Practice Monograph*, no. 1.

Michigan Department of Education, "What Research Says About Parent Involvement in Children's Education," 2002.

Joseph W. Labrie, et al., "Parents Know Best, But Are They Accurate? Parental Normative Misperception and Their Relationship to Students' Alcohol-Related Outcomes," *Journal of Studies on Alcohol and Drugs*, July 2011.

Anne-Marie Ambert, "An International Perspective on Parenting Social Change and Social Construct," *Journal of Marriage and Family* 56 (3) August 1994, 529–543.

Child Welfare League of America, *Parenting*, February 2005.

Chen Zeng-yin and Howard B. Kaplan, "Intergenerational Transmission of Constructive Parenting," *Journal of Marriage and Family* 63 (1) February 2001, 17–31.

Kathleen V. Hoover Dempsey, et al., "Why Do Parents Become Involved? Research Findings and Implications," *Elementary School Journal* 106 (2), 2005.

Nancy L. Marshall, et al., "It Takes an Urban Village: Parenting Networks of Urban Families," *Journal of Family Issues* 22 (163), 2001.

K. H. Bogan, "Yolanda Parenting in the 21st Century: A Return to Community," *Negro Educational Review* 55 (April–July 2004), 2–3.

Selma H. Fraiberg, *The Magic Years: Understanding and Handling the Problems of Early Childhood* (New York: Fireside, 1996).

Anne Marie Durham, *The Gifts of Community: Changing Your Life by Changing Your World* (Bloomington, IN: Balboa Press, 2012).

acknowledgments

I would first and foremost like to acknowledge the many millions of parents just like me, who love their kids dearly and strive to raise them in the best way they know how. In this day and age, we are all faced with myriad challenges in the most simple of circumstances. Whether it be mitigating or monitoring their technology use or making sure they are eating healthy, or figuring out how best to handle the circumstances of a divorce. This book and toughLOVE.com will help us all to become the parents we want to be, to learn how to instill the values in our children that we strive for in ourselves, to navigate the wonderful world of parenthood, preparing kids for adulthood while protecting them from growing up too quickly. As parents, we are the most important factors in helping our children be the best they can be in all of their endeavors.

Many people worked long, tiring days and months in order for us to launch toughLOVE.com and get this book to you. Our author-experts, you are eighteen in a million. Intuitive, smart, and caring, you are truly the parenting thought leaders for this generation. Thank you for your hard work and your priceless parenting guidance and wisdom. Thank you to Lisa Stiepock, Amy Iorio, and Lori Gottlieb for the unbelievable effort and determination it took to coordinate our great experts and edit this book. The quality of work is truly beyond compare.

I am grateful to all of my family and friends who have been so supportive and shared my passion to launch toughLOVE. They understood how impactful toughLOVE will be as a cutting-edge new-media social movement. We are building the twenty-first-century village that it takes to raise a child and we are fostering a worldwide discussion on modern parenting.

Lastly, I need to thank my daughter, Carolina, the inspiration for my dedication to this movement and for working so hard to be the best parent I can be. Thank you for keeping me on my toes on a daily basis. I love you!

Igal J. Feibush
CEO, Digital Family Media Group
toughLOVE.com

about the authors

LISA BELKIN is the chief national correspondent for *Yahoo! News*, writing about American social issues. She joined Yahoo! after three years as a senior columnist at the *Huffington Post*, covering life, work, and family. Belkin spent most of her career at the *New York Times*, where she was a Houston-based national correspondent, a medical reporter, a contributing writer for the *New York Times Magazine*, and the creator of the "Life's Work" column and the *Motherlode* blog. The author of several books, including *Life's Work: Confessions of an Unbalanced Mom*, Belkin was also the host of "Life's Work with Lisa Belkin," on XM Radio, as well as a regular contributor on parenting topics to Public Radio's *The Takeaway* and NBC's *Today* show.

MICHAEL J. BRADLEY, EDD, is a practicing psychologist, award-winning author, and nationally acclaimed speaker specializing in the treatment and parenting of adolescents. He has authored four books, which include the bestselling *Yes, Your Teen Is Crazy! Loving Your*

Kid Without Losing Your Mind. As an expert on adolescent behavior, Bradley is frequently quoted in the press and has appeared on hundreds of TV and radio programs, including *Good Morning America*, the *Today* show, *CNN World News Tonight*, the Fox News Network, and National Public Radio. In addition to being a licensed clinical psychologist, he is certified both as a specialist in substance abuse disorders by the American College of Professional Psychology and as a forensic examiner by the American Board of Forensic Examiners. Beyond that, he offers as his best credential being the parent of a twenty-four-year-old son and a seventeen-year-old daughter, two people he incessantly worries might grow up to be just like him.

SANDRA BRYSON, MFT, a marriage and family therapist for the past thirty years, helps individuals, couples, and families successfully navigate some of life's most difficult challenges. She speaks to parents, educators, and therapists about helping children grow up healthy in the age of online technology. It is her belief that parents hold the primary responsibility to raise children to become good digital citizens. She established parentmindfully.com to empower parents with practical advice about technology in the areas of screen time, cyberbullying, and Internet safety. She teaches parents to teach their children to behave in self-protective and considerate ways when using technology, while still making it accessible, understandable, and useful. Sandra has a private practice in the Rockridge area of Oakland, California.

JILL CASTLE, MS, RDN, has practiced as a registered dietitian/nutritionist in the field of pediatric nutrition for more than twenty-four years, including private practice. She is the coauthor of *Fearless Feeding: How to Raise Healthy Eaters from High Chair to High School*, and creator of *Just the Right Byte*, a childhood nutrition blog. She is currently writing her second book, *Eat Like a Champion: Performance Nutrition for Your Young Athlete,* due out in 2015. Castle is the food allergies expert for About.com, and regularly contributes to USA Swimming, US Rowing, the National Alliance for Youth Sports blog, *Sporting Kid* magazine, and Bundoo.com as a childhood nutrition expert. Castle has spoken to a wide variety of groups, from parent groups to national organizations, and is regularly quoted in popular print and online publications as a leading childhood nutrition expert. She lives in New Canaan, Connecticut, with her husband, four children, and two dogs.

ANN CORWIN, PHD, MED, has made it her life's work to develop practical parenting programs for parents and children. With a PhD in marriage, family, and child therapy, a master's degree in education, and more than thirty years of experience in parenting consulting and child development education, she is a much-sought-after trainer and lecturer, particularly in the field of emotional literacy. Her program, Pocket Full of Feelings, teaches parents and children how to recognize and deal with feelings in order to change behavior. She believes the root cause of childhood behavior is linked to the way kids feel and strives to make the teaching and development of emotional literacy a fundamental part of raising children.

Corwin grew up in the Midwest and relishes the joy of her close-knit family: both her grandparents and parents were/have been married for more than sixty years. Her two fantastic kids and husband of thirty-seven years are very enthusiastic about her work and passionate about her parenting programs. Find out more about those programs and Dr. Ann at pocketfulloffeelings.com and theparenting doctor.com.

PEGGY DREXLER, PHD, is a research psychologist and Assistant Professor of Psychology in Psychiatry, Weill Medical College of Cornell University, and a former gender scholar at Stanford University. She has spent her career researching what it means to be a family. She is the author of *Our Fathers, Ourselves: Daughters, Fathers, and the Changing American Family* and *Raising Boys Without Men.* She has appeared on and written for a wide range of national and international media, including: the *Today* show, *Good Morning America*, NPR, *Dr. Oz*, *The Good Life*, the *New York Times*, the *Wall Street Journal*, CNN.com, and *Parents* magazine and writes regular columns for *Forbes*, *Psychology Today*, and the *Huffington Post.* She has raised a son and daughter and is now at work on three yellow Labrador retrievers.

ELLEN GALINSKY, MS, president of Families and Work Institute (FWI), is a founder of the work-life field. Her more than one hundred books and reports and three hundred articles include the bestselling *Mind in the Making: The Seven Essential Life Skills Every Child Needs, Ask the Children*, and the now classic *The Six Stages of Parenthood.* At FWI, the Mind in the Making study is an unprecedented effort to share the science of children's learning with the general public, families, and professionals who work with them. Galinsky was a presenter at the 1997 White House Conference on Child Care, the 2000 White House Conference on Teenagers, and the 2014 White House Summit on Working Families. She appears regularly in the media and is the recipient of many awards, including the 2004 Distinguished Achievement Award from Vassar College, the Seven Wonders of the Work-Life World from *Working Mother* magazine, and the 2014 Friend of Children Award from the Southern Early Childhood Association.

KENNETH R. GINSBURG, MD, MSED, is a pediatrician specializing in adolescent medicine at the Children's Hospital of Philadelphia and a professor of pediatrics at the University of Pennsylvania School of Medicine. He also serves as director of health services at Covenant House Pennsylvania, an agency that serves Philadelphia's homeless and marginalized youth. The theme that ties together his clinical practice, teaching, research, and advocacy efforts is that of building on the strengths of teenagers by fostering their internal resilience. He strives to translate the best of what is known from research and practice into practical approaches parents, professionals, and communities can use to build resilience. Core to this model is understanding that youths choose behaviors that manage stress in their lives, and that if we are to reduce worrisome youth behaviors, we need to address those stressors. His most recent book is *Building Resilience in Children and Teens: Giving Kids Roots and Wings*, published by the American Academy of Pediatrics. He is the editor and coproducer of the multimedia textbook for youth-serving professionals *Reaching Teens: Strength-Based Communication Strategies to Build Resilience and Support Healthy Adolescent Development*. He works closely with the Boys and Girls Club of America, which serves over five million youths, to incorporate resilience-building strategies into its programming. He has also been honored to work on behalf of those who serve America, preparing military parents, health professionals, counselors, and teachers to incorporate stress reduction and resilience-building strategies as they care for the nation's nearly two million military-affiliated children. But his greatest honor is to be the parent of two teenage daughters.

LORI GOTTLIEB, MFT, is a psychotherapist and parenting consultant and the *New York Times* bestselling author of *Marry Him: The Case for Settling for Mr. Good Enough*. She speaks nationwide to schools and corporate audiences on raising kids to be thriving adults and started a worldwide conversation with her article "How to Land Your Kid in Therapy: Why Our Obsession with Our Kids' Happiness May Be Dooming Them to Unhappy Adulthoods." Gottlieb is a contributing editor for the *Atlantic* and regularly appears as a relationship and parenting expert in media including the *Today* show,

Good Morning America, The Early Show, CNN, MSNBC, *Oprah*, and NPR.

AMY IORIO, MED, is a digital media executive with extensive experience in building online content and community across multiple platforms. Most recently she has worked with Lisa Stiepock and Lori Gottlieb to bring together a community of parenting experts for toughLOVE. As a VP at Yahoo! Media, Iorio launched *Shine*, Yahoo!'s first women's online magazine, which rapidly grew to 30 million unique monthly viewers. In the rapidly colliding worlds of computer technology and learning, Iorio created an award-winning digital series from the beloved Magic School Bus franchise at Microsoft, taking full advantage of her BA in computer science from Dartmouth College and master's in education from Harvard University. She extended her success into the realm of linear film media as the director of an award-winning short film *Seven's Eleven* through the American Film Institute. She is the extremely proud mother of one son who is the owner of a ragdoll cat and kittens. The arrival of the kittens inspired Iorio to develop a series of apps and board books called Kitten Preschool, which are currently in development.

LYNNE KENNEY, PSYD, is a mother of two, a practicing pediatric psychologist, and the author of *The Family Coach Method*. She has advanced fellowship training in forensic psychology and developmental pediatric psychology from Massachusetts General Hospital/Harvard Medical School and Harbor-UCLA/UCLA Medical School. Kenney speaks internationally about enhancing executive function and social and academic skills with motor movement. Her new book with Wendy Young, *Bloom: 50 Things to Say, Think and Do with Anxious, Angry and Over-the-Top Kids*, came out in paperback in spring 2015. Kenney's work is featured in *Real Simple, Parents, Parenting,* and

People. Kenney has spoken with more than four thousand parents and teachers in the past twenty years. Combining her love for motor movement and brain development, Kenney's newest endeavor, *Play Math*, is helping children ages six through eleven learn their math facts with playground balls and Hula-Hoops for better algebraic thinking. For more visit www.lynnekenney.com.

MADELINE LEVINE, PHD, has been a practicing psychologist in Marin County with close to thirty years of experience and is the author of two *New York Times* bestsellers. *The Price of Privilege* explores reasons why teenagers from affluent families are experiencing epidemic rates of emotional problems. *Teach Your Children Well* tackles our current narrow definition of success—how it unnecessarily stresses academically talented kids and marginalizes many more whose talents are less amenable to measurement. Levine is also co-founder of Challenge Success, a project of the Stanford University Graduate School of Education. Levine is highly sought after as a lecturer and keynote speaker for parents, educators, and business leaders, both nationally and internationally. She lives just outside San Francisco with her husband and is the (extremely) proud mother of three sons.

LOGAN LEVKOFF, PHD, is a nationally recognized sexologist and sexuality educator. She designs and implements sexuality education programs across the country for audiences of all ages. Levkoff appears frequently on television, including on *Good Morning America*, the *Today* show, and CNN. She is the author of several books, most recently, *Got Teens? The Doctor Moms' Guide to Sexuality, Social Media, and Other Adolescent Realities* (written with Dr. Jennifer Wider). Levkoff's work with parents and teens has been profiled by many publications, including the *New York Times*. She received her PhD in human sexuality, marriage, and family life education from New York University. She lives in New York City with her husband, son, and daughter.

ROBERT J. MacKENZIE, EDD, is a family therapist, educational psychologist, and nationally recognized parent educator and staff development trainer with more than twenty-five years of experience helping parents and teachers solve children's learning and behavior problems. He is the author of *Setting Limits, Setting Limits in the Classroom,* and *Setting Limits with Your Strong-Willed Child,* which has spent 4,300 days in Amazon's top 100. His newest book is *Setting Limits with Your Strong-Willed Teen* (Three Rivers Press). Dr. MacKenzie received his MA in educational psychology from the University of California at Davis and his doctorate in counseling and educational psychology from the University of San Francisco. He writes for magazines and educational journals and consults privately with schools, hospitals, and colleges. Dr. MacKenzie has two adult sons. He says his youngest is very strong-willed and "the inspiration for most of my professional work."

CHRISTINA McGHEE, MSW, from Tulane University, is an internationally recognized divorce coach, speaker, and author of the highly acclaimed book *Parenting Apart: How Separated and Divorced Parents Can Raise Happy and Secure Kids.* McGhee, dubbed the "divorce coach" by the UK press, gained worldwide attention for her work with three British families in the Channel 4 documentary *How to Divorce Without Screwing Up Your Kids.* She has been featured on television, radio, and in print around the US and abroad, including the BBC, HLN with Kyra Phillips, Fox Family, *LA Talk Radio,* the *Dr. Laura Berman Show, Parents* magazine, and *The Times.* Today she spends much of her time doing outreach, promoting, and speaking around the documentary *SPLIT.* Released in 2014, this compelling film about how divorce affects kids inspired McGhee to become involved as subject matter expert and creative team member. McGhee is both a stepmom and a mom of four. She's been married for twenty years to a man whose work takes him out of the home and on the road. There are many days when she feels like a single mom challenged by crisis management, constant negotiation, deep breathing, and loving without limits.

DAN PETERS, PHD, is a licensed psychologist who has devoted his career to working with children and families. His practice focuses on the assessment and treatment of children, adolescents, and families with diverse challenges, including overcoming worry and fear, learning differences, and issues related to giftedness and twice-exceptionality. Peters is passionate about creating healthy communities by helping parents and teachers engage children in the classroom, at home, and in life so that they can realize their full potential. As the father of three children, he understands the daily challenges of parenting in today's complicated world, as well as the importance of teaching children of all ages coping skills, problem solving, and resilience. Peters is cofounder and executive director of the Summit Center, where he is available for consultation, with offices in the San Francisco Bay area and Los Angeles. He is the author of *Make Your Worrier a Warrior: A Guide to Conquering Your Child's Fears* (winner of a 2014 IPPY Gold Award and the 2014 Legacy Award for best parenting book) and the companion book for children, *From Worrier to Warrior: A Guide to Conquering Your Fears*. In addition, he is coauthor (with Dr. Susan Daniels) of *Raising Creative Kids* (winner of the 2013 Legacy Award for best parenting book). Peters is a regular contributor to the *Huffington Post* and *Psychology Today* and is a frequent media guest. He writes and lectures frequently on topics related to parenting, anxiety, learning differences, giftedness, and twice-exceptionality. See www.DrDanPeters.com.

JAMES P. STEYER, JD, is founder and chief executive officer of Common Sense Media, the nation's leading nonpartisan organization dedicated to improving media and technology choices for kids and families. He is also a founding board member of the Center for the Next Generation, as well as author of *Talking Back to Facebook* and *The Other Parent: The Inside Story of the Media's Effect on Our Children.* Prior to launching Common Sense Media, Steyer was chairman and CEO of JP Kids, a leading educational kids' media company. Before that, he was the founder and president of Children Now, the highly respected national advocacy and media organization for children, which he founded in 1988. Steyer also teaches at Stanford University as a consulting professor and appears regularly on national radio programs as an expert commentator and children's advocate. Last, but most important, he's a dad of four.

LISA STIEPOCK, MS, is a cross-platform editor, writer, and content curator specializing in the areas of parenting, family, teenagers, pets, wildlife, food, travel, and tourism. Most recently she has worked with Amy Iorio and Lori Gottlieb to bring together a community of parenting experts for toughLOVE. She spent many years spearheading innovative projects and publications for families as a creative development director at Disney, leaving that position to become the editor of the provocative and award-winning *Wondertime* magazine for parents. She was a senior editor with *Family Fun* magazine and edited a series of Family Travel guides for Disney Editions and in another life was an innkeeper and restaurateur. She lives on Block Island, Rhode Island, with her husband, fourteen-year-old daughter, two dogs, two cats, and a bunny.

JANET TAYLOR, MD, is a community psychiatrist in New York City. She is on the front line battling the emotional and economic impact of mental illness. She holds an MD from the University of Louisville, completed her psychiatric residency at New York Medical College, and obtained an MPH from Columbia University's Mailman School of Public Health in health promotion and disease prevention. She has a column in *Family Circle* magazine, "Ask Dr. Janet." Dr. Taylor is also frequently featured on CBS's *Early Show* and NBC's the *Today* show, and ABC's *Good Morning America*. She is a former host of the Discovery Health/OWN series *Facing Trauma* and was the guest care director for *The Jeremy Kyle Show*, a syndicated talk show. She is the proud mother of four daughters.

JIM TAYLOR, PHD, is internationally recognized for his work in the psychology of performance in business, sport, and parenting. Taylor has been a consultant for the US and Japanese ski teams. He is a clinical associate professor in the Sport & Performance Psychology graduate program at the University of Denver. Taylor received his bachelor's degree from Middlebury College and earned his master's degree and PhD in psychology from the University of Colorado. He is currently an adjunct faculty member at the University of San Francisco and the Wright Institute in Berkeley. He has appeared on the *Today* show, Fox News, CBS5, and NPR, among other radio and on-air programming.

FRAN WALFISH, PSYD, is the leading Beverly Hills child, family, and relationship psychotherapist; an author; and an expert panelist on the WE television series, *Sex Box*. In addition to her thriving private practice, Walfish was on the clinical staff in the department of child psychiatry at Cedars-Sinai Medical Center for fifteen years. She was a school psychologist and served a four-year term as chair of the board of the Early Childhood Parenting Center founded at Cedars-Sinai in Los Angeles. Walfish is featured in every online issue of Parents.com's "Ask the Experts" column and in her weekly Q&A in the *Beverly Hills Courier*. She is an expert contributor to many media outlets, including *NBC Nightly News with Brian Williams,* CBS2 News local affiliates, Fox News *Live at Five, The Doctors* on CBS, the *Wall Street Journal,* Turner Broadcasting, the *Chicago Tribune, Forbes* magazine, CNN.com, the *New York Times, Family Circle* magazine, *Ladies' Home Journal,* Momlogic.com, iVillage.com, and *People* magazine. Walfish's current book, *The Self-Aware Parent: Resolving Conflict and Building a Better Bond with Your Child,* is published by Palgrave Macmillan/St. Martin's Press. Although she has no children of her own, Walfish has raised thousands of kids in her private practice, as well as cared for her baby sister and beloved nephews and nieces. You can visit her on her website at www.DrFranWalfish.com.

index